REPORT OF
THE COMMITTEE OF INQUIRY
INTO HUNTING WITH DOGS
IN ENGLAND & WALES

Presented to Parliament by the Secretary of State for the Home Department
by Command of Her Majesty
June 2000

CM 4763

£32.50 (inc VAT in UK)

The Rt. Hon Jack Straw MP
Secretary of State for the Home Department
50 Queen Anne's Gate
London SW1A 0AA

9 June 2000

You appointed us in December 1999 to carry out an inquiry into hunting with dogs, with the following terms of reference:

"To inquire into:

- the practical aspects of different types of hunting with dogs and its impact on the rural economy, agriculture and pest control, the social and cultural life of the countryside, the management and conservation of wildlife, and animal welfare in particular areas of England and Wales;
- the consequences for these issues of any ban on hunting with dogs; and
- how any ban might be implemented.

To report the findings to the Secretary of State for the Home Department."

We now have pleasure in enclosing our report.

Without doubt, conducting the inquiry has been a challenging experience. This is a complex issue that is full of paradoxes. We were helped by the terms of reference, which asked us to concentrate on the factual and analytical background to hunting. We have addressed those issues and we have not attempted to answer the question of whether or not hunting should be banned. In particular, we have not sought to find a compromise solution, which we regarded as outside our terms of reference.

The result is a report that might appear long on analysis and short on solutions. But we believe that it will help to inform the debate that will follow the publication of our report.

We have travelled widely throughout England and Wales and listened to many people. We were left in no doubt about the sensitivity of the issue or the passion that it arouses. We have sought to conduct the inquiry in a very open manner. We have made as much as possible of our evidence available on the inquiry website. Our oral evidence sessions have been in public and transcripts have also been posted on the website as quickly as possible. We commissioned research papers, which were made available in draft and discussed at seminars, also open to the public.

In the process we believe that we have gone some way to reach a wider agreement about the analysis of the issues, although some important differences remain. Some of these differences could be narrowed further with more research conducted over a longer time period. Others are likely to remain because they are not capable of being resolved in this way.

We would like to record our thanks to the staff of the Committee. They have worked tirelessly against very tight deadlines to cope with the huge amount of material we received, to prepare it for publication on the website and to organise a complex series of visits, oral evidence and seminars. In particular, we would like to recognise the important role of Brian Caffarey, the Secretary to the Committee. We have only been able to complete our task within the tight timetable given to us because of Brian's planning and organisational strengths, his ability to communicate quickly and sensitively with people on all sides of this debate and because of his drafting skills.

LORD BURNS (Chairman)

DR. VICTORIA EDWARDS

PROFESSOR SIR JOHN MARSH

LORD SOULSBY OF SWAFFHAM PRIOR

PROFESSOR MICHAEL WINTER

Acknowledgements

We would like to thank all those who helped us in our inquiry, including all the organisations and individuals who submitted evidence to us. We are particularly grateful to representatives of the Countryside Alliance and Deadline 2000, the hunts and other groups whom we visited, the research teams, participants at our seminars, the Home Office, Professor David Macdonald and Mr Michael Fordham, who assisted us, respectively, on scientific and legal matters and our stenographer, Cheryl Slater.

Footnotes

References such as "MDHA 1" refer to 'first round' evidence. References such as "IFAW 2" refer to 'second round' evidence. Other details refer to the paragraph numbers in the evidence unless otherwise stated.

CD Rom

The CD Rom in the back cover of this Report contains the following material: terms of reference; letter of 19 January 2000 inviting 'first round' evidence; evidence submitted by the main organisations and a number of individuals; details of visits made by the Committee; details of the research commissioned by the Inquiry; draft research reports; transcripts of the seminars held to discuss the draft research reports; final research reports; transcript of a seminar on the legal aspects of implementing a ban, plus supporting papers; notes of 'by invitation' meetings held with supporters of the Countryside Alliance and Deadline 2000; letter of 17 April 2000 inviting 'second round' evidence; all the responses received to that invitation; and the Committee's report.

CONTENTS   PAGE

SUMMARY AND CONCLUSIONS

Chapter 1   INTRODUCTION

1   The Committee was asked to inquire into the practical aspects of different types of hunting with dogs and its impact on the rural economy, agriculture and pest control, the social and cultural life of the countryside, the management and conservation of wildlife, and animal welfare in particular areas of England and Wales; the consequences for these issues of any ban on hunting with dogs; and how any ban might be implemented.

2   We were asked to focus on the hunting with dogs of foxes, deer, hares and mink. The use of dogs solely to locate or retrieve quarry was excluded from our terms of reference. We were not asked to recommend whether hunting should be banned. Nor were we asked to consider moral or ethical issues.

3   The Committee gathered information through an open process of written and oral evidence, research reports, seminars, meetings and visits.

Chapter 2   HUNTING

4   Hunting with dogs is a diverse activity.

5   There are about 200 registered packs of hounds (mainly foxhounds but also some harriers) in England and Wales which hunt foxes, plus a number of unregistered packs in Wales. Most packs have mounted followers but a number, including the Fell packs in Cumbria and the footpacks in Wales, are followed on foot only. The Welsh gunpacks use dogs to flush foxes to waiting guns.

6   The registered packs are estimated to kill some 21,000-25,000 foxes a year. About 40% of the foxes killed by the registered packs are killed in the autumn/cub hunting season. In Wales and other upland areas, a high proportion of foxes are dug out, using terriers, and shot. Outside the registered packs, many more foxes are dug out and shot or are killed by people using lurchers or other "long dogs". Some of these activities are carried out by farmers, landowners and gamekeepers. Others involve trespass.

7   There are three registered staghound packs in the Devon and Somerset area. They kill about 160 red deer a year in total, excluding injured deer which they dispatch. This probably represents about 15% of the numbers which need to be culled in the area to maintain a stable population.

8   There are about a hundred registered packs of hounds (beagles, bassets and harriers) which hunt hares. They kill about 1,650 hares a season, a very small percentage of the number killed by shooting.

9   There are some 24 registered hare coursing clubs, which kill about 250 hares a year in total, and a small number of other unregistered clubs. But there is a good deal of illegal hunting/coursing in some areas.

10   The 20 minkhound packs kill somewhere between 400 - 1,400 mink a season. The number is thought to be considerably smaller than that killed by trapping and shooting.

Chapter 3   HUNTING AND THE RURAL ECONOMY

11   Hunting, especially in its organised form, needs to be seen in a wider economic and social context. The population of rural areas is increasing and new service industries have been established. But agriculture has been in serious decline, and the new jobs tend to be in less remote areas.

12   There is a complex set of relationships between hunting and a diverse range of other economic activities, mostly in rural areas, and largely horse-related, that either directly serve hunting or are in some way dependent on it.

13   There have been widely varying estimates given in recent years for the loss of jobs which would result from a ban on hunting.

14   The research which we commissioned attempted to estimate the jobs (full-time equivalents, FTEs) which currently depend on hunting, either directly or indirectly.

15   It is relatively straightforward to estimate the number of jobs which the hunts provide. It is much more difficult to estimate the other jobs which depend, directly or indirectly, on hunting. Identifying the number of participants and allocating their expenditure between hunting and other equestrian activities is particularly problematic.

16   Estimating the effects of a ban is also complex. It is necessary to take account of other factors such as the extent to which alternative activities would replace hunting, how the money currently used would be spent, other changes taking place in the rural economy and the differential impact in different areas.

17   It is difficult too to estimate the effects of a ban on hunting on individuals. These must take into account the extent to which the people concerned would be able to switch to other available employment, as well as the part-time and seasonal nature of many jobs.

18   We estimate that somewhere between 6,000 and 8,000 full-time equivalent jobs presently depend on hunting, although the number of people involved may be significantly higher. About 700 of these jobs (involving some 800 people) result from direct employment by the hunts. Another 1,500 to 3,000 full-time equivalent jobs (perhaps involving some 2,500 to 5,000 people) result from direct employment on hunting-related activities by those who are engaged in hunting. The remaining

jobs, in a wide variety of businesses, are indirectly dependent on hunting. Of these, many will be in urban, rather than rural, areas. (Paragraph 3.43)

19   In view of all the uncertainties, it is not possible to give a precise figure for the number of jobs which would be lost if hunting were banned. In terms of national employment statistics, the short-term loss would be limited, and extend not much further than those employed by the hunt, and some employed by those hunt followers who immediately reduced their use of horses. In the medium term, say three to five years, more losses would occur as hunt followers brought their horse numbers into line with current use. Losses would also arise in the wider rural economy, in particular the horse economy, although in part they would be offset by other changes, including expenditure being diverted into other activities. In the long term, say seven to ten years, most (if not all) of the effects would be offset as resources were diverted to new activities and the rural economy adjusted to other economic forces. (Paragraph 3.72)

20   In terms of national resource use, the economic effects of a ban on hunting would be unlikely to be substantial, especially in the context of the drastic changes taking place in the agricultural sector. However, at least in the short and medium term, the individual and local effects would be more serious. Most jobs that are directly dependent on hunting are in the land-based sector. Some of those directly affected have specialised skills which would not transfer easily, and they would find it hard to find alternative employment. For these people especially, the adjustment process could be painful. Some thought would have to be given to the possibilities for re-training and acquiring new skills. (Paragraph 3.73)

21   For some businesses that are on the borderline of viability, the loss of revenue could lead to a bigger impact than the direct effect may suggest. For a small number of local communities which depend to a significant extent on hunting, and where there are limited alternative employment opportunities, the effects could also be more serious. (Paragraph 3.74)

22   Farmers would lose the benefit of a recreation they value. In addition, many of them would feel that they had suffered an economic loss since a free "pest control" service would have been removed; they would expect more predation of lambs, poultry, piglets and game birds; and they would lose the "fallen stock" service provided by many hunts. The negative impacts of a ban would be particularly resented because they would be viewed as unnecessary by many of those affected, and as an avoidable addition to other problems facing the farming community. (Paragraph 3.75)

Chapter 4   SOCIAL AND CULTURAL ASPECTS

23   It is commonly argued that hunting plays a critical role in the social and cultural life of rural communities. Hunting is itself a social activity, and hunts organise a wide range of social and sporting events. But it is also important to see hunting, especially

9

organised hunting, in its wider context. It is a highly co-operative social activity taking place in a rural setting. Different people value different aspects but farmers and landowners are at its heart. Rural communities are diverse and changing but farmers, as a group, feel that their interests and way of life are not understood by central government and the urban majority.

24   The research which we commissioned examined the relative importance of hunting to the social and cultural life of four rural communities where hunting is actively pursued. Among the findings were that there were higher levels of support for hunting than previous surveys have suggested; that support tends to be based not so much on importance to the individual - although this was true for hunt participants and some farmers - but a belief that hunting had greater significance for the community as a whole and for others living there; that hunt-based social activities play a significant part in the social life of these communities, but are not as significant as those of the local pub or church; that support for hunting, and a belief in its importance to individuals and to the local community, was particularly strong in the Devon and Somerset study area; and that a significant minority who were opposed to hunting would welcome its abolition.

25   It is not possible simply to extrapolate these findings since the areas studied deliberately focused on those in which organised hunting actively takes place, rather than rural communities in general.

26   **Rural communities are diverse. Many, especially those near urban centres, have experienced substantial changes in recent years as agriculture has declined in importance, communications have improved and people have moved in from towns. The part played by hunting in the social and cultural life of rural communities varies greatly, depending on factors such as their proximity to urban centres and the type of hunting taking place. (Paragraph 4.52)**

27   **The social activities organised by the hunts form an important feature of the social life of those communities in which hunting is actively pursued. For a significant minority, notably hunt participants and farmers in more isolated rural communities, the hunts play a dominant role. The loss of these activities, if that were the outcome of a ban on hunting, would be keenly felt. For those who take part, hunting is itself partly a social event, particularly during the winter months when alternative activities are scarce. For others, the social activities organised by the hunts are significant, but less so than those organised by other groups, in particular the pub and the church. Even those who would not feel greatly, at a personal level, the loss of the hunts' social activities consider that it would have a detrimental effect on the social life of others and on community life in general. A number would also feel that it would mark the end of an important, living cultural tradition. The precise balance between these different responses would vary from region to region and area to area. Generally, however, the impact would be felt most strongly in the more isolated rural areas. In areas of greater population density where there are more alternative activities available, and where the**

population is more socially diverse, a ban would make less of a social impact. (Paragraph 4.53)

28   It is clear that, especially for participants in more isolated rural communities, hunting acts as a significant cohesive force, encouraging a system of mutual support. Farmers and other landowners - many of whom feel increasingly isolated - are both the linchpins and the main beneficiaries of the system. Many of them also value hunting as an expression of a traditional, rural way of life and would strongly resent what they would see as an unnecessary and ill-informed interference with it. As a result it would increase their sense of alienation. (Paragraph 4.54)

29   For another group, the hunt itself seems divisive, intrusive and disruptive. (Paragraph 4.55)

30   Because the organisation of point-to-points relies heavily on voluntary labour supplied by hunt followers and supporters, there could be difficulties in running these events. Pony clubs also often depend heavily on hunt followers and supporters. To a lesser extent these too could be affected by a ban. These activities should be able to continue provided alternative forms of organisation develop. (Paragraph 4.56)

Chapter 5   POPULATION MANAGEMENT AND CONTROL

Foxes

31   The pre-breeding population of foxes in England and Wales is thought to number some 217,000. They are perceived as pests mainly because of predation on lambs and game birds, although there are marked regional variations. Farmers and gamekeepers consider that they need a range of methods to control foxes. There is little information about the numbers of foxes which are killed and by what methods. Shooting is the most common method, but the use of dogs is particularly prevalent in sheep-rearing upland areas.

32   In most areas of England and Wales farmers, landowners and gamekeepers consider that it is necessary to manage fox populations in view of the damage which foxes can cause to farming and game management interests. (Paragraph 5.40)

33   Methods involving guns probably account for the greater part of those foxes which are deliberately killed, but there are marked regional variations. (Paragraph 5.41)

34   In lowland areas hunting by the registered packs makes only a minor contribution to the management of the fox population, and terrierwork, especially by gamekeepers, may be more important. In these areas, in the event of a ban,

other means of control have the potential to replace the hunts' role in culling foxes. (Paragraph 5.42)

35   In upland areas, where the fox population causes more damage to sheep-rearing and game management interests, and where there is a greater perceived need for control, fewer alternatives are available to the use of dogs, either to flush out to guns or for digging-out.   (Paragraph 5.43)

Deer

36   There are estimated to be about 4,000-6,000 red deer in the areas hunted by the three registered packs in Devon and Somerset. About 1,000 deer need to be culled each year to maintain a stable population. The hunts kill about 160 deer each year, excluding the "casualty" deer which they dispatch.

37   The population needs to be managed, mainly because of the damage which deer cause to agricultural, forestry and conservation interests and because the numbers would otherwise increase substantially. Apart from hunting, the only other method of culling deer is by stalking/shooting.

38   It is generally accepted that red deer numbers in Devon and Somerset need to be controlled. Hunting with dogs presently accounts for about 15% of the annual cull needed to maintain the population at its present level. However, because of the widespread support which it enjoys, and consequent tolerance by farmers of deer, hunting at present makes a significant contribution to management of the deer population in this area. In the event of a ban, some overall reduction in total deer numbers might occur unless an effective deer management strategy was implemented, which was capable of promoting the present collective interest in the management of deer and harnessing such interest into sound conservation management. (Paragraph 5.75)

Hares

39   There are about 630,000 brown hares in England and Wales. They are most abundant in eastern England, where high numbers are often encouraged for shooting purposes. Hares are regarded, at most, as a minor agricultural pest. About 1,650 hares are killed by hunting by the registered packs and about 250 by the registered coursing clubs. Much larger numbers are killed by shooting and illegal coursing.

40   There is little or no need to control overall hare numbers and, indeed, they are a Biodiversity Action Plan species. However, the distribution of hares is uneven: they are abundant in some areas, mainly in the east of England, and scarce in much of Wales and the West Country. Hare hunting and coursing are essentially carried out for recreational purposes and have a relatively small direct impact on hare numbers. A ban would therefore have little effect in practice on agriculture or other interests. (Paragraph 5.94)

41 **Because hare numbers tend to be maintained at high levels in areas where hunting/coursing occurs, the impact of a ban might well be that, in the absence of other changes, the population would decline in those areas. This would partly result from a loss of suitable habitat but also, in a few areas, from the shooting of hares to deter poaching and illegal coursing. However, in comparison with the impact of organised shooting on hare numbers, a ban on hare hunting and coursing would have a negligible effect. (Paragraph 5.95)**

Mink

42   Mink are not a native species. Following their introduction to Britain mink rapidly increased in their distribution and abundance. However, over the last 10 years mink populations have declined substantially, and are now an estimated 18,000 in England and Wales. Mink prey on a wide variety of mammals, birds and fish. Trapping is the main method of killing mink, but mink hunts probably account for between 400-1,400 mink a year.

43 **Mink can cause localised damage to poultry, gamebirds, fishing and wildlife interests. Because mink hunts kill relatively small numbers of mink, and because of their high fecundity and ability to disperse, hunting does not have any significant effect on the mink population at a national or regional level. It can, however, lead to temporary reductions in the mink population in specific localities. (Paragraph 5.121)**

44 **Trapping is potentially an effective means of control but it needs to be carried out fairly intensively from January to April every year to have a lasting impact. It is therefore relatively costly. Hunting can be helpful in providing a free service to farmers and others that identifies where mink are located, enabling them to target trapping efforts more effectively. (Paragraph 5.122)**

Chapter 6   ANIMAL WELFARE

45   The issues of cruelty and animal welfare are central to the debate about hunting. Animal welfare is essentially concerned with assessing the ability of an animal to cope with its environment: if an animal is having difficulty in coping with its environment, or is failing to cope, then its welfare may be regarded as poor. This judgment is distinct from any ethical or moral judgments about the way in which the animal is being treated.

46   Except in relation to deer, little scientific work has been done to assess the impact of hunting on the welfare of the four quarry species. Because it is not possible to ask an animal about its welfare, or to know what is going on inside its head, it is necessary to draw up some indicators which enable one to make a judgment. The precise nature of these indicators will vary depending on the animal concerned but they will usually comprise a mixture of physiological indicators and behavioural indicators. But, because they are only indicators, there is often room for argument about the extent to which a

particular finding indicates poor welfare as opposed to, for example, exertion that can be regarded as falling within natural limits. It is also necessary to consider whether the assessment of welfare should be on an absolute or comparative basis.

47   Animal welfare is concerned with the welfare of the individual animal, not the management of the wider population. In assessing the impact of hunting on animal welfare we are persuaded that it is necessary to look at it on a relative, rather than an absolute, basis. It should not be compared with only the best, or the worst, of the alternatives. Nor is it right to justify hunting by reference to the welfare implications of illegal methods of control. (Paragraph 6.12)

48   In the event of a ban on hunting, it seems probable that farmers and others would resort more frequently to other methods to kill foxes, deer, hares and perhaps mink. There would be a mixture of motives: pest control; the value of the carcass; and the recreational value to be derived from shooting. It follows that the welfare of animals which are hunted should be compared with the welfare which, on a realistic assessment, would be likely to result from the legal methods used by farmers and others to manage the population of these animals in the event of a ban on hunting. (Paragraph 6.13)

Deer

49   The hunting of a red deer typically comprises a series of intermittent flights in which the deer exerts itself maximally in order to escape from the hounds. An average hunt which ends in the killing of the deer lasts about 3 hours. Scientific studies show that, at the end of a chase, deer have very low levels of carbohydrate (glycogen) in their muscles and that this largely explains why they are forced to stop.

50   There is a lack of firm information about the wounding rates which arise from stalking/shooting deer. Comparing the welfare implications of hunting and stalking/ shooting deer is a complex matter, requiring the balancing of the welfare of all the deer that are hunted against the welfare of the numbers of shot deer which are wounded.

51   Although there are still substantial areas of disagreement, there is now a better understanding of the physiological changes which occur when a deer is hunted. Most scientists agree that deer are likely to suffer in the final stages of hunting. The available evidence does not enable us to resolve the disagreement about the point at which, during the hunt, the welfare of the deer becomes seriously compromised. There is also a lack of firm information about what happens to deer which escape, although the available research suggests that they are likely to recover. (Paragraph 6.33)

52   Stalking, if carried out to a high standard and with the availability of a dog or dogs to help find any wounded deer that escape, is in principle the better method of culling deer from an animal welfare perspective. In particular, it obviates the need to chase the deer in the way which occurs in hunting. (Paragraph 6.39)

14

53 A great deal depends, however, on the skill and care taken by the stalker. It is unfortunate that there is no reliable information on wounding rates, even in Scotland where stalking is carried out extensively. In the event of a ban on hunting, there is a risk that a greater number of deer than at present would be shot by less skilful shooters, in which case wounding rates would increase. Consideration should be given to requiring all stalkers to prove their competence by demonstrating that they had undertaken appropriate training. (Paragraph 6.40)

Foxes

54 The three main aspects of foxhunting which give rise to concern on welfare grounds are: the chase; the "kill" by the hounds above ground; and digging-out/terrierwork.

55 There is a lack of scientific evidence about the welfare implications of hunting, although some post mortem reports have been received. The welfare implications of hunting need to be compared with those which arise from other methods such as shooting, and snaring.

56 The evidence which we have seen suggests that, in the case of the killing of a fox by hounds above ground, death is not always effected by a single bite to the neck or shoulders by the leading hound resulting in the dislocation of the cervical vertebrae. In a proportion of cases it results from massive injuries to the chest and vital organs, although insensibility and death will normally follow within a matter of seconds once the fox is caught. There is a lack of firm scientific evidence about the effect on the welfare of a fox of being closely pursued, caught and killed above ground by hounds. We are satisfied, nevertheless, that this experience seriously compromises the welfare of the fox. (Paragraph 6.49)

57 Although there is no firm scientific evidence, we are satisfied that the activity of digging out and shooting a fox involves a serious compromise of its welfare, bearing in mind the often protracted nature of the process and the fact that the fox is prevented from escaping. (Paragraph 6.52)

58 It is likely that, in the event of a ban on hunting, many farmers and landowners would resort to a greater degree than at present to other methods to control the numbers of foxes. We cannot say if this would lead to more, or fewer, foxes being killed than at present. (Paragraph 6.58)

59 None of the legal methods of fox control is without difficulty from an animal welfare perspective. Both snaring and shooting can have serious adverse welfare implications. (Paragraph 6.59)

60 Our tentative conclusion is that lamping using rifles, if carried out properly and in appropriate circumstances, has fewer adverse welfare implications than

hunting, including digging-out. However, in areas where lamping is not feasible or safe, there would be a greater use of other methods. We are less confident that the use of shotguns, particularly in daylight, is preferable to hunting from a welfare perspective. We consider that the use of snaring is a particular cause for concern. (Paragraph 6.60)

61   In practice, it is likely that some mixture of all of these methods would be used. In the event of a ban on hunting, it is possible that the welfare of foxes in upland areas could be affected adversely, unless dogs could be used, at least to flush foxes from cover. (Paragraph 6.61)

Hares

62   There are two areas of welfare concern in respect of hare hunting and coursing: the chase and the "kill". Although no scientific studies have been carried out, there is evidence that, in the case of coursing, there can be a significant delay before a hare which has been caught by the dogs is dispatched.

63   There is a lack of firm scientific evidence about the effect on the welfare of a hare of being closely pursued, caught and killed by hounds during hunting. We are satisfied, nevertheless, that although death and insensibility will normally follow within a matter of seconds, this experience seriously compromises the welfare of the hare. (Paragraph 6.67)

64   We are similarly satisfied that being pursued, caught and killed by dogs during coursing seriously compromises the welfare of the hare. It is clear, moreover, that, if the dog or dogs catch the hare, they do not always kill it quickly. There can also sometimes be a significant delay, in "driven" coursing, before the "picker up" reaches the hare and dispatches it (if it is not already dead). In the case of "walked up" coursing, the delay is likely to be even longer. (Paragraph 6.68)

65   In the event of a ban on hunting and coursing hares, it seems likely that a few more would be shot than at present. There are concerns about the welfare implications of shooting hares because of wounding rates. (Paragraph 6.69)

Mink

66   There have been no scientific studies of the welfare implications of hunting in relation to mink.

67   There is a lack of firm scientific evidence about the welfare implications of hunting mink. There seems reason to suppose, however, that being closely pursued, caught and killed by hounds, or being dug out or bolted, seriously compromises the welfare of the mink. The kill, by the hounds or by shooting, is normally quick once the mink is caught. In the absence of hunting, more mink would probably be killed by shooting and, mainly, trapping. These methods involve welfare implications but

16

we do not have sufficient evidence to conclude how they compare with those raised by hunting. **(Paragraph 6.71)**

The welfare of other animals incidentally affected by hunting

68 Concerns have been expressed about the welfare of wildlife incidentally affected by hunting and of farm animals and pets.

69 **There is some evidence that hunting incidentally affects the welfare of wildlife. In particular, we have been informed about the stopping-up of badger setts and a few isolated cases of disturbance to otter – both of which are protected species - and wildfowl during mink hunting. The frequency of such incidents is disputed. (Paragraph 6.75)**

70 **The welfare of pets which are attacked by hounds is clearly compromised, and their owners often suffer great distress. (Paragraph 6.76)**

The welfare of the hounds and horses

71 Concerns have been expressed about the welfare of hounds and the horses involved in hunting. These have tended to focus on injuries or deaths of hounds on roads or railway lines; injuries to terriers during terrierwork; and the common practice of putting hounds down at the end of their working lives. In relation to horses, concerns are sometimes expressed about the injuries received during hunting.

72 **We have received evidence of injuries to terriers during terrierwork. This clearly involves some compromise of the terrier's welfare when it occurs. (Paragraph 6.84)**

73 **We have received no evidence that hunting, in general, raises greater concerns about the welfare of the horses and dogs involved than other activities such as horse racing or greyhound racing, except for small number of deaths or injuries to hounds which result from straying on roads or railways lines. There are other concerns about the hunts' practice in putting down hounds which are considered too old to hunt and about the numbers of hounds which might be put down in the event of a ban. Similarly, there are concerns over the fate of surplus horses if hunting were to be banned, and of retired racehorses. Strictly speaking, these matters do not raise animal welfare concerns provided that the hounds and horses are destroyed humanely. Rather, they raise ethical issues, which are outside our terms of reference. But any need to put down hounds or horses, in the event of a ban, could be minimised if there was a suitable lead-in time before it was implemented. (Paragraph 6.85)**

Chapter 7   MANAGEMENT AND CONSERVATION OF HABITAT AND OTHER WILDLIFE

74   The hunts argue that hunting has played, and continues to play, an important role in creating, managing and conserving habitat which is valuable for plant and animal life.

75   Hunts are involved in activities such as managing woodland, scrub and hedgerows, as well as helping to carry out censuses of deer and hares. A judgement about the importance of these activities needs to be made in the context of major changes in agricultural land use and practice, the introduction of agri-environment schemes and any evidence of negative impacts arising from such matters as the disturbance caused to habitat and wildlife by hunting.

76   **It is difficult to distinguish the effect that hunting has had on influencing land management practices from the broader impact of game management for shooting. Foxhunting has undoubtedly had a beneficial influence in lowland parts of England in conserving and promoting habitat which has helped biodiversity, although any effect has been in specific localities. In the case of hare hunting and coursing, it seems clear that those interested in these activities have helped to maintain habitats which are favourable to the hare and to a number of other species. (Paragraph 7.32)**

77   **Hunting has clearly played a very significant role in the past in the formation of the rural landscape and in the creation and management of areas of nature conservation. Nowadays, however, hunting with dogs is likely to form only a relatively minor factor in determining farmers' and landowners' land management practices. It still plays a role, though, in certain localities in respect of woodland planting and management. (Paragraph 7.42)**

78   **Hunting exerts much less influence than agricultural market and policy trends, the management of game for shooting or incentives under agri-environment schemes. With the possible exception of hare conservation, a ban on hunting with dogs would be unlikely to have a major impact from a conservation perspective. In the case of the hare, on those estates which favour hare coursing or hunting, rather than shooting, a ban might lead farmers and landowners to pay less attention to encouraging hare numbers. The loss of habitat suitable for hares could have serious consequences for a number of birds and other animals. (Paragraph 7.43)**

Chapter 8   DRAG AND BLOODHOUND HUNTING

79   Drag and bloodhound hunting involve following a man-made trail, either an artificial scent or the scent of a human being. It is frequently argued that they could provide a very satisfactory replacement for live quarry hunting, enabling hunters, followers, hounds and horses to switch from one activity to the other.

80   The research which we commissioned, and the evidence which we heard, indicates that the picture is more complicated than this. There are potential difficulties over such matters as the availability of suitable land, the relative "predictability" of these sports compared with live quarry hunting, the lack of attraction for non-mounted followers, the problems in producing interesting "houndwork" and the fact that they tend to appeal most at present to those who want concentrated riding and jumping.

81   **Drag and bloodhound hunting are different from live quarry hunting. In particular, they involve the laying of a man-made trail. They lack the unpredictability and, consequently, some of the interest associated with a live quarry. The hound work, especially in the case of the draghounds, is less subtle and complex. (Paragraph 8.44)**

82   **There would be greater incentive, in the event of a ban, to expand the number of drag and bloodhound packs and the level of participation in both sports. Because bloodhounds are in short supply, and are not easy to breed, any growth in the short term would mainly come from using foxhounds for draghunting. The scope for expansion is impossible to predict with any accuracy at present because the existence of hunting as a complementary activity means that there has been little motivation in practice to develop the sports. The popularity of horse riding, however, suggests that greater efforts would be made to develop substitute activities in the event of a ban on hunting. The kinds of opportunities that drag and bloodhound hunting already offer in some areas might be expanded. There is some scope for adjusting the level of skill required in drag and bloodhound hunting to riders of different ability levels. There is also possible scope for developing other forms of cross country riding, possibly on a fee-paying basis. (Paragraph 8.45)**

83   **Some of the evidence we received suggested that there would be considerable reluctance on the part of farmers to make available sufficient, suitable contiguous land and that this could considerably limit the growth of these sports. It is questionable whether the possibility of making payments to farmers would overcome these difficulties. A payment system would not be easy to devise and operate and would be likely to increase significantly participants' costs. (Paragraph 8.46)**

84   **A few of those who presently take part in live quarry hunting already go drag or bloodhound hunting as well. In the event of a ban, some more would take up one or other of these sports. And, no doubt, if more diverse types of draghunting were developed, some new recruits would come from those who do not presently hunt live quarry. But others would either not give these sports a try or would not persevere with them. In particular, they offer little attraction to non-mounted participants and followers. Evidence from elsewhere, in particular Germany, suggests that draghunting and bloodhound hunting would not change materially or experience a major upsurge in popularity. Instead it would be simply one - and not necessarily the most important - of a number of equestrian activities to which participants in mounted hunting might turn in the event of a ban. (Paragraph 8.47)**

85   In the event of a ban on live hare coursing, drag coursing might have some appeal, especially to those owners of greyhounds who are essentially interested in racing their dogs. It would have less appeal for those people who particularly enjoy the contest between the hare and the dog. (Paragraph 8.52)

86   It is unlikely that either drag and bloodhound hunting or drag coursing would of themselves mitigate to any substantial extent any adverse effects on the rural economy or the social life of the countryside arising from a ban on hunting. (Paragraph 8.53)

Chapter 9   PRACTICAL ASPECTS OF HUNTING: THE CONCERNS

87   There are a number of aspects of the way that hunting is carried out which give rise to particular concern. (Paragraph 9.2)

Trespass, disruption and disturbance

88   There are complaints of trespass, disruption and disturbance by the hunts. These include trespass on roads and railway lines, invasion of people's property and blocking of roads and lanes. There is also concern about the way in which hunts sometimes deal with complaints.

89   There are too many cases of trespass, disruption and disturbance. These are most common where hunts operate too close to residential areas and interfere with the movement of traffic on roads. We do not want to exaggerate these problems but they can cause distress to the individuals and families involved. To some extent hunts could avoid these problems themselves, by being more selective about the areas in which they hunt. This would be likely to lead to fewer hunts. Steps that might be taken, in the absence of a ban, include: restricting hunting in certain parts of hunts' countries; reducing or amalgamating the number of hunts; requiring permission to be obtained in writing on a regular basis from farmers and landowners; penalising trespass, or repeated trespass, over land where permission has not been given; and improving means of seeking and obtaining redress. (Paragraph 9.8)

Openness

90   Concerns about hunting are exacerbated by a sense that it is not really open to public scrutiny.

91   In the absence of a ban, organised hunting should be conducted on a more open basis than at present in order to provide greater reassurance that approved procedures are being followed. One possible option would be the appointment of individuals as independent monitors who would have the freedom to take photographs and video evidence. Their task would be to observe organised hunting and to take up with the hunt, and others as necessary, any concerns that they might have about the way in which it is being conducted. They might also serve as a channel for complaints by others. It would no doubt be helpful if monitors were appointed by a reputable, independent body. (Paragraph 9.10)

Autumn/cub hunting

92   Autumn/cub hunting takes place in the late summer/early autumn. It is argued that it is important in reducing the numbers of foxes; that it disperses the young foxes; and that it serves to train young hounds. These arguments are not wholly persuasive. Moreover, the practice of "holding up" (i.e. driving foxes back into the wood or coppice) causes concern.

93   In the absence of a ban, consideration could be given to a number of options for responding to the concerns about autumn/cub hunting. These options include: prohibiting the practice entirely; introducing a closed season for hunting foxes, so that hunting would start at a later date than it does at present; permitting it only in those areas where it was clearly necessary as a means of controlling fox numbers; and prohibiting the practice of "holding up". (Paragraph 9.16)

Digging-out and bolting/Terrierwork

94   There is concern about terrierwork. It is felt that a fox, once it has gone to ground, should not be dug out. There are also reports of injuries caused in fights between terriers and foxes underground. On the other hand, it is argued that terrierwork is important in controlling fox numbers, especially in upland sheep-rearing and game management areas.

95   Digging-out and bolting foxes is a complex issue because of the perceived needs in different parts of England and Wales. In the absence of a ban, serious consideration could be given as to whether this practice should be allowed to continue and, if so, under what conditions. Possible options would be to ban it altogether; confine it to those areas where it is considered necessary as a means of controlling fox numbers or in the interests of animal welfare; make the practice subject to the general legislation on cruelty by removing the present exemptions for hunting; or improve monitoring by the hunts and by any independent monitors. (Paragraph 9.20)

Stopping-up

96   There are complaints that hunts are not complying with the legal requirements governing the way in which they may stop up badger setts. Some people also object to the stopping up of foxes' earths.

97   There have been many suggestions put to us that, at times, hunts and others contravene the law relating to the stopping-up of badger setts. One option, in the

absence of a ban on hunting, would be to remove the present exemption for hunts. In the case of stopping-up of foxes' earths, there are a number of possible options which could be considered in the absence of a ban. These include: prohibiting the practice entirely; confining it to those areas where it is considered necessary in the interests of controlling fox numbers; or otherwise limiting the circumstances in which it may be done or the way in which it can be carried out. (Paragraph 9.24)

Use of artificial earths

98   Artificial earths have been used by hunts to provide shelter for foxes and to provide shelter for foxes and to encourage them to live in suitable places.

99   The active use of artificial earths, with a view to hunting, is inconsistent with the stated objective of controlling fox numbers through hunting. In the absence of a ban, hunts could be required, or encouraged, to end this practice. (Paragraph 9.27)

Deliberately interfering with the quarry's flight

100   There is concern about deliberate direct interference by people with the quarry's flight. In the absence of a ban, action could be taken to amend, where necessary, the rules of the relevant associations and to ensure that such interference does not take place unless it is in the interests of the safety of the people or animals involved. In particular, provision could be made to ensure that there was no interference with the flight in order to prolong the chase, prevent the quarry escaping or to prevent it entering land where the hunt did not have permission to go. (Paragraph 9.30)

A closed season for hares

101   There is no closed season for culling hares.

102   There is understandable concern that the seasons for hare coursing and hunting are too long in relation to the hare's breeding season. In the absence of a ban on hunting, an option would be to introduce a closed season. Consideration would also need to be given to whether a closed season should apply to shooting. (Paragraph 9.33)

Hunting hinds with calves

103   Hunting hinds with a calf gives rise to understandable concern. It puts the hind in a position of having to choose between saving itself and staying with the calf. We are not able to say how often this situation occurs but action could be taken to end this practice in the absence of a ban. (Paragraph 9.35)

Legislative action

104   In the event of a ban on hunting, the various concerns would be resolved, in principle, subject to any exemptions or exceptions permitted in the legislation. There would be no need, therefore, to consider separate action. In the absence of a ban, one possible legislative approach would be to remove the present exemptions for hunting in the Wild Mammals (Protection) Act 1996. This would be an important signal and give opponents of hunting a clearer opportunity to test their views about cruelty in the courts. In practice, this might have only a limited effect since the activities penalised by that Act have little relevance to hunting. (Paragraph 9.39)

Hunting practised outside the registered hunts and coursing clubs

105   A great deal of hunting takes place outside the regulatory framework of the registered hunts and coursing clubs. Consideration would have to be given, in the absence of a ban, to the way in which any changes made should apply to these activities.

106   If action is taken to address any of the concerns about the way hunting is carried out, it would be important to consider whether, and if so how, it could be applied to hunting undertaken by those operating outside the registered hunts and coursing clubs. (Paragraph 9.42)

Licensing and regulation

107   Many other countries have licensing systems to cover hunting, governing such matters as the suitability of the applicant and their knowledge of hunting. In the absence of a ban, consideration could be given to establishing such a system here.

108   The fact that hunting (of all kinds) is not subject to some form of licensing contrasts markedly with the position in a number of other countries. (Paragraph 9.52)

109   The existing self-regulation operated by the various hunts and coursing associations has been adapted over the years to deal with emerging concerns and evidence of damage to animal welfare. It will be strengthened by the establishment of the Independent Supervisory Authority for Hunting. None of this regulatory activity applies, however, to hunting carried out by those outside this regulatory framework. It is a reasonable assumption that any adverse impact on animal welfare is greater in the case of the latter than it is with hunting under the auspices of the various self-regulatory bodies. In the absence of a ban, consideration could be given to strengthening the supervision of these forms of hunting. It is for consideration whether, in that event, there would be advantage in establishing some form of licensing system to control all forms of hunting with dogs. (Paragraph 9.53)

Further research

110   There are a number of issues which would probably benefit from further research work, if a ban on hunting was not introduced.

111   Consideration could be given, in the absence of a ban on hunting, to commissioning research on a number of topics.   (Paragraph 9.56)

Chapter 10   IMPLEMENTING A BAN

Compatibility with the European Convention on Human Rights

112   It has been argued that a ban on hunting would be incompatible with the European Convention on Human Rights. The arguments principally centre on whether a ban can be regarded as an interference with "respect for private life" and, if so, whether this is justified under the terms of the Convention; and on whether a ban can be regarded as an interference with property rights and, if so, whether this is justified in the "general interest".

113   Legislation to ban hunting might be open to challenge under Article 1 Protocol I (property rights) and, possibly, Article 8 (respect for private life) of the European Convention on Human Rights.   We are not qualified to express an opinion on whether any challenge along these lines would succeed. Key questions would be whether the undoubted interference with property, and possibly with private life, was justified under Convention principles, bearing in mind the nature of the interference and the latitude enjoyed by the national authorities.   An important consideration would be whether legislators could point to unnecessary suffering or some other reference point beyond mere disapproval, to reflect the general interest (or, to the extent necessary, the protection of morals and pressing social need).   A relevant issue would be the form of the Bill: one which required proof of unnecessary suffering, or some similar test, would be less open to argument than one which banned hunting per se. (Paragraph 10.17)

Scope and form

114   In preparing legislation to ban hunting consideration would have to be given to the precise scope of the Bill; the need for exemptions or exceptions; whether the prohibited activities can be defined sufficiently clearly; whether the main offence should be defined closely or be cast in broad terms; what the mental element of the offence should be; the need for secondary offences and enabling powers; and its geographical coverage.

115   Consideration should be given to whether any ban would be manifestly unjust, bearing in mind the activities caught and not caught by it. (Paragraph 10.28)

116 Consideration should be given to whether any ban could be framed sufficiently clearly to enable people to regulate their conduct. A central issue would be whether a Bill would need to have a detailed definition of the prohibited offence and any exceptions or exemptions. (Paragraph 10.29)

117 It would be necessary to consider the form of exceptions that should apply in particular areas, especially sheep-rearing upland areas, and for particular cases, such as the pursuit of injured deer or dealing with orphaned foxes underground or for research purposes. It would be necessary to establish the number and type of dogs that should be permitted for this purpose. (Paragraph 10.30)

118 Unless there was a good reason on objective grounds, we do not think it would be satisfactory to have different legislative provisions in force in different regions of the country. (Paragraph 10.31)

Timing

119 There are three options in respect of the implementation of a ban: implementing it at an early fixed date; implementing it at a later fixed date; and providing an order-making power to allow various provisions to be brought into force subsequently.

120 It would be feasible to implement a ban quickly. This would have the advantage of certainty, encouraging those concerned to get on as rapidly as possible with making any necessary adjustments. There are stronger arguments for allowing a reasonable period of adjustment. This would enable more time, for example, to reduce naturally the number of hounds; to develop draghunting and other activities; to put in place new population management strategies; and to mitigate wherever possible any social and economic consequences of a ban. (Paragraph 10.35)

121 A strong objection to a delay in implementing a ban would be that, in the meantime, various practices which opponents of hunting view as particularly objectionable would be allowed to continue. It might be possible to meet some of these objections by taking action in the meantime to ban or curtail some of these activities by considering the options discussed in Chapter 9. (Paragraph 10.36)

Enforcement

122 It is argued that the police might have some difficulties in enforcing, and in giving sufficient priority to, a ban on hunting.

123 Legislation implementing a ban might well pose some enforcement difficulties for the police. These matters should be considered by Parliament when examining a Bill. (Paragraph 10.41)

Controls on hunting

124   There are various matters relating to other methods of control which might be considered in the event of a ban on hunting.

125   In the event of a ban on hunting, consideration should be given to the training of stalkers, the use of snares and the possible case for a closed season for culling hares. (Paragraph 10.46)

Other population management measures

126   Other than in relation to hares, there are no arrangements for monitoring or managing mammal populations.

127   Consideration should be given to the possibility of developing arrangements for monitoring and managing the populations of the four quarry species and other mammals. A ban on hunting would make it necessary to review the existing arrangements for managing deer in the Devon and Somerset area in order to ensure that an effective strategic management system is in place. (Paragraph 10.49)

Encouraging other activities

128   The extent to which drag and bloodhound hunting would be taken up, in the event of a ban, would depend on its appeal in comparison with other leisure activities. The Jockey Club and others would no doubt consider the future of point-to-pointing. No central government action would seem to be necessary.

129   In the event of a ban on hunting, there is no specific action which central government should take to promote other activities such as drag or bloodhound hunting. (Paragraph 10.53)

Financial, economic and employment aspects

130   Local action might be needed to deal with the employment and economic consequences of a ban. It would be necessary to consider whether any action was required in respect of the fallen stock service and the destruction of hounds.

131   In the event of a ban on hunting, consideration would need to be given to possible action in respect of the fallen stock service provided by many hunts and to whether there would be a case for compensation if hounds had to be destroyed and hunts had no further use for their kennels. (Paragraph 10.60)

CHAPTER 1

INTRODUCTION

Terms of reference

1.1   This chapter sets out our terms of reference and describes how we went about our work.

1.2   The Committee's terms of reference were:

"To inquire into:

- the practical aspects of different types of hunting with dogs and its impact on the rural economy, agriculture and pest control, the social and cultural life of the countryside, the management and conservation of wildlife, and animal welfare in particular areas of England and Wales;

- the consequences for these issues of any ban on hunting with dogs; and

- how any ban might be implemented.

To report the findings to the Secretary of State for the Home Department".

1.3   The Home Secretary made clear that he intended that the Committee should focus on the hunting with dogs of foxes, deer, hares and mink. He also indicated that he regarded the use of dogs to retrieve dead or injured quarry as being outside our terms of reference.

1.4   It is important to stress that we were not asked to recommend whether hunting[1] should be banned. Nor were we asked to consider moral or ethical issues. Instead, our task was to set out as clearly as possible the impact of hunting on certain matters, the effects of a ban on those matters and how a ban might be implemented. Chapter 2 discusses the scope of our work in greater detail.

1.5   We were appointed in December 1999 and were asked to report by "late spring". This meant that we had about six months to complete our inquiry.[2] Inevitably, this placed some limitations on the way we went about our work: for example, there was not time - even if we had wished to do so - to take extensive oral evidence. Nor could we follow up in great detail any matters which, though of interest, were not central to our inquiry. We hope, nevertheless, that the open way in which we approached our work,

---

[1] For the sake of simplicity, the term "hunting" is normally used in this report to describe the activities with which the Committee was concerned. See paragraphs 2.66 to 2.70 for a description of other types of hunting with dogs, which were outside our terms of reference. In other countries, "hunting" often has an even broader meaning, encompassing shooting.

[2] We note, in passing, that the Scott Henderson Committee - admittedly with a wider remit (see footnote 3) - took two years to report.

which we describe below, enabled all the interested parties to contribute fully despite the tight timetable.

Background to the Inquiry

1.6   The immediate background to the setting-up of our inquiry was continuing debate, in Parliament and elsewhere, about a possible ban on hunting. This followed the failure of a Bill, introduced by Mr Michael Foster MP in November 1997, to make progress beyond Report Stage in the House of Commons.

1.7   Mr Foster's Bill is one of a succession of Bills which have been introduced since the last full-scale inquiry into hunting, undertaken by the Scott Henderson Committee, reported in 1951.[3] These Bills have either sought to ban hunting with dogs in general or specific activities such as foxhunting or hare coursing. Even while we have been undertaking our work, two further Private Member's Bills have been introduced, Lord Watson has introduced a Bill before the Scottish Parliament and amendments have been tabled to the Countryside and Rights of Way Bill.

Approach

1.8   Our examination, in the rest of our report, of the issues surrounding hunting inevitably leaves us open to the inference that we support a ban; that we are opposed to it; or that we favour some "middle way". We need to make the position clear. We have reached no view on these matters - because we were not asked to do so - and nothing in the rest of our report should be construed to the contrary.

1.9   In carrying out our work we tried to be as open and as even-handed as possible. For example, we made available on our website as much as possible of the written evidence which we received from the main organisations and a number of individuals.[4] We were also accompanied on visits by representatives of the two main "pro" and "anti" organisations: the Countryside Alliance and Deadline 2000.[5] This helped to provide reassurance to us and to others that we were seeing hunting activities as they would normally take place.

1.10   The following paragraphs describe the main ways in which we collected evidence.

---

[3] The Scott Henderson Committee had a wider remit than our inquiry, being asked to inquire into practices or activities which might involve cruelty to all British wild mammals, whether at large or in captivity, but excluding such matters as the killing of captive animals for food or use in scientific experiments. *Report of the Committee on Cruelty to Wild Mammals.* June 1951. Cmd 8266

[4] The Scott Henderson Committee took all its oral evidence in private and did not publish any of its written evidence.

[5] The Countryside Alliance (CA) represents the following organisations: Association of Masters of Harriers and Beagles (AMHB), Central Committee of Fell Packs (CCFP), Federation of Welsh Packs (FWP), Masters of Basset Hounds Association (MBHA), Masters of Deerhounds Association (MDHA), Masters of Foxhounds Association (MFHA), Masters of Mink Hounds Association (MMHA), National Coursing Club (NCC) and National Working Terrier Federation (NWTF). Deadline 2000 comprises the International Fund for Animal Welfare (IFAW), the League Against Cruel Sports (LACS) and the Royal Society for the Prevention of Cruelty to Animals (RSPCA).

Written evidence

1.11   We issued a request for written evidence on 19 January 2000 inviting responses by 21 February. This request was sent to 247 organisations and placed on the Committee's website. We received written evidence from 317 organisations and 53 individuals. A list of the main organisations which responded is at Appendices 1 and 2.[6] [7] Appendix 3 contains an analysis of the written evidence sent to us by members of the public. We subsequently issued a further request for written evidence on 17 April 2000. This invited brief observations on evidence which had already been submitted and on other material which we had posted on our website. This request was sent to those organisations which had submitted evidence on the first round and was also posted on our website. We received 79 responses, all of which were placed on our website.[8]

Oral evidence

1.12   We took oral evidence from the Countryside Alliance and Deadline 2000 on 6 and 10 April 2000. These sessions were held in public and transcripts were placed on the website.[9]

Research

1.13   We commissioned research on the following topics:

- hunting with dogs: expenditure and numbers employed by hunts and their followers

- the direct and indirect effects of hunting with dogs on the rural economy and the longer-term effects of a ban

- the effects of hunting with dogs on the social and cultural life of the countryside

- management of the population of foxes, deer, hares and mink and the impact of hunting with dogs

- methods of controlling foxes, deer, hares and mink

- the effects of hunting with dogs on the welfare of foxes, deer, hares and mink

- drag and bloodhound hunting.

---

[6] The bulk of this evidence, barring material such as published reports, is available on a CD Rom published with this report.
[7] Several anti-hunting bodies declined to co-operate with our Inquiry.
[8] This evidence is also on the CD Rom.
[9] The transcripts of the proceedings are on the CD Rom.

Further details of the research are given in Appendix 4.

1.14   Draft final reports of the research were made publicly available prior to our holding seminars to discuss the findings.[10] These seminars also took place in public and transcripts were made available on the website. Each seminar took the form of a discussion between the researchers, the Committee, representatives of the Countryside Alliance and Deadline 2000 and other expert contributors. Following the seminars the researchers produced their final reports. These reports are discussed in later chapters. We also held a seminar on implementing a ban on hunting: this issue is discussed in Chapter 10 of our report.[11]

1.15   We also commissioned the following pieces of background briefing and research:

- an interpretative account of foxhunting by Dr Garry Marvin of the Roehampton Institute, University of Surrey, on which we have drawn in Chapter 2

- post mortem reports on four foxes killed by hunts - discussed in Chapter 6[12]

- post mortem reports on twelve hares killed during hare coursing - also discussed in Chapter 6[13]

- a survey of Farming and Wildlife Advisory Group advisers - discussed in Chapter 7[14]

- information about hunting in other countries, compiled by Professor S.R. and D.F. Harrop of the University of Kent - summarised in Appendix 9.

Visits

1.16   We thought it important to see at first hand as wide a range of hunting activities as possible, including drag and bloodhound hunting and drag coursing. Our visits included seeing a demonstration drag hunt in Germany. Because of the time of year, however, we were not able to observe autumn/cub hunting: see paragraph 2.29. We also observed lamping i.e. shooting at night using a bright spotlamp. Details of our visits are at Appendix 5. On our visits, in addition to observing hunting, we spent time talking to those present about their views on hunting and the impact of a ban. We also visited some hunt kennels and stables, a wildlife hospital and a sanctuary run by the League Against Cruel Sports.

---

[10] The draft and final versions of the research reports mentioned in paragraph 1.14, plus the transcripts of the seminar proceedings, are also on the CD Rom.

[11] The papers produced for this seminar by the Countryside Alliance and Deadline 2000, plus the transcript of the proceedings, are on the CD Rom.

[12] The post mortem reports are on the CD Rom.

[13] The post mortem reports are on the CD Rom.

[14] Summary on the CD Rom.

Meetings

1.17 We considered holding fully open public meetings. However, discussions with the Countryside Alliance and Deadline 2000 suggested that joint meetings would not be productive. We therefore held four meetings with Countryside Alliance supporters in Exmoor, Coventry, Builth Wells and Leeds, and three meetings with Deadline 2000 supporters in Taunton, Wrexham and York. Each organisation was responsible for issuing invitations to its own supporters. Summaries of the issues raised at these meetings were placed on our website.[15] In addition, we attended two informal gatherings with Deadline 2000 supporters. These took place in Taunton and London and were intended to provide the same opportunities to talk informally to us as hunt supporters had enjoyed during our visits.

Scientific and legal assistance

1.18 In the latter stages of our work we appointed Professor David Macdonald and Mr Michael Fordham to assist us, respectively, on scientific and legal issues.

---

[15] Also on the CD Rom.

CHAPTER 2

HUNTING

2.1   The main purpose of this chapter is to describe the different types of hunting covered by our terms of reference. We also give a brief summary of the legal position. And we say something about the way organised hunting is run and financed and what it costs. Finally, we give some information about other types of hunting, involving the use of dogs, which fall outside our terms of reference and about hunting-related activities such as point-to-point and National Hunt racing.

Introduction

2.2   Hunting with dogs covers a wide range of activities. The following paragraphs summarise the main types of hunting with dogs with which we are concerned.

2.3   The main ways in which foxes are hunted with dogs are:

- on horseback by registered[16] packs of foxhounds and harriers

- on foot by the registered and affiliated foxhound packs in the Lake District (the 'Fell packs') and by registered and unregistered packs in Wales

- by registered and unregistered gunpacks in Wales, which use hounds mainly to flush out foxes to waiting guns

- by the use of terriers, in conjunction with the above packs or by other groups or individuals such as gamekeepers, in order to locate or kill the fox underground and to dig it out or bolt it to nets, guns or lurchers or other "long dogs"

- by the use of lurchers and other "long dogs" at night to kill foxes caught in the beam of a powerful lamp.

2.4   Deer are hunted on horseback by the three registered packs hunting red deer in the south west of England and by at least two unregistered packs hunting roe deer.

2.5   Hares are hunted on horseback by the registered packs of harriers and, on foot, by the registered packs of beagles and basset hounds.

2.6   Hare coursing is practised by registered coursing clubs using greyhounds or other dogs and by other groups and individuals using lurchers or other "long dogs".

---

[16] "Registered" means registered with, or affiliated to, one of the hunting or coursing associations: see Appendix 6 for further details of these bodies

2.7   Mink hunting takes place by the registered packs of mink hounds and by the use of terriers in conjunction with these packs.

2.8   The best known, and most visible, types of hunting come under the auspices of various bodies such as the Masters of Foxhounds Association (MFHA). But a good deal of hunting takes place outside this regulatory framework, sometimes involving trespass on private land. It is impossible to quantify accurately how much hunting takes place informally, but the fact that it is extensive has considerable implications for estimating the effects of hunting, the impact of a ban and how a ban might be implemented. We return to this aspect in later chapters of our report.

Legal Position

2.9   The registered packs and coursing clubs operate a system of self-regulation,[17] but there is no body of legislation in England and Wales which is specifically concerned with hunting. The Wild Mammals (Protection) Act 1996 prohibits the carrying out of various acts with intent to cause suffering to wild mammals. There is an exception, however, in respect of hunting and coursing provided that an animal is killed "in a reasonably swift and humane manner" and provided that the individual concerned is not trespassing. There is a further exception in respect of acts done by a dog used for the purposes of killing or taking any wild mammal. There are also specific provisions in the Protection of Badgers Act 1992 which allow registered hunts to stop up badger setts provided that certain conditions are met. In addition, there are various provisions in other pieces of legislation, summarised in Appendix 8, which deal with such matters as the prohibition on the sale of hare during the breeding season.

Hunting : a description

<u>Fox hunting</u>

Hunting by registered packs

(i)   Background

2.10   Organised traditional mounted foxhunting in England and Wales has a relatively short history compared with the hunting of hares and deer. By the late thirteenth century, King Edward I had a royal pack of foxhounds but it was not until several centuries later that foxhunting was generally taken up by the nobility.[18] Today there are some 175 foxhunting packs in England and Wales registered with the MFHA.[19] There are also nine fell packs registered with, or affiliated to, the Central Committee of Fell Packs (CCFP).[20] In addition, there are seven packs of harriers, registered with the Association of Masters

---

[17] See Appendix 6
[18] *Foxes*. David Macdonald. Colin Baxter Photography, Grantown-on-Spey, Scotland. 2000
[19] MFHA letter to the Inquiry
[20] CCFP1,2.2

of Harriers and Beagles (AMHB), which mainly hunt foxes, under MFHA rules. There are also another two harrier packs which are registered to hunt foxes.[21]

2.11 The position in Wales is less clear and more fluid. There are 48 foxhunting packs registered with the Federation of Welsh Packs (FWP), which include 27 Welsh-based packs of the MFHA, and 30 registered with the Welsh Farmers' Fox Control Association (WFFCA), although some of these are also registered with the FWP.[22] However, both these bodies have been formed fairly recently and represent only a proportion of the total number of packs in Wales. Some estimates put the number of unregistered packs in Wales at two or three times those of registered packs.[23]

2.12 Hunting by the registered packs takes place from August/September until March/April. The hunting season in a particular area depends on local circumstances, especially the need to avoid damaging crops or disturbing livestock. In total there are some 15,000 meets throughout the season. Most hunts go out twice a week but some of the larger hunts go out more frequently. According to a survey commissioned by the Countryside Alliance, there are about 67,000 subscribers and hunt supporters, the great majority of whom would be involved in foxhunting.[24]

2.13 About 14,000-15,000 foxes a year are killed by MFHA packs and a further 7,000-10,000 by other registered packs.[25] About a third of the foxes killed by MFHA hunts are dug out and shot but the percentages vary significantly in different parts of the country, ranging from 18% in the East Midlands to 77% in mid-Wales.[26]

2.14 Those hunts covered in a Produce Studies survey[27] kill, on average, 79 foxes over 74 hunting days. This amounts to just over 1 fox per day's hunting, averaged over the year. The number of foxes killed per hunting day does not vary a great deal by region, the lowest being 0.8 per day in the North and the highest 1.3 per day in Wales.

2.15 A typical MFHA pack has an income of £73,000 a year, although there are some important regional variations. The average in the Midlands and East Anglia region is £125,000, in contrast to £35,000 in Wales. On average, there are 120 subscribers per hunt and 200 members of supporters' clubs.[28] [29]

2.16 About 40 to 50 per cent of the hunts' income goes on employment costs. On average, a typical hunt employs 2.5 full-time and 1.4 part-time staff (excluding employed Masters), although this varies with the size of the hunt. On average, they look after four

---

[21] MFHA letter to the Inquiry
[22] FWP 1, 4.01; MFHA letter to the Inquiry; WFFCA1, Appendix E1
[23] FWP – telephone conversation
[24] Countryside Alliance (CA) 2,7.7.1
[25] Macdonald et al, 5.2.3,5.2.4 (See Chapter 5 for full reference to research report by Macdonald et al.)
[26] Macdonald et al, 5.2.5
[27] Produce Studies Research National Survey of Hunts
[28] Ibid
[29] For further details of hunts' income and expenditure by quarry species, see Appendix 7

horses that are owned by the hunt, 31 couple of entered hounds and nine couple of unentered hounds.[30] [31]

2.17   Putting on a day's hunting costs an average of £1,000 after all overheads have been allocated.[32]   Again, there are regional variations. The number of days' hunting is similar across regions and the differences in income are reflected in differences in the average cost of putting on a day's hunting. In the Midlands and East Anglia it is £1,500 per day, compared with £500 per day in Wales.[33]

2.18   Averaging out over the year and across all foxhunts, each fox killed costs £930. Looking at it by region, the cost per fox killed varies from almost £1,500 in the South to £380 in Wales. Looking at the figures for the individual hunts, the range is much bigger. There are six hunts, mainly in Wales, which have a cost per fox of under £100. At the other end of the spectrum, seven hunts have a cost per fox of over £3,000. In large part this reflects the extent to which hunting can be seen as a recreational activity or, alternatively, as efficient pest control. If anything, these figures probably understate the full cost, particularly with the hunts with a lower income, as some labour is provided on a voluntary basis. On the other hand, there will have been some additional "lambing" calls when the hunt will have gone out without the field and which are not included in these figures for the number of days' hunting.

2.19   The following paragraphs briefly describe the main features of a day's foxhunting with mounted followers.

(ii)   A day's hunting

2.20   In the days leading up to a hunt the Master or Huntsman[34] is expected to contact farmers and landowners in the area to discuss any potential difficulties such as growing crops or fields in which livestock are being held. Many hunts take steps the night before, or early on the day of the hunt, to block up the entrances to earths, badger setts and artificial places such as drains. This is to ensure that foxes stay above ground after they have hunted during the night and to prevent them from going to ground once the hunt has started. Where earths have been stopped they are required by the MFHA rules to be opened up again at the end of the day's hunting.

2.21   Typically, riders, hounds and followers gather together at the meet at about 11:00 am. This is usually held at a farm or outside a public house or on a village green. After refreshments and any announcements, the Huntsman, the hunt staff and hounds will "move off" to the place where it is planned to start hunting. The mounted field, typically 30 at a mid-week meet and 50 at weekends, led by the Field Master, will follow at a

---

[30] Produce Studies Research National Survey of Hunts

[31] "Entered hounds" are those that have hunted. "Unentered hounds" have yet to hunt for the first time

[32] The costs quoted here and elsewhere in this chapter are in relation to the hunts' income and expenditure and exclude the sums paid by those who follow hunts, either mounted or on foot

[33] Produce Studies Research National Survey of Hunts

[34] The terms 'Master' and 'Huntsman' are used by those involved to cover both sexes. We therefore use them in our report

distance. A similar number of other followers will set off, often in vehicles, for a suitable vantage point.

2.22   The hounds will be encouraged to spread out to "draw" (search) for a fox in woodland or rough ground. If they find a scent, the hounds will "speak" (give voice excitedly) and follow the "line". Sometimes the hounds will come across a fox and kill it immediately ("chop" it) before it has had a chance to flee. In other cases, the hounds, followed at a distance by the mounted field, who may have to take an indirect route, will pursue the fox or, rather, its scent. Often, the hounds will lose the scent altogether, as a result of the scenting conditions or the fox's movements. They may have to "check" in order to rediscover it. If the hounds are successful in their pursuit, they will get close enough to the fox to see it and will then catch it up, kill it and usually tear at the carcass ("break it up"). The length of the chase may vary considerably, from a few minutes to well over an hour or even longer, but the average is some 15 to 20 minutes. The distance covered may be anything up to six or seven miles, in a circular or twisting line.[35]   The Huntsman, once he or she has caught up with the hounds, will call them off. The tail ("brush") of the fox, or possibly its feet, may be removed and given to one of the followers. Generally, few riders and followers will be present at the kill.[36]

2.23   Quite frequently, instead of being caught by the hounds, the fox will go to ground, typically in a fox earth. According to the rules of the MFHA, if the fox has gone to ground in a natural earth, it may be dug out and killed if the farmer or landowner has requested that any foxes going to ground on his or her land should be dug out.[37] It cannot be released to be hunted again. The decision whether to dig out is for the Master to take and may turn on the difficulty of doing so or the damage which might be caused in the process. If, however, the fox has taken refuge in a man-made structure, or in a place such as rocks where it cannot be dug out, the fox may be "bolted", by putting a terrier down, and hunted again. The MFHA rules require that the fox must be given a sporting chance to escape before the hounds are "laid on".

2.24   The same rules about digging-out apply to MFHA-registered members of the FWP and to those AMBH packs which hunt foxes. The CCFP's rules also require that the MFHA procedures should be followed, although we understand that more discretion is permitted because of the nature of the terrain and the greater emphasis on 'pest control'.

2.25   The task of dealing with a fox that has "gone to ground" falls to the terrierman.[38] In the case of the MFHA and related associations, the terrierman must be on the register of terriermen kept by the MFHA and must also hold a current licence from them.[39] If the fox is to be dug out, they will close, or net off, other possible exits and then put a terrier (usually with a radio tracking device) down the hole in order to locate the fox. The terrier

---

[35] MFHA 1,13

[36] We received a couple of letters referring to the practice of "blooding" i.e. smearing blood on the faces of new participants. It appears that this has now largely died out

[37] CA2, 8.4.2

[38] There are a few terrier women. The terms 'terrierman' and 'terriermen' are used by those involved to cover both sexes. We therefore use them in our report

[39] The WFFCA keeps its own list of terriermen, who are authorised to work only on a "meet by meet" basis

will either bolt the fox or drive it back to a stationary position. In the case of the latter, the terriermen will then block any exits from the earth and dig down to the fox, remove the terrier and shoot the fox in the head with a specially-adapted pistol. If the fox runs into a net, it will be held still and shot. The MFHA rules state that only one or two people should assist the terrierman when digging out or bolting and that the Master in charge, or someone of authority personally appointed by them, must supervise any digging-out or bolting operation.[40] In the meantime the hunt will usually have moved on to begin hunting elsewhere.

2.26   For the rest of the day there will be a similar process of drawing, scenting and pursuit. Mounted followers may change horses.

2.27   A typical day's hunting for a fell pack - and for foot packs in Wales - is quite similar except that no horses are involved and, because of the terrain, the hounds tend to work at a greater distance from the Huntsman.

2.28   The Welsh gunpacks, however, operate rather differently. Typically, the hounds will be sent into forested areas to drive out foxes to waiting shotguns. These tend to be stationed near routes which foxes leaving the wood are likely to take. The foxes will often move out quite slowly, perhaps having been merely disturbed by the noise of the hounds some distance away in the wood. Some foxes will be "chopped" in the forest; others may escape the guns and then be pursued by the hounds; some may go to ground and be dug out. There is no firm information on the numbers killed by these different means.

2.29   Starting in late August or September, many packs engage in "autumn" or "cub" hunting. The object is to kill or disperse foxes, whose numbers will have increased during the breeding season, and to introduce the young hounds to hunting foxes. Soon after daybreak the Huntsman and a few others on foot or horseback will surround a small wood or coppice and send the hounds in. Foxes will either be killed in the wood or will escape, sometimes pursued by the hounds. Those present will attempt to deter fleeing foxes by making as much noise as possible. Autumn/cub hunting is not advertised in the meet card and there are usually very few people present. About 40% of the foxes killed by MFHA packs are killed during autumn/cub hunting.[41]

Other hunting of foxes

2.30   Although there has been little research carried out on the subject, it is generally accepted that the number of foxes killed with the use of dogs by other groups and individuals is higher than those killed by the registered packs. We include in this category both legal hunting and illegal activities i.e. those involving trespass because prior permission has not been obtained from the landowner.

---

[40] CA2, 8.4.2
[41] CA2, 8.5.1 See also paragraphs 9.11 to 9.16

2.31   Terrierwork is the most widespread. It is practised by some individual farmers and gamekeepers as a means of pest control, and by individual or "gangs" of terriermen, as a sport, or in response to a request for help in pest control. The National Working Terrier Federation (NWTF) consists of 26 clubs and has about 3,000-4,000 individual members. It has drawn up regulations and a code of conduct. However, much terrierwork is carried out by non-members. There is no accurate estimate of the numbers of foxes killed with the use of terriers outside registered hunting.

2.32   The use of lurchers or other "long dogs", though not as widespread as terrierwork, is nonetheless significant. Some are used for pest control by farmers and gamekeepers, most often in the context of lamping. There are also many other lurcher owners in the country, a small minority of whom use their dogs for catching foxes. The Association of Lurcher Clubs has a set of regulations and a code of conduct for their membership, which, though growing in number, represents only a minority of the total number of lurcher owners. Numbers of foxes killed by the use of lurchers are impossible to estimate with any precision.

International information

2.33   Foxes are hunted with dogs and guns in many other countries. Mounted 'English-style' foxhunting is also widely practised, including by 10 packs in the Scottish lowlands and a number of packs in Ireland, the USA and Canada.[42]

Deer hunting

Hunting by registered packs

2.34   There are now three registered packs of hounds in Britain which hunt red deer, all based in Devon and Somerset: the Devon & Somerset, the Quantock and the Tiverton Staghounds. The New Forest Buckhounds, which hunted fallow deer, were disbanded in 1997.[43] [44]

2.35   The three packs hunt on a total of about 290 days each season and have a total income of £360,000 a year. The average cost of putting on a day's hunting, at £1,250, is about 25 per cent higher than for the average fox hunt and reflects the larger number of hounds in the pack and the greater number of horses that are owned by the hunt.[45]

2.36   The three packs are of very different size, with the result that average figures for members and followers are less meaningful. However, the three hunts have mounted fields averaging about 50 at mid-week meets and 90 at weekends. The number of unmounted followers is put at 150 for mid-week meets and 300 at weekends.[46]

---

[42] For a fuller account of hunting with dogs in other countries, see Appendix 9
[43] Macdonald et al, 3.3.1
[44] Deerhunting does not take place in Scotland
[45] Produce Studies Research National Survey of Hunts
[46] Ibid

2.37   The season is divided into three phases. Mature stags are hunted in August, September and October. Hinds are hunted from the beginning of November to the end of February. "Spring stags", usually two to four years old, are hunted in the last two months of the season, March and April.   The numbers killed over the seasons are evenly distributed both between stags and hinds and, among stags, between mature and "spring". Over the last five years the packs have killed about 160 deer each season in total. They also deal with about 80 "casualty" deer each year. The latter are deer which have been injured, for example in road accidents, and which the hunts are called out to dispatch. The total number of deer killed by the packs, excluding casualties, is thought to represent about 15% of the number which it is estimated[47] need to be killed to prevent the population increasing in the area.   The average cost per deer for the hunt comes to £2,300, excluding "casualty" deer, and £1,500 per deer if "casualties" are included.

2.38   A major difference between deer hunting and fox and hare hunting is that, in the case of the stags at least, the hunt aims to select, hunt and kill a particular deer. It is the role of the "harbourer", following discussion with farmers in the area, to select a particular stag for the hunt to pursue.   The harbourer and assistants will track the individual deer's whereabouts the previous day and return there early in the morning of the hunt to make sure it is still in the same place.   The harbourer will then advise the Huntsman, who will take a small number of experienced hounds (called "tufters") to flush out the stag. The stag will then be given a head start before the whole pack sets off in pursuit.

2.39   The selection of a hind to hunt is usually more random since they are difficult to distinguish from each other.   In this case the tufters will usually be sent to disperse a small herd, with the intention of separating one from the others.

2.40   The length and duration of the chase can vary considerably. The chase may last less than an hour or it can even last all day. Recent research indicates that, in the case of deer that are killed, the average duration of the hunt is about three hours and that the distance travelled is about 18 kilometres.[48]   The chase will usually take the form of a series of intermittent flights by the deer as the hounds come near, followed by periods when the deer will move more slowly or even lie low. Sometimes the hounds will lose the scent altogether and have to cast around for it.   About half the deer which are separated from the herd and hunted subsequently escape.[49]

2.41   Eventually, if the hounds are successful in following the deer, the stag ceases to run and confronts the hounds by turning and facing them ("standing at bay").   (Hinds similarly stop and may lie down.) In Exmoor this quite often takes place in a river or stream.[50] The hounds will surround the stag until the Huntsman and gun carrier arrive. The hounds are trained not to attack the deer but biting occasionally occurs.

---

[47] Macdonald et al, 5.4.4
[48] Bateson and Harris, 3.2 (See Chapter 6 for full reference to research by Bateson and Harris)
[49] Ibid, 3.2
[50] Ibid, 6.2.2

2.42   Since the last war, the preferred method of ensuring a quick kill has been a 12 bore shotgun.[51] A shot to the head is always used, and the marksman will get as close to the deer as possible. The recommended maximum distance is seven yards in order to ensure an "instant knockdown". A second shot is occasionally required. Each hunt will also have several members who carry, and are trained in, the use of firearms known as a "humane killer" (normally a .32 pistol). The nearest available gun carrier will be expected to shoot the quarry if, for example, it is known to be lying down or otherwise concealing itself in such a manner that the marksman does not have a clean shot. On occasion, the deer may be held by the antlers or neck.

2.43   After the kill, the deer is cleaned and the offal (with the exception of the liver) is fed to the hounds. Slots and antlers are retained and subsequently mounted. The carcass is butchered and distributed free of charge to farmers and landowners in the area where the deer was found.

Other hunting of deer by dogs

2.44   Roe deer are also hunted by at least two unregistered buckhound packs in parts of the staghound hunt countries. The hounds used to hunt roe deer are usually either basset/harrier crosses or beagles. Buckhounds commonly pursue their quarry followed only by a small core of mounted followers (Huntsman, Master and whipper-in), with the remainder of followers on foot. The way in which roe deer are hunted is similar to that described for hind hunting. An average hunt which results in a kill normally lasts about an hour to an hour and a half. At the end of the chase, roe deer tend to lie down, rather than being brought to bay, and are then dispatched with a modified shotgun or humane killer. Hunting of male roe deer usually takes place between the end of August and the end of October, and also from April to early May. Females are hunted from October to February. Each of the two packs usually hunts once a week during the season, with a total of around 35 meets per pack. The main purpose of roe deer hunting is to provide sport. It is estimated that about 30-40 roe deer in total are killed each year by the two packs.[52]

International information

2.45   In Germany, the use of hounds for hunting deer has been forbidden since 1936. Trained dogs are, however, commonly used for tracking and following wounded deer. In Sweden, hunting of roe deer with shotguns and driving deer with hounds is permitted. The use of dogs for driving deer is also still permitted in France and Belgium. In France, La Grande Vénerie (mounted hunting with dogs), is particularly popular, with about 120 registered packs hunting red or roe deer.[53] In Spain, the traditional hunting method

---

[51] The gun has a maximum twenty-four inch barrel length to comply with the working of the Deer Act (1963). The load used in the cartridge is Special S.9. Buckshot
[52] Macdonald et al, 3.3.1.6
[53] Association Française des Equipages de Vénerie 1, page 2

known as the 'Monteria' is still practised, which involves the use of dogs, beaters, and sometimes also horse-mounted riders, to drive deer towards guns.

Hare hunting

Organised hare hunting

2.46   Hunting hares with hounds dates back some 2000 years. Nowadays, in England and Wales, three different types of hounds are used: beagles, bassets and harriers.

2.47   There are 72 registered packs of beagles in England and Wales, 10 packs of bassets and 20 packs of harriers. (Seven of the harrier packs hunt mainly foxes and two hunt foxes and hares). Beagles and bassets are followed on foot, while harriers are followed on horseback. Beagle and harrier packs are registered with the AMHB and the basset packs are governed by the Masters of Basset Hounds Association (MBHA). The packs have an average income of £17,000 a year and, on average, hunt over some 50 days a year at an average cost of £325 per day. Typically, there are reported to be about 30 followers present at weekend meets. The packs kill about 1,650 brown hares in total or, on average, less than 20 hares per pack.[54]

2.48   There is no statutory closed season for hare hunting but the AMHB rules forbid hunting after the end of March[55] to coincide with the onset of the breeding season. The season begins in late August or early September. The way in which hunting by packs of harriers and bassets is carried out is broadly similar to foxhunting by a mounted hunt, although hares generally travel much shorter distances and tend to follow a circular route. In addition, since hares live entirely above ground, earth stopping and digging-out are not practised.

Other hare hunting

2.49   In addition to the registered packs of hounds, there are a small number of privately-owned packs which hunt hares.

2.50   Much more significant, though, in terms of the numbers of hares killed are the activities of various other groups and individuals who use dogs to kill or course hares: see paragraph 2.56 below.

International information

2.51   Hunting hares with registered packs, as opposed to using dogs for driving or retrieving, is not practised widely elsewhere in the world with the exception of France, where "Petit Vénerie" (foot pack hunting) is widespread. There are currently 115 registered packs in France which hunt hares.[56]

---

[54] Association of Masters of Harriers and Beagles (AMHB) 1, 67
[55] See also paragraphs 9.31 to 9.33
[56] Association Française des Equipages de Vénerie 1, page 2

<u>Hare coursing</u>

Organised hare coursing

2.52   Hare coursing has a long history, going back to the Egyptian and Greek empires. It seems likely that it was introduced to Britain by the Romans. It became very popular in the late 19th and early 20th centuries when there were some 300 coursing clubs and large crowds attended the Waterloo Cup, the premier hare coursing event.

2.53   There are now some 24 greyhound coursing clubs affiliated to the National Coursing Club (NCC), as well as clubs for other breeds such as whippets and salukis. Some dogs also run on the greyhound track. The NCC has a set of rules which affiliated clubs are required to observe. It also licenses key officials, including coursing inspectors, whose duties are to ensure that the rules are observed at each event. In the 1998/1999 season, 90 days' coursing took place, involving some 1,600 courses. About 250 hares have been killed each year in recent seasons.[57]

2.54   Coursing by registered clubs takes place from 15 September to 10 March. The object is to test the skills of two greyhounds in a knock-out competition. Typically, a day's coursing will involve some 32 dogs competing against each other in a series of rounds, with the final two dogs challenging for a cup and a cash prize. A mounted judge awards the dogs points for their speed and skill in making the hare turn. A maximum of one point is awarded in the event of a dog catching a hare.

2.55   Typically, beaters move in from neighbouring fields, encouraging hares onto the coursing field, one at a time. (In "walked-up", as opposed to "driven", coursing the participants walk in a line through a field and release the dogs from the middle of it when the hare sits up.) The slipper, who is holding the two greyhounds on a leash, is expected to allow the hare a minimum of some 80 yards before releasing the dogs. The dogs quickly gain ground on the hare, but the latter twists and turns and has much more stamina. Because greyhounds hunt by sight alone, once the hare reaches cover or a hedge, the chase is over. An average course lasts about 40 seconds. If a hare is caught, one of the pickers-up is expected to get to it as quickly as possible and to ensure that it is dead. This is done by breaking the hare's neck. The number of hares killed averages between one in six and one in eight overall, but the proportion varies considerably between coursing events.

Unregulated coursing

2.56   In terms of the number of hares killed, unregulated coursing, including illegal coursing, where the landowner's permission has not been obtained, is thought to be very significant. The actual numbers killed can only be inferred from the estimated number of working lurchers, which, at its lowest, is put at 70,000 and, by another survey, at over 200,000. The fact that hare populations are concentrated in specific areas of southern and

---

[57] White et al, C, 5.5.3 (See Chapter 5 for full reference by White et al.)

eastern England probably serves to limit the number killed by unregistered coursing rather more than the figures for lurcher ownership would indicate. Hunting hares for the pot is also carried out with dogs but there is no reliable evidence of the numbers killed.

2.57   Illegal coursing is sometimes accompanied by threats or physical violence to landowners, leading some farmers and landowners to "shoot out" hares in order to deter illegal coursers and poachers.[58]

International information

2.58   Coursing is a popular greyhound sport in Ireland. Most of the coursing that takes place is "park", in which the coursing occurs within enclosures and the greyhounds are muzzled. There is also open coursing on the English model, for which the greyhounds are not muzzled. Open coursing is also popular in Spain, and park coursing is being reintroduced in Portugal, after hare numbers on the estates had been decimated during the 1970s. Coursing is also popular in Pakistan, and greyhounds are often shipped out from this country for the purpose. The position in the USA varies state by state but open coursing is still practised in California, Wyoming and Montana. Live hare coursing is no longer permitted in Australia.[59]

Mink hunting

Organised mink hunting

2.59   Mink hunting is a relatively recent development. North American mink were introduced into this country in 1928 and subsequently spread widely as the result of escaping, or being released, from mink farms. Following the ban on the killing of otters introduced in 1975, the former otterhound packs switched entirely to hunting mink. The Masters of Minkhounds Association (MMHA) was formed in 1978 and now represents 20 mink hunts in England and Wales, some of which are privately run. Some five to 15 couple of hounds are used for hunting. These are often kennelled at neighbouring foxhunts. The average income for a mink hunt is reported as £4,500.

2.60   The mink hunting season usually runs from April to early October. Hunts go out, on average, once or twice a week, with about 35 followers present at weekend meets,[60] although the number of people following a mink hunt varies from a handful to as many as 150.[61] The hunts manage, on average, about 42 days' hunting in each season, killing some 400-1,400 mink a year in total.[62] The hunts also respond to calls at short notice from people suffering from mink depredation. In 1999 these represented just over 10% of the total meets.[63]

---

[58] NCC - letter to the Inquiry
[59] NCC - letter to the Inquiry
[60] Produce Studies Group National Survey of Hunts
[61] MMHA 1,5
[62] Ibid; Macdonald et al, 5.6.2
[63] MMHA - telephone conversation

2.61   A day's mink hunting is conducted in a similar fashion to other types of hunting on foot, although of course it takes place mainly along rivers and streams. The hounds will draw a river bank or stream. Occasionally, a mink, once discovered, may be killed quickly ("chopped") by the hounds. More often the hounds will pursue its scent, checking to rediscover it as necessary. The mink will either be caught by the hounds or, if it has climbed a tree, it may be shot or dislodged so that it falls to the hounds.[64] As with fox hunts, mink hunts may make use of terriers for bolting mink and for the purposes of digging-out.[65]

Other hunting of mink by dogs

2.62   There is no information about whether other hunting of mink by dogs takes place.

International information

2.63   Trained dogs are sometimes used in Iceland to sniff out occupied mink dens, from which the mink may be captured.

Other types of hunting with dogs

2.64   As we mentioned in Chapter 1, we were asked to examine hunting with dogs of foxes, deer, hares and mink. The Home Secretary also indicated that he regarded the use of dogs to locate or retrieve quarry as being outside our terms of reference.

2.65   We thought that it would be helpful, nevertheless, to describe briefly other hunting activities involving dogs, since they might be affected by any future legislation to ban hunting with dogs.

Ratting

2.66   It is common in rural areas to use terriers, and other dogs, in an attempt to control rat populations, particularly on agricultural properties and where gamebirds are found. Ratting is largely conducted on an informal basis and is regarded as being a useful contribution to pest control. Whilst there is a social component to ratting, it appears to be viewed mainly as a means of pest control where poison cannot be used safely.[66]

Falconry

2.67   Dogs (spaniels and pointers) are used extensively with hawks and falcons to flush quarry such as rabbits for the bird to give chase. We received representations from those involved in falconry to say that they believed that any ban on hunting with dogs, on the

---

[64] Macdonald et al, 3.5.1
[65] Ibid, 3.5.1
[66] Rat Hunting 1, Anon

lines of the Bill introduced by Mr Michael Foster MP, would have a direct and serious effect on the continuation of falconry as a sport and as a means of pest control.[67]

Rabbiting

2.68   The use of dogs for hunting rabbits is widespread and involves a large number of breeds/types of dog, the lurcher appearing to be the type most commonly used. This activity is carried out as a sport and as a means of pest control and can take several forms, for example in conjunction with ferrets to put up the rabbit; in lamping; and in coursing. Terriers are also used, often in conjunction with ferrets, with the terrier being used to mark the warren before the ferret is introduced.[68]

Deer stalking

2.69   In stalking deer, use is made of dogs to scent the deer and provide advance warning to the stalker of the presence of deer. A dog (or dogs) may also be used to locate a deer that has been shot or wounded, enabling the stalker to dispatch it or, in the case of a fatally wounded deer which has run before death, to locate the carcass.[69]

Driving gamebirds

2.70   Gamebirds are often driven towards guns by a combination of human beaters and dogs. We have received representations which stress that such dogs, no matter how well trained, may pursue other animals that are put up in the course of a beat. Concern has been expressed to us that any legislation to ban hunting should take this into account.[70]

Hunting - related activities

Point-to-pointing

2.71   Point-to-pointing is an amateur form of steeplechasing, regulated by the Jockey Club. To qualify to race in a point-to-point a horse must have hunted a minimum of seven times in the current season. Certification to this effect is issued by the relevant hunt and lodged with the Jockey Club. A total of 4,106 horses qualified with 190 hunts in 1999. Each point-to-point rider is required to be a member of, or a subscriber to, a recognised hunt. In 1999, the Jockey Club issued 1,084 riders' qualification certificates.

2.72   Point-to-points are designed in part to raise funds for the organising hunt, but also to provide a competitive arena for the participants and an enjoyable day out in the countryside for spectators. They attract around 700,000 people every year. In 2000 there are 209 meetings programmed, being held at around 120 different venues around the country.

---

[67] British Falconers' Club 1, page 2
[68] Essex Ferret Welfare Society 1, un-numbered
[69] British Association for Shooting and Conservation (BASC) 1, un-numbered
[70] BASC 1, un-numbered

2.73   Point-to-points are generally regarded as the training ground for both horses and riders prior to National Hunt racing, with young horses learning their trade. Around 10% of National Hunt runners have previously been point-to-pointing. At the same time, many National Hunt horses are able to enjoy a healthy and active retirement by being ridden in point-to-point and in the hunting field.

National Hunt racing

2.74   Hunter chases, for horses which have hunted in the current season, make up 10% of the National Hunt steeplechase programme.

CHAPTER 3

HUNTING AND THE RURAL ECONOMY

3.1   This chapter discusses that part of our remit which required us to consider the impact of hunting, and of a ban on hunting, on "the rural economy".

The wider context

3.2   It is important to see the arguments in this chapter, and the following chapter, in the wider context of the economic and social changes which have taken place, and are taking place, in the countryside.

3.3   Hunting is set in the rural economy. Within the areas classified as 'rural', the population has been growing.   The population of districts in England with a predominantly rural character grew faster between 1984 and 1998 (10.3%) than that of the country as a whole (5.3%).[71] Rather more than a fifth of rural residents receive incomes in excess of 150% of the national average. However, the incomes of almost one-fifth are below 50% of the national average. Unemployment in rural areas is generally lower than in the country as a whole: 4.2% in rural districts compared with 6.1% in England in 1998. There is also evidence that rural businesses are more vibrant.[72] Thus, in many rural areas, poverty exists cheek by jowl with affluence.[73]

3.4   Within this buoyant rural economy traditional industries have been in long-term relative decline. There has been a continuing long-term decline in the agricultural labour force and some shift in composition with the number of full-time workers falling more rapidly than the casual or part-time. The process has accelerated recently and the number of jobs has decreased sharply in the last few years. During the twelve months to June 1999 more than 7% of jobs were lost.[74]

3.5   The decline in the number of people engaged in agriculture has been accompanied by a long-term downward trend in the aggregate income of the sector. However, in the last few years, the fall in real income has been much more dramatic. Between 1995 and 1998 an index of Total Income from Farming more than halved.[75]

3.6   Faced with a situation in which many farms are operating at a loss, there is a strong pressure to reduce costs. Apart from shedding hired labour, farmers seek to reduce all other forms of expenditure, including investment in replacement machinery and equipment. There are already signs that this will be insufficient to enable all the current farm businesses to survive.

---

[71] *State of the Countryside 2000.* Countryside Agency. 2000
[72] Ibid
[73]*Rural Economies.* Performance and Innovation Unit. 1999. (PIU report)
[74] *Agriculture in the United Kingdom (AUK)*, various editions, MAFF; and MAFF Statistics News Release, 12 January 2000
[75] MAFF AUK 99

3.7   The growth in employment which has taken place in the rural economy is largely in service industries, including banking, finance and insurance and other services.[76] This is strongest in those regions with easy access to centres of business. In the remoter areas, that is not the case. Here, the service industries which may create new jobs tend to be linked to small scale processing and the tourism sector. Many of the jobs created are part-time and seasonal.

3.8   Hunting, as an economic activity, is so small as to be almost invisible in terms of national aggregates. However, it often takes place in these remoter regions where farming is vulnerable and there are few alternative jobs close at hand. In these areas the impact of a ban on hunting would be much more severe in terms of employment and, from the viewpoint of some upland farmers, in relation to the viability of their businesses.

3.9   Within both agriculture and hunting much work is of a part-time seasonal nature. The activities are often complementary, hunting having its largest need for labour during the winter months when work on most farms may be at a low level. This points to the danger of relying only on estimates couched in the language of Full-Time Equivalents (FTEs). These are needed to make comparisons with the overall labour use in the sector. However, in many rural situations, the loss of part-time jobs may seriously affect the capacity of relatively poor households to survive within their communities.

3.10   This background helps to explain why there has been so much debate in the last few years about the job losses which would result from a ban on hunting. The effect on jobs and on the rural economy has been one of the main planks of the arguments put forward by those who are opposed to a ban on hunting. It is interesting to note, in passing, that this is in contrast to the position when the Scott Henderson Committee reported, when there was little mention of possible job losses.[77]

The jobs and economic activity that are supported by hunting

3.11   There are four main categories of paid employment which need to be calculated in order to estimate the present number of jobs which depend on hunting:

- direct employment by the hunts themselves - it is relatively easy in principle to collect good quality information by carrying out surveys of the hunts

- direct employment by hunt followers - mainly grooms. This information is very much harder to collect since the precise number of hunt followers is not known and because it involves estimating what proportion of employees' time is divided between hunt and non-hunt activities and whether the motivation/reason for keeping a horse at all is related to hunting

---

[76] PIU report Chart 5.1. Table 5.1

[77] *Report of the Committee on Cruelty to Wild Animals*, paragraphs 133-137. Cmd 8266

- indirect employment by suppliers of goods and services to hunts and hunt followers - this information is also very difficult to collect. One approach is to use surveys of a sample of businesses which supply the inputs needed by hunts. An example is the BETA survey.[78] Again, most of these businesses supply non-hunting activities as well as hunts and followers, so some division has to be made. An alternative is to work backwards from the expenditure of hunts and followers, using a coefficient which estimates the employment content of these purchases in the supplying businesses

- induced employment - this is employment which results from the spending of their wages by all the direct and indirect employees identified in the previous three categories.

Research

3.12   In order to throw more light on potential job losses we commissioned some research from Public and Corporate Economic Consultants (PACEC). As we explain in more detail below, PACEC's work[79] has been helpful on a number of counts. First of all, it has highlighted some of the methodological issues that have to be resolved in calculating the jobs which are dependent, directly or indirectly, on hunting. Secondly, it has produced an estimate for the number of jobs which the hunts themselves provide (710 full-time equivalents) which, we think, will be generally accepted as being broadly accurate. Thirdly, it has served to narrow down - but not to define precisely - the parameters for the other jobs which presently depend on hunting. The fact that we are not able to give firmer figures reflects a number of difficulties Some of them are methodological and some are more to do with the inherent problems in identifying accurately all the participants in hunting, especially the mounted followers, and in allocating their expenditure between hunting and all the other equestrian activities in which they may take part.

3.13   Many different estimates have been produced of the jobs dependent on hunting, ranging from about 4,000 to over 22,000.[80]

3.14   As PACEC note, these reflect differences of approach in, for example:

- the treatment of part-time and seasonal jobs

- calculating the number of participants

- allocating expenditure by hunts and followers to direct and indirect effects

[78] *National Equestrian Survey 1999.* British Equestrian Trade Association (BETA)
[79] *The Economic Effects of Hunting with Dogs.* Public and Corporate Economic Consultants (PACEC), 49-53 Regent Street, Cambridge CB2 1AB ('PACEC')
[80] PACEC, Table 2.1

- distinguishing the proportion of horse-related expenditure and employment which should be allocated specifically to hunting as opposed to other equestrian activities[81]

3.15　We describe in the following paragraphs the approach which PACEC followed in attempting to estimate the direct and indirect employment from hunting. We discuss the qualifications which need to be attached to the approach which they adopted and the figures which they produced. Finally, we consider the different - but equally difficult - question of how many jobs would actually be lost if a ban on hunting was introduced.

Methodology used by PACEC

3.16　The approach used by PACEC was to develop a "social accounting matrix" i.e. an input-output table of the hunting economy and how it relates to the rest of the economy. This table, which is reproduced below in summary form, shows all the relevant income and payment flows, as well as the number of FTE jobs which are either known or are estimated to result from the different types of expenditure. (The figures should not be regarded as precise but as indicating orders of magnitude).

Table 3.1[82]　Social accounting matrix for the Hunting Economy - Summary Transactions Table

	← Payments by (£m) →					
↓ Income to (£m) ↓	Followers	Hunts	Associated social & sporting events	Rest of the economy	Employees	Total income
Followers						
Hunts	8.1	0.2	5.9	1.4		15.6
Associated social & sporting events	11.9					11.9
Rest of the economy	49.1	9.3	5.1	94.7	48.6	206.8
Employees	12.0	6.1	0.9	45.8		64.8
Total expenditure	81.1	15.6	11.9	206.8	64.8	380.2
Balancing item (surpluses, imports, deductions etc)		0.0	0.0	64.9	16.2	
No of FTE jobs reported / assessed	1,497	621	89	3,517		5,724
Average annual wage as calculated (£)	8,035	9,806	9,806	13,026		11,321

---

[81] Ibid,2.4.4 and 2.4.5
[82] Ibid, Table 1.1

Direct effects - income, expenditure and employment of the hunts

3.17   We, and the researchers, were fortunate that the Countryside Alliance had already commissioned Produce Studies to carry out a survey of hunts in order to collect this information and that they were willing to make it available. We are grateful for this. We asked PACEC to validate and "clean-up" these data. They did this, in part, by carrying out telephone surveys of hunt masters/treasurers where there appeared to be inconsistencies, although in general they were small. The survey was also used as a means of collecting more detailed information on hunts' employment, income and expenditure.[83]

3.18   As a result of this work PACEC were able to produce "grossed-up" figures for the 302 registered hunts in England and Wales. Inevitably, this covered only recorded cash in-flows and out-flows. Voluntary labour and in-kind income are not included. The figures are shown in the following table.

Table 3.2[84]   Grossed-up and adjusted estimates of employment, income and expenditure of all hunts (Preferred estimates, based on findings of the PACEC follow-up survey, and other adjustments)

Employment	Full-time:	609	jobs
	Part-time:	202	jobs
	Total:	811	jobs
Full-time equivalent employment, where 2PT=1FT:		710FTEs	
Income	£15.6 million		
Revenue / operating expenditure	£14.2 million		
Capital expenditure	£2.4 million		
Cost of collecting fallen stock	£3.8 million		
Income from collection of fallen stock*	£1.4 million		

* not examined in the Countryside Alliance questionnaire.

3.19   As can be seen, total income was £15.6 million. The following table shows that just over half of this sum came from payments by members, subscribers and others following the hunt. Closely-related sporting and recreational events contributed nearly 40 per cent. Total revenue expenditure came to £14.2 million. Nearly 40 per cent was accounted for by staff costs.

---

[83] Ibid, 1.2.8
[84] Ibid, Table 3.3

Table 3.3[85]   Breakdown of hunts' income and expenditure

Item:	% of total
Source of Income	
Subscriptions, donations, caps and gifts	51
Social events (e.g. Balls, dances, race nights etc.)	25
Equestrian events (e.g. point-to-points, hunter trails etc.)	12
Dog events (e.g. puppy shows, kennel open days)	1
Other / unspecified	11
Type of Revenue / operating expenditure	
Staff costs	39
Property costs	11
Utilities and communications	11
Goods purchased	9
Services purchases	8
Surpluses / unallocated	21
Type of capital expenditure	
New building work	20
Vehicles	37
Other plant and machinery	43

3.20   There is little doubt that PACEC's estimate that the hunts employ the equivalent of 710 full-time employees in 811 jobs is close to the mark. It is broadly consistent with the figure of 835 jobs in the National Survey of Hunts.[86] Nearly all the other studies produce similar figures.[87]

3.21   The most significant feature about the spread of these jobs is that some 28% of the employment is based in the south west of England.

<u>Direct effects - expenditure and employment of hunt followers</u>

3.22   As we mentioned in paragraph 3.11, information about direct employment by hunt followers is very much harder to collect than that for direct employment by the hunts themselves. Some of the difficulties are :

- there is no accurate information about the numbers of hunt subscribers, followers and supporters - and, indeed, confusion about the precise meaning of each of these terms makes it hard to gather reliable data

- some people will subscribe to more than one hunt but, equally, it is possible to follow hunts without becoming a member: the National Survey of Hunts indicated that 40% of the total number of days spent on organised hunting

---

[85] Ibid, Table 3.4
[86] CA2, 2.1.3
[87] PACEC, Table 2.1

each year comprised "visitor days", that is, attended by visitors who do not pay an annual subscription to the particular hunt[88]

- many hunts do not collect annual subscriptions from farmers on whose land they hunt[89]

- it is not easy to calculate precisely how much horse-related expenditure and employment can properly be ascribed to <u>hunting</u>. For example, if someone buys a horse primarily in order to use it for hunting, but then also uses it for other activities, should all the expenditure/employment be counted or only that proportion which reflects the time the horse spends hunting?

3.23   Using information derived from the National Survey of Hunts, their telephone survey and elsewhere, PACEC produced estimated totals of 8,839 subscriber/member households and 9,826 "other supporter" households. They then sought to estimate the amount spent by households on horse-related activity and what proportion could be ascribed to hunting. Based on telephone interviews with a sample of subscriber/members and followers, PACEC calculated the total amount spent on all horse-related activity as some £124 million a year.[90] On the basis of information derived from their survey about the use made of horses for hunting and other activities, PACEC calculated that 51% of this expenditure could be regarded as hunting-related.

3.24   In the Countryside Alliance's view, the approach adopted by PACEC underestimates the amount of horse-related activity associated with hunting. First, they argue that it underestimates the number of subscribers/members, followers and the number of households. They consider, in particular, that it overestimates the extent of multiple membership and that it confuses following a hunt with membership or subscription to that hunt.[91] In their view, Produce Studies' estimate of 16,700 subscriber/member households is more likely to be accurate.[92] Second, they argue that the figure of 51% used for hunting-related expenditure is too low, on the basis that time spent hacking or point-to-pointing should not necessarily be viewed as an entirely separate activity from hunting.[93]

3.25   The breakdown of expenditure in the PACEC analysis is shown in the following table.

---

[88] CA2, 2.2.15
[89] Ibid, 2.2.15
[90] PACEC, 1.2.6 and Table 4.1
[91] CA2, 2.2.15-2.2.16
[92] Ibid, 2.2.19
[93] Ibid, 2.2.23

Table 3.4[94]   Breakdown of followers' expenditure on hunting

	Horse-owning households		Other supporter households	
	£000	%	£000	%
Payments to Hunts	7,000	10.0	1,100	27.2
Spending on hunt-related social & recreational activities	10,124	14.4	1,795	44.4
Wages to employees	12,006	17.1	23	0.6
Horse feed & bedding	6,989	9.9	0	0.0
Stabling/livery fees	3,905	5.6	0	0.0
Vets' bills	4,367	6.2	0	0.0
Farriers	7,073	10.1	0	0.0
Tack & riding clothes	3,448	4.9	278	6.9
Horse transport	8,223	11.7	0	0.0
Other	7,200	10.2	850	21.0
Total	70,334	100.0	4,047	100.0

3.26   PACEC's next step was to estimate the number of FTE jobs and the average full-time equivalent wage, based on their estimate of hunt followers' expenditure on wages. This was done by using information from the sample survey, which implied that each FTE employee could look after an average of 16.9 horses and would be paid a full-time equivalent wage of £8,000. They also estimated that the total number of horses involved in hunting was 50,000, which compares with BETA's estimate that 56,000 horses are used primarily for hunting.[95][96]

3.27   On the basis of their figures, PACEC estimate that the number of FTE employees paid by followers is 1,497 and that they would be paid a full-time equivalent wage of £8,000.[97]

3.28   This figure compares with Produce Studies' estimate of 6,100 jobs. PACEC argue that the discrepancy is much lower if the latter figure is expressed as FTEs. Depending on the precise method used for converting jobs to FTEs, it would translate to between 2,200 and 2,850 FTEs. Thus, the difference between the two sets of figures is some 700-1,350 FTEs.

3.29   The Countryside Alliance argue that there is a flaw in the methodology used by PACEC to calculate the number of FTE grooms and the estimate of the total number of

---

[94] PACEC, Table 4.2
[95] PACEC, 4.3.2
[96] BETA 1, 3.03
[97] PACEC, 4.4.3

hunting horses. And that, when this is combined with the underestimation of expenditure by followers on hunting, PACEC understate the number of FTEs attributable to hunting who are employed by members/subscribers. They also dispute the PACEC calculation which translates the number of jobs in the Produce Studies data into FTEs and continue to argue that the difference between the two sets of figures is bigger than claimed by PACEC.[98]

Reconciling participants' expenditure with hunt income and expenditure

3.30 We suspect that the PACEC analysis understates the amount of economic activity that goes into supporting hunt followers. In part, this reflects the extent to which much of the work is unpaid or is difficult to allocate to different activities. However, it is in the nature of social accounts that incomes and expenditures need to balance. In this case the bulk of the participants' expenditure goes on horses but they also make payments direct to hunts for subscriptions and social activities. It is a useful check to see how far the estimate of expenditure by followers coincides with the estimate of the hunts' income from followers.

3.31 There were two categories where reconciliation was necessary. There was a difference of some £3.3 million between the income which the hunts reported receiving from followers (£8.0 million) and the sums which followers themselves estimated that they had spent (£11.3 million). PACEC decided that the hunts' figure was more likely to be reliable, mainly because the survey of hunts was much more extensive than that of followers.[99] This left the problem of how to treat the remaining £3.3 million of estimated expenditure. The researchers decided to treat half of it as a reporting error and to allocate the other half to the remaining expenditure categories, which we are about to discuss.[100]

3.32 The second discrepancy (£6.8 million) is between the amount which followers reported spending on hunts' social and recreational activities and the income (mainly gross, according to the returns) which hunts themselves reported as receiving. PACEC consider that the discrepancy can largely be explained by the fact that the participants' gross expenditure would include items like travel and food and drink which would not normally be included in the hunts' gross income figures. In line with their experience of other voluntary organisations, the researchers decided to allocate to the hunt about half of supporters' gross expenditure on balls and point-to-points, and 60% of the expenditure on other animal or sporting events.[101]

3.33 Although we suspect that the analysis, if anything, understates the impact of the horse-owning activities of hunt followers on the local economy, these calculations provide some reassurance that the outcome of the calculation of expenditure by hunt followers is plausible.

---

[98] CA2, 2.11.4
[99] PACEC, 5.2.3
[100] Ibid, 5.2.4
[101] Ibid, 5.2.5-5.2.7

3.34   In order to estimate the expenditure and employment generated indirectly through the spending by those businesses directly supplying hunts and their followers, PACEC carried out a survey of over 150 businesses known to be particularly strongly linked to hunting.[102] This produced a certain amount of information but its usefulness was limited by reluctance on the part of some of them to reveal sales and operating expenditure.[103] This information was therefore considered in conjunction with information available nationally about expenditure in these sectors on employment costs. Employment impacts were then estimated for two groups of businesses: those with a heavy emphasis on horses or hunting and those which were more like the generality of the economy. PACEC estimated that this produced a total of 680 FTE jobs in the first category and 400 FTE jobs in the second.[104]

3.35   PACEC then calculated the "second and subsequent round" expenditure and employment derived from hunting. This comes from the expenditure/jobs which are created further back in the economy by the money spent by the suppliers to hunts and hunt followers on, for example, raw materials. This was done by applying the average UK ratio of sales to employment for the various industries and apportioning it between urban and rural-based businesses.[105] This resulted in an estimated 710 jobs, producing an estimated total of 1992 FTEs dependent on the direct and indirect result of purchases by hunts and followers.[106]

Induced employment

3.36   The final category of employment which PACEC had to calculate was induced employment i.e. the jobs created in turn by the expenditure by all the direct and indirect employees of their wages. They estimated that these totalled 1,525 FTEs. It should be noted that a smaller proportion of these jobs are likely to be in rural areas since the expenditure concerned will be spent on goods and services across the UK and abroad.

Summary of calculations of employment dependent on hunting

3.37   Pulling all these figures together, we can see that PACEC's calculations produce the following figures.

---

[102] Ibid, 5.3.1
[103] Ibid, 5.3.2
[104] Ibid, 5.3.8
[105] Ibid, 5.3.10
[106] Ibid, 5.3.12

Table 3.5

Type of employment	FTEs
Direct employment by hunts	710
Direct employment by followers	1,497
Indirect employment by suppliers of goods and services to hunts and hunt followers	1,992
Induced employment from the salaries spent by direct and indirect employees	1,525
Total	**5,724**

Conclusions

3.38. We mentioned in paragraph 3.15 that we needed to attach some qualifications to the estimates produced by PACEC and, indeed, it will have been clear from the account we have just given that a number of the assumptions and figures which they have used are capable of being challenged.

3.39 We consider that the "social accounting matrix" approach which PACEC adopted (see paragraph 3.16) is a useful approach but it has its limitations. In particular, it relies heavily, like all models, on the accuracy of the data which is inputted. There are particular problems in applying a model of this kind to a very small sector of the economy, like hunting, and especially one which operates in many respects in quite an informal way. For example, many businesses do not keep separate accounts of their receipts from different types of customer. So, payments by people for horse-related equipment which they may or may not use for hunting are unlikely to be distinguished in the records of the retailers. Similarly, those who buy items may use them for a number of purposes. Electricity bought to light the stables will not be paid separately from that used for the farm as a whole. Grass grazed by horses may not be separate from that used by sheep. Horses which are used to train may be regarded as part of hunting expenditure where the aim is to enable a child to join the hunt, or as part of riding expenditure where hunting is not particularly in mind. Moreover, because it is difficult to use national average data to check on a sector that has a distinctive and different pattern of resource use, one is driven to relying more heavily on the quality of the data that is collected through surveys - with all the difficulties which we have just described.

3.40 Another limitation of the "social accounting matrix" approach is that it is essentially a financial model. In order to translate the financial figures into employment it is necessary to use some factor which represents payment per job. This can be done only in terms of FTEs. However, in the rural sector generally, and in hunting in particular, part-time work is likely to supply a large part of the total input. This means that the number of jobs affected will be substantially greater than the FTEs, although we do not know how much greater.

3.41 A more fundamental point, in some ways, is that a "social accounting matrix" approach cannot take account of the fact that, in common with many rural recreation activities, many followers of hunts make an unpaid input into hunting from their own land and by their own labour. This includes the voluntary activities of hunt members. Some examples are looking after dogs in kennels, organising and managing fund raising activities, tending horses kept at home and supplying part of their food. These activities will often be carried out, within an overall farm business, without being separately identified from general farm expenditure. Sometimes these inputs are rewarded by payment in kind: for example, volunteers who look after horses may be allowed to ride them without payment. This part of the employment generated by hunting cannot be precisely measured, even by those who supply it. Equally, it is not clear how much of it would be redirected to other activities should hunting cease. Despite this, in coming to a view on the totality of land and labour used in hunting, those who take part recognise it as significant. Although these activities cannot be covered in studies of formal paid employment, they nevertheless form part of the real resources devoted to hunting.

3.42 For all these reasons we think that, despite the contribution which PACEC's work has made in clarifying some of these issues, it is not possible to give any very precise estimate of the numbers of jobs/FTEs which can be regarded as being dependent on hunting. There is general agreement that the number of FTEs directly employed by the hunts is about 700. But, as we have explained, it is very difficult to produce an accurate figure for the number employed by those who take part in hunting and, consequently, for those jobs which flow from other, indirect and induced, expenditure and employment. Nonetheless, even allowing for all the uncertainties, we are satisfied that the number of FTE jobs dependent on hunting is fewer than 10,000 and that it is probably somewhere in the region of 6,000-8,000. In terms of the total number of people affected the figure could be significantly higher. The Countryside Alliance cite the Produce Studies' estimate that some 70% of the people employed by hunt followers work part-time, work for only part of the year, or work part-time for part of the year. Applying the principle that two part-time or part-year employees equates to one FTE, the total number of people employed by hunt followers might be some 70% higher than the number of FTEs.[107]

3.43 We estimate that somewhere between 6,000 and 8,000 full-time equivalent jobs presently depend on hunting, although the number of people involved may be significantly higher. About 700 of these jobs (involving some 800 people) result from direct employment by the hunts. Another 1,500 to 3,000 full-time equivalent jobs (perhaps involving some 2,500 to 5,000 people) result from direct employment on hunting-related activities by those who are engaged in hunting. The remaining jobs, in a wide variety of businesses, are indirectly dependent on hunting. Of these, many will be in urban, rather than rural, areas.

---

[107] CA2, 2.11.13

The effects of a ban

Factors to be considered

3.44   It is one thing to estimate the number of jobs, direct or indirect, which are dependent on hunting. It is an entirely different matter, however, to estimate what the effects would be on those jobs - and, more importantly, on the people involved - if hunting was banned.

3.45   Factors which need to be taken into account are:

- the extent to which other activities, especially equestrian activities, would serve as a replacement for hunting

- the extent to which other changes in the rural economy would offset losses in expenditure and employment

- how the money presently spent on hunting would be expended

- the extent to which the impact would be increased, or reduced, by the part-time and seasonal nature of much of the work

- the extent to which other economic activities related to hunting or using hunt labour, such as point-to-point, National Hunt and riding schools would be affected

- the impact on pubs, hotels and so on of lost trade from those visitors who come to the area to take part in, or to observe, hunting

- the significance of unpaid and voluntary work

- the uneven nature of the impact in different rural areas

- the timescale over which changes would occur

- the nature of the adjustment that would be needed.

3.46   It is impossible to predict with any certainty what would happen in practice. What we can say with some confidence is that, even on a worst case scenario, not all the jobs presently dependent on hunting would be lost. In particular, we believe that only a small proportion of horse owners would immediately seek to get rid of their horses if a ban was introduced. It is much more likely that many would take up other equestrian activities, reduce the use of their horses or not buy new horses when the time came to replace them. Any reduction in jobs flowing from decreased use of horses for hunting would therefore be gradual rather than immediate.

3.47　It is also important to note that a proportion of the induced employment which is dependent on hunting does not form part of the rural economy at all. It relates to goods and services which are supplied by urban providers, some of which will be based outside the UK.

3.48　We can also be confident that there would be some job losses if hunting was banned. Even if drag and bloodhound hunting expanded - and we argue in a later chapter that these activities would be unlikely to see major growth in the short term - they would take up only some of the slack. In particular, because drag and bloodhound hunts use fewer hounds, there would be a need for fewer kennelmen. It is also likely that there would be fewer non-mounted followers since both sports appeal primarily to riders.

Changes in the rural economy

3.49　As we noted in paragraph 3.8, hunting forms an extremely small part of the national economy.

3.50　It is true to say that, from a macro-economic perspective, the number of jobs which are presently dependent on hunting is very small compared with the jobs which, as we noted in paragraph 3.4, have been lost in agriculture or for that matter, in other sectors such as mining or shipbuilding. We know that, although agricultural employment has declined, it has been more than compensated for by increases in other sectors: rural employment increased by nearly 600,000 in the 1980's and 1990's. This trend is expected broadly to continue, as illustrated in the following table.

Table 3.6[108]　Employment trends and change in England and Wales

Type of area:	Actual / Projected Levels ('000s)				Change ('000s)			Change (%)		
	1980	1990	2000	2010	80-90	90-00	00-10	80-90	90-00	00-10
Remote rural	1,670	1,859	1,989	2,112	189	130	123	11	7	6
Accessible rural	3,661	4,062	4,529	4,926	401	467	397	11	11	9
All rural areas	5,331	5,921	6,518	7,038	590	597	520	11	10	8
[Ex] Coalfield	305	278	269	279	-27	-9	10	-9	-3	4
Urban	6,157	6,298	6,589	7,063	141	291	474	2	5	7
Metropolitan	8,512	7,846	7,824	8,169	-666	-22	345	-8	0	4
All areas	20,305	20,343	21,200	22,549	38	857	1,349	0	4	6

Source: ONS (NOMIS), PACEC, Annual Employment Survey (to 1997)

3.51　The following table also shows that employment in all rural areas in England and Wales is projected to go on increasing, including in the south west region.

---

[108] PACEC, Table 6.7

Table 3.7[109]   **Regional breakdown of employment trends and change in rural areas**

Rural areas in:	Actual / Projected Levels ('000s)				Change ('000s)			Change (%)		
	1980	1990	2000	2010	80-90	90-00	00-10	80-90	90-00	00-10
South East	1,167	1,365	1,538	1,705	198	173	167	17	13	11
Eastern	760	846	944	1,036	86	98	92	11	12	10
South West	888	1,004	1,127	1,216	116	123	89	13	12	8
West Midlands	504	547	601	637	43	54	36	9	10	6
East Midlands	693	729	838	909	36	109	71	5	15	8
Yorks/Humber	310	357	376	395	47	19	19	15	5	5
North West	570	597	607	638	27	10	31	5	2	5
North East	79	83	85	88	4	2	3	5	2	4
Wales	362	393	400	415	31	7	15	9	2	4

Source: ONS (NOMIS), PACEC, Annual Employment Survey (to 1997)

3.52   However, as we noted in paragraph 3.7, the growth in employment which has been taking place in the rural economy has largely been in service industries and has been strongest in those areas within easy reach of urban centres.

3.53   It was suggested to us that job losses might be mitigated through increased tourism and recreation in the countryside as a result of improved public access resulting from the Countryside and Rights of Way Bill currently before Parliament. It seems to us, however, that there is little available evidence to suggest that significant numbers of people are currently constrained from visiting the countryside because of lack of public access (or, indeed, because of objections to hunting, as was also suggested in evidence). The UK Day Visits Survey, undertaken by Social and Community Planning Research, showed that, in 1998, 34% of households in England did not visit the countryside at all.[110] The reasons given did not relate to hunting or to lack of access.

3.54   Similarly, a recent survey by MVA Ltd showed that the majority of the respondents (69%) did not think than an extension of their access rights to open country would lead to a change in their use of the countryside.[111] Curry and Ravenscroft suggest that, when the data are grossed up to reflect the entire population, the findings show that approximately 2% of England's population would spend an extra one to two hours in the countryside, particularly in woodlands and along watersides, if access to open country became law.[112]

---

[109] Ibid, Table 6.8
[110] *U.K. Day Visits Survey.* Social and Community Planning Research
[111] *Access to the Open Countryside: Measuring Potential Demand.* Report to the Countryside Agency
[112] *Assessing the Demand for Countryside Recreation: A Case Study in the County of Surrey,* Draft Final Report to the Countryside Agency, London, Curry N and Ravenscroft N (2000)

3.55　It is important to note too that job losses would not be evenly spread across all rural communities.[113]　It is highly probable, therefore, that, in particular localities such as some of the villages in Exmoor, they would not be compensated for, at least in the short term, by projected employment growth.

Effect on farmers

3.56　Many farmers too would no doubt feel that they had suffered a financial loss if hunting was banned.　They would no longer be able to use the local hunt as a free "pest control" service or to use the hunt's volunteer labour for mending fences and gates. In addition, they would expect, rightly or wrongly, to experience more predation of lambs, poultry, piglets and game birds or more damage to their crops.

3.57　Those farmers who currently use the "fallen stock" service presently provided by many hunts would also be faced with potential additional costs.　This service involves the collection from farms of unsaleable dead farm animals or injured or sick animals.　The 200 hunts surveyed in the Produce Studies National Survey of Hunts indicated that they had handled some 336,000 carcasses in the previous 12 months.　Because of the different methods of calculating throughput, it is not easy to say what proportion of the total business this represented.

3.58　The fallen stock service used to be provided free of charge but, because of increased costs, mainly resulting from the additional restrictions imposed as a result of the BSE crisis, many hunts now charge small fees.　These charges, however, are substantially lower than those which would be charged by a licensed knacker's service. The evidence we received from the Countryside Alliance and the hunts indicated that this service would cease almost entirely, in the event of a ban on hunting.

3.59　It is not clear, in any case, whether all the hunts would be able to continue the fallen stock service even if hunting was not banned.　The EU Waste Incineration Directive introduces new requirements for hygiene and for incinerators.　PACEC's report indicated that up to 19% of hunts had said that they would either upgrade their incinerator and continue a fallen stock collection or that they had been told that their incinerator already met the new requirements.[114]

3.60　In the event of a ban, it seems plain that a large part , at the very least, of the existing service would cease.　This would clearly have financial consequences for farmers if they had to use a licensed knacker's service instead.　Although it has been argued that this cost would not be significant, this would not necessarily be true for those farmers who had come to rely on the service provided by hunts.　Moreover, the cost would need to be seen against the backcloth of the depressed livestock industry.

---

[113] PACEC, 6.4.5
[114] PACEC, 3.7.4

3.61   A reduction in the fallen stock service would also have potential implications for the environment since farmers might resort more frequently than at present to burning or burying carcasses. The latter carries a serious risk of contaminating water courses.

Effect on other businesses

3.62   The extent to which businesses supplying goods and services to the hunts and hunt followers would be affected by a ban on hunting would be determined by their relative dependency on hunting in relation to their overall supply and to the financial state of their business. For some businesses which are only just viable, the loss of revenue, even if only representing a small proportion of total income, might be critical. This could force some businesses to close, with a knock-on effect for local communities. Because of the more remote location of some of these businesses, it cannot be assumed that custom lost by a specific individual or business would necessarily be picked up by another.

Effect on the horse economy

3.63   Hunting as an economic and social activity is intrinsically intertwined with other activities within the horse and countryside economy. The horse economy is large, with an estimated 2.4 million participants in horse riding and 900,000 horses.[115] As we note in the following chapter, related activities and events include point-to-points, National Hunt, pony clubs and agricultural and country shows. Other related interests include riding schools, veterinary surgeons, horse breeders, farmers and all the businesses which depend to a greater or lesser extent on hunting. It is possible that, in the event of a ban on hunting, these businesses could be dealt a double blow. Not only might they suffer a loss of income from hunting but, if the related activities were also affected, they might lose income from those activities too.

3.64   Among the points which were put to us were:

- the Association of British Riding Schools told us that their part of the equestrian industry has been struggling financially since the early 1990s and that livery for hunting and the hire of horses for hunting in many rural (and urban) areas is an essential part of riding schools' business.[116] A survey of riding schools, recently conducted by the Association, found a dramatic decline in the number of schools in business, due to increases in the Uniform Business Rate, district council licensing fees, veterinary fees, insurance premiums and the cost of complying with new Health & Safety requirements

- the British Equine Veterinary Association estimates that several hundred veterinary surgeons deal regularly with horses involved in hunting, although many more may deal with them occasionally.[117] A recent poll amongst veterinary practices in Gloucestershire revealed that 36 out of 40 treat horses

---

[115] National Equestrian Survey, 1999
[116] Association of British Riding Schools 2
[117] British Equine Veterinary Association 1, Para 1,2

regularly and that in 9 of these practices equine work accounts for 75% of their caseload

- the Farriers Registration Council estimates that, in the worst case scenario, there would be a loss to the industry of around 32% of business. It notes that, whatever the take-up of drag hunting or bloodhound hunting in the event of a ban, the frequency of shoeing for horses engaged in such activities is less than that for foxhunting.[118]

3.65 In the event of a ban on hunting, there could also be a significant impact on point-to-pointing, National Hunt racing and other equestrian interests. Among the points which were put to us were:

- the British Horse Racing Board has estimated that, at a minimum, at least one quarter of point-to-point venues would close as a consequence of a ban in hunting.[119] Such a shrinkage is estimated to lead to a drop of at least 25% in the total numbers of people and horses participating in the sport

- in terms of National Hunt, Hunter Chases, for horses which have hunted in the current season, make up 9-10% of the National Hunt steeplechase programme and these races would obviously be affected, with subsequent effects on employment

- there would be a loss in the breeding, training and trading of hunting, point-to-point and National Hunt horses, as well as general horse-related services and specialist services specifically related to this sector of the industry, including insurance and transportation. In the event of a ban on hunting, there might be a decline in breeding activity as dressage and showjumping horses are imported at high prices from the Continent

- current employment associated with point-to-points is obviously predominantly rural, involving some 660 trainers, 1,000 stable staff, vets, farriers, transporters, feed and forage merchants and a variety of other services, including breeders, stud staff and agents.[120] A reduction in the volume of point-to-pointing might lead to job losses in these businesses

- in addition, there might be a knock-on effect on the professional racing industry. Of the 523 professional licensed trainers (employing over 5,300 stable staff), 56% are located away from the five main training centres (Newmarket, Lambourn, Middleham, Malton and Epsom). These trainers rely on local suppliers whose economic viability depends on the existence of sufficient demand, part of which arises from the local hunt

[118] Farriers' Registration Council, 1,3
[119] British Horse Racing Board 1 and 2
[120] Ibid 18

- the UK is the centre of the "eventing" world, which also has its roots in hunting. The British Equestrian Trade Association predicts a decline in eventing over the longer term as fewer young people grow up in a hunting environment[121]

- as other equestrian activities declined in popularity following a ban on hunting, BETA predicts that showjumping would become more popular, but large indoor facilities would be in much greater demand and unaffiliated showjumping events held in farmers' fields would become less frequent.[122]

3.66   In addition to various consequential effects of a ban on hunting on other equine sporting events, there might be similar changes to dog shows and other canine events. For example, the Hound Trailing Association told us that a ban on hunting could lead to them losing permission to run on some landowners' courses.[123]

3.67   In summary, a ban on hunting ban could set in train a series of interlocking reactions which would affect a wide range of equestrian activities and businesses and might alter the structure of the equestrian industry as a whole. BETA predicts that, without hunting to sustain it, equestrian activity would be likely to change to a more elitist model, akin to that which exists in Germany, over a generation or so. As the rural riding school sector continued to decline, exacerbated by the loss of hunting livery income, riding centres would become more like clubs, with good facilities and a more affluent customer base, and would be concentrated in the suburbs of the larger conurbations. They note that even now many of the major equestrian establishments are not in rural areas. This would lead to a growing interest in indoor equestrian activity, particularly in dressage. Concurrently, there would be an increase in less well-managed establishments, offering low cost options with lower standards to cater for a declining lower end of the market. As riding became more elitist, BETA predicts that fewer people would take part, with a decline to around 1.4m riders. In such a reduced market place, surviving businesses would be larger and more profitable and the breeding industries would produce predominantly dressage horses.[124]

Effect on individuals

3.68   Another very important factor to bear in mind is that the people who would be displaced from the jobs which are dependent on hunting would not necessarily be suitable for the new jobs being created. This was a point emphasised to us by the TGWU and the Union of Country Sports Workers in their evidence to us.[125] [126] Most of the people employed by hunts and hunt followers fall into an employment group which is expected to decline over the next ten years. Many of those displaced would not have - or would

---

[121] BETA 1, un-numbered
[122] Ibid, un-numbered
[123] Hound Trailing Association, Ltd 2, un-numbered
[124] BETA 1, un-numbered
[125] Rural & Agricultural and Allied Workers (TGWU) 1, un-numbered
[126] Union of Country Sports Workers 1, 4(a)

find it difficult to acquire - the skills and qualifications needed.[127]   Some thought would need to be given to ways in which the people concerned might be re-trained.

3.69   Research in other areas suggests that, while some of those who are displaced would find jobs almost immediately, a larger number would not do so for some time or might drop out of the labour market altogether.   The process of adjustment could be severe for the individuals involved, their families and, in some cases, for local communities.

3.70   Another important factor is that a person's income may be made up of a number of different income sources.   For example, someone may have seasonal employment or supplement their income from work during the week with money earned at weekends.   In this situation, if one of these elements is put at risk, the individual's financial situation as a whole can be endangered.   How serious this would turn out to be in practice would depend on the actual jobs available to that person, not the total number of vacancies available in the region.   To people who would be displaced by hunting, this makes the state of the related employment sectors - farming, tourism, horse-related recreation and forestry - of particular importance.   Here, again, the use of aggregated data, even those used for remote rural regions, may not really shed much light on the way in which individuals would actually be affected by a ban on hunting.

3.71   As we noted earlier on, too, the rural economy involves a good deal of unpaid work in which people either give up their time voluntarily or for payment in kind.   It is very difficult to predict what the effects would be of a ban on employment of this kind and how much of it would be redirected to other activities.

Conclusions

3.72   In view of all the uncertainties, it is not possible to give a precise figure for the number of jobs which would be lost if hunting were banned.   In terms of national employment statistics, the short-term loss would be limited, and extend not much further than those employed by the hunt, and some employed by those hunt followers who immediately reduced their use of horses.   In the medium term, say three to five years, more losses would occur as hunt followers brought their horse numbers into line with current use.   Losses would also arise in the wider rural economy, in particular the horse economy, although in part they would be offset by other changes, including expenditure being diverted into other activities.   In the long term, say seven to ten years, most (if not all) of the effects would be offset as resources were diverted to new activities and the rural economy adjusted to other economic forces.

3.73   In terms of national resource use, the economic effects of a ban on hunting would be unlikely to be substantial, especially in the context of the drastic changes taking place in the agricultural sector.   However, at least in the short and medium term, the individual and local effects would be more serious.   Most jobs that are

---

[127] PACEC, 6.4.6

directly dependent on hunting are in the land-based sector. Some of those directly affected have specialised skills which would not transfer easily, and they would find it hard to find alternative employment. For these people especially, the adjustment process could be painful. Some thought would have to be given to the possibilities for re-training and acquiring new skills.

3.74   For some businesses that are on the borderline of viability, the loss of revenue could lead to a bigger impact than the direct effect may suggest. For a small number of local communities which depend to a significant extent on hunting, and where there are limited alternative employment opportunities, the effects could also be more serious.

3.75   Farmers would lose the benefit of a recreation they value. In addition, many of them would feel that they had suffered an economic loss since a free "pest control" service would have been removed; they would expect more predation of lambs, poultry, piglets and game birds; and they would lose the "fallen stock" service provided by many hunts. The negative impacts of a ban would be particularly resented because they would be viewed as unnecessary by many of those affected, and as an avoidable addition to other problems facing the farming community.

CHAPTER 4

SOCIAL AND CULTURAL ASPECTS

4.1   This chapter considers the impact of hunting, and of a ban on hunting, on the "social and cultural life of the countryside". We have taken this to include sporting and social events associated with hunting.

4.2   Although in the last few years the economic arguments about hunting have come to the fore, its proponents have also continued to stress its importance to the social, cultural and sporting life of rural communities. Indeed, it has often been argued that organised hunting plays a vital role in binding rural communities together. The Countryside Alliance, in their evidence to us, said that "hunting provides the social glue in many communities because it provides a valid purpose for socialising".[128]   By contrast, opponents of hunting have argued strongly that hunting, far from engendering social cohesion, is divisive and gives rise to social tensions within rural communities.[129]

4.3   What was less clear to us, though was what were the views of people living in rural communities. How important is hunting to the social lives of those who participate? And what about people who do not take part? How were their lives affected, if at all, by hunting and its related activities? Were there, for example, other social networks which operated in their case? What would be the impact on them if hunting was banned? We were also aware that some of those opposed to hunting felt that their lives were adversely affected by hunting, especially if conflict arose because they refused to allow hunts on their land.

4.4   In the following paragraphs we begin by setting out what we see as the broader social and cultural context in which hunting, especially organised hunting, takes place. We then describe some of the social, cultural and sporting activities which hunts and their supporters arrange. We summarise the ways in which, it is argued, they contribute to life in rural communities and the views of those who believe that hunting has a detrimental effect on the lives of people in these areas. We then go on to describe the findings of some research which we commissioned on these matters from Dr Paul Milbourne and his colleagues in the Department of City and Regional Planning, Cardiff University.[130] Their report has helped us to reach a better understanding of the complexities which, as so often, underlie issues of this kind.

---

[128] CA1, 9.2

[129] League Against Cruel Sports (LACS) 1, 9

[130] *The effects of hunting with dogs on the social and cultural life of the countryside in England and Wales.* Paul Milbourne, Andrew Norton and Rebekah Widdowfield, Department of City and Regional Planning, Cardiff University. ('Milbourne et al')

The wider context

4.5   We think it is important, both for the purposes of this chapter and for our report as a whole, to set out what we have come to see as the wider context in which hunting - in particular, hunting by the registered packs - takes place. We believe that appreciating the social and cultural significance of hunting, especially in its organised forms, may be helpful in understanding why it seems to assume greater significance than an analysis of the sum of its parts may suggest is warranted.

4.6   We think that the key to this is two fold: that it is a highly co-operative activity and that, as we emphasised in the previous chapter, it takes place essentially in a rural setting. It is clear from the figures which we give in Chapter 2 and Appendix 7 about the costs of the registered packs that a good deal of the traditional mounted hunting which takes place is not cost effective - in the sense that no one individual would be likely to pay these sums to kill a single fox, deer or hare. This confirms that these activities are seen as serving a wider purpose and providing different 'outputs' which are of value to different participants. Indeed, there are few other activities which involve such an extensive degree of co-operative effort.

4.7   Farmers (and landowners) are at the heart of this activity. As a group, they are clearly in favour of hunting. They participate in significant numbers. They provide the land on which hunting takes place. They benefit from pest control to the extent that it matters. They believe that they understand best what is good for the countryside.

4.8   It is clear from the letters we received that others enjoy participating for a variety of reasons.[131] Some like riding horses and are willing to pay subscriptions and daily charges ('caps') to take part in the hunt: about 60% of the hunts' income comes from subscriptions, donations and caps. Some like watching hounds work. Some simply enjoy the social life and being out in the countryside. Some do not actively take part but support hunting in various ways because they see it as part of the local community and as a traditional country pursuit. This includes attending hunt social events: about 30% of the hunts' income comes from various fund-raising activities. Even those who hunt essentially for recreational purposes, though, usually believe their enjoyment is ultimately in a good cause managing the population of the animal concerned. However, there are no doubt a few people - mainly away from public gaze and often illegally – who hunt simply because they enjoy using their dogs to kill animals.

4.9   Organised hunting also gains support from a whole host of other interest groups who benefit in some way from it: the equestrian trade, the farriers, rural pubs and so on.

4.10   Organised hunting is therefore an intricate and complex social activity which is intimately linked to other features of rural life and which rests on a foundation of overlapping mutual interests, with the farmer/landowner at the hub. As we indicated in the previous chapter, though, farmers in particular see themselves as a group facing great pressures as a result of the recent serious decline in the agricultural sector. The fact that

---

[131] See Appendix 3 for analysis of the letters we received from members of the public.

hunting is under threat simply adds to the sense that they are an embattled, isolated group, whose interests and way of life are not really appreciated by central government and the urban majority.[132]

4.11   But we also need to recognise that, as we noted in the previous chapter, rural communities are diverse and are changing in character. Many, especially those near urban centres, have experienced major changes in recent years as agriculture has declined in importance, communications have improved and new people, and new types of employment, have moved in from the towns. As the research by Dr Milbourne and his colleagues tends to confirm, the part played by hunting in the social and cultural life of rural communities varies greatly, depending on factors such as their proximity to urban centres and the type of hunting which takes place.

4.12   Living, sometimes uncomfortably, in rural communities - or visiting the countryside - are those who are opposed to hunting. They fall into several categories. There are those who have a moral objection to hunting and who are fundamentally opposed to the idea of people gaining pleasure from what they regard as the causing of unnecessary suffering. There are also those who perceive hunting as representing a divisive social class system. Others, as we note below, resent the hunt trespassing on their land, especially when they have been told they are not welcome. They worry about the welfare of the pets and animals and the difficulty of moving around the roads where they live on hunt days. Finally there are those who are concerned about damage to the countryside and other animals, particularly badgers and otters.

Social, cultural and sporting activities

4.13   Hunting is, of course, a social event in its own right, as we have already mentioned in Chapters 2 and 3. For those who participate, organised hunting has a strong social - even ritual - element.[133] This social element takes on a formal character at the opening meet but, as we have seen on our visits, it is also an enjoyable and valued part of the rest of the day. This social interaction can take many forms, including the opportunity for the mounted field to chat while the hounds work and for car followers to pass the time of day by the roadside as they scan the hills trying to follow the course of the hunt.

4.14   We do not underestimate the importance, for those who take part, of the opportunities for social interaction provided by hunting. Especially for those living in remote rural areas, it can help to counter the isolation that is often felt by farmers and others, particularly during the long winter months.

---

[132] Professor Peter Midmore of the University of Wales, Aberystwyth, argued in written evidence that economic pressures are contributing to increasing psychological morbidity in farming and rural communities.

[133] Dr Garry Marvin , an anthropologist who provided us with an interpretative account of foxhunting, has examined these ritual aspects in detail. See 'The problem of foxes: legitimate and illegitimate killing in the English countryside'. Forthcoming in Knight J (ed) 2000 The Politics of Wildlife: Anthropological Perspectives, Routledge, London.

Social Events

4.15   The hunts organise numerous social events, many of which are designed to raise money to defray their costs. In their evidence to us, the Countryside Alliance and the hunts gave many examples of the events they organise. These included dinners, dances, discos, hunt balls, barbecues, dog shows, hunter trials, coffee mornings, coach trips, point-to-points, pantomimes, hedge-laying competitions, cricket matches, pub evenings, talks/presentations, barn dances, darts matches, midnight steeplechases, horse trials, quiz nights, antiques days, skittles evenings, wine and cheese evenings, garden parties, hunt suppers, clay pigeon shoots and young supporters' parties.[134] The Produce Studies report on the National Survey of Hunts estimated that hunts organise nearly 4,000 functions a year, which are attended by over one and a quarter million people.[135]   The Produce Studies separate survey of hunt supporters' clubs estimated a further 800 events each year, with a total attendance of between 250,000 and 500,000. As the Farmers' Union of Wales also pointed out, the use made by hunts of local facilities, such as village/church halls and local pubs, helps to maintain these facilities.[136]

4.16   Many of these social events, such as coffee mornings and barbecues, are not exclusive to the hunts. They are typical of the kind of event organised up and down the country by a whole host of groups such as pubs, churches, football clubs and the Women's Institute. We discuss below, in the context of the research outcomes, the respective part played by hunts and other groups in organising such events. However, some of the events that take place are, by their nature, much more closely linked with the hunt. The most notable examples are point-to-points, puppy shows, pony clubs and country fairs and shows.

Point-to-points

4.17   We have already noted, in the previous chapter, the potential implications for point-to-point racing of a ban on hunting. Point-to-point races are regulated by the Jockey Club but are run almost exclusively by the hunts. The Countryside Alliance told us that, of the 209 listed point-to-point meetings, 189 are organised by the hunts.[137]   Some 700,000 people attend events each year.[138]   The most important aspect of the hunts' involvement is that much of the voluntary labour needed to run point-to-point meetings is supplied by the hunt. There is, of course, an incentive for hunt members and supporters to offer their services, since point-to-points are an important source of funds for the hunt. Another aspect, though, is that landowners or farmers will often charge a reduced fee for the use of their land because they themselves support the hunt.

---

[134] CA1, 99
[135] CA1, 10.4
[136] Farmers' Union of Wales 1,46
[137] CA1, 9.13
[138] The British Bloodstock Agency plc 1, un-numbered

Puppy shows

4.18 The organisation of puppy shows is another activity which is strongly linked with the hunts, providing an opportunity to show the young hounds as part of a social gathering. These shows are popular social events, for example in the Fells.[139]

Pony clubs

4.19 Most hunts run pony clubs. These provide an opportunity for children to learn to ride under the guidance of people associated with the hunt. The cost tends to be lower than attending a riding school.

4.20 The Pony Club has stated that its origins are in hunting and that nearly all branches of the Pony Club are named after the hunt in their area. Although Pony Clubs might be able to survive in the event of ban, hunting with dogs sustains them by offering a non-competitive equestrian activity for children and in fostering equestrian skills.[140]

Country and Agricultural Shows

4.21 Country and agricultural shows seek to promote the countryside and encourage the link between the rural and urban populations. Horses, horse breeding, horse showing including jumping, both show jumping and working hunter, and farrier work are an integral part of shows, as are the many country pursuits such as hedging, conservation and forestry which are all part of the countryside and its way of life.

4.22 Evidence submitted by the Association of Show & Agricultural Organisations, which has just over 200 members, and by several individual show societies, suggests that certain events other than the display of hounds by hunt staff, such as horse classes, both breeding and jumping, and farrier classes, might be affected by a ban on hunting.[141] In addition, the take-up of trade stands from equestrian suppliers would decline and sponsorship might suffer. Many shows emphasised that they depend on hunts and their followers to provide the stewarding of such events and other vital volunteer labour.

4.23 Show societies varied in their estimation of the extent to which a ban on hunting would affect the number of people attending their events as spectators, participants, volunteers and traders. The Newbury and District Agricultural Society quoted as much as a 50% loss to their programme of events, and the Tavistock Country Show stated that it would be forced to stop in the event of a ban on hunting.

4.24 Our evidence suggests that there is a reservoir of hunting people who contribute to running and assisting in the management of all of the above activities and that, although it is difficult to quantify the effects of a ban on hunting on such contributions, there would be likely to be at least a temporary reduction in such volunteer labour.

---

[139] CA1, 9.11
[140] CA1, 9.19
[141] Association of Show and Agricultural Organisations 1, un-numbered

Cultural matters

4.25 The Countryside Alliance and others also drew our attention to the contribution which hunting has made to literature, art, music and architecture. This is perhaps best known through the work of Stubbs and, more popularly, the work of numerous other artists who have made, and continue to make, paintings, pictures and prints focusing on hunting scenes. Many of these adorn the walls of pubs and restaurants in rural areas. Hunting has also featured in literature through the centuries.[142]

Evidence about negative social effects

4.26 Deadline 2000 and its supporters provided evidence of a very different nature, both in its formal submissions and at the meetings we attended with opponents of hunting.[143]

4.27 This evidence fell into two broad related categories. The first consisted of complaints about trespass, disruption and disturbance and the way in which hunts responded to representations made about these matters. We discuss this aspect in greater detail in Chapter 9 of our report. The second reflected concern about the tensions and divisions in rural communities that can be caused by hunting and the fact that those opposed to hunting could be ostracised if they complained or could feel that they could not speak openly about their views. This is touched on in the research undertaken by Dr Milbourne and his colleagues.

4.28 A national survey undertaken for IFAW by MORI, and submitted to us just before we were due to report, revealed that only 28% of those living in the middle or the edge of the countryside (as defined by respondents themselves) were aware of hunting taking place in their local area. However, nearly all of that group (25%) were aware of one or more listed types of hunt havoc taking place locally (ranging from 4% awareness of trespass on railway lines to 12% awareness of trespass on private land). In the absence either of any information on the actual geographical locations of respondents or of what is meant by awareness of particular activities, it is hard to assess the full meaning of these figures. In particular, the respondents were not asked whether their awareness was based on personal experience, newspaper reports or hearsay.

Research outcomes

Methodology

4.29 The research focused on a number of parishes/communities in four rural areas in different parts of the country, all of which are covered by particular hunts. The areas chosen were in West Cumbria, Devon and Somerset (Exmoor), Leicestershire and Powys.

---

[142] CA1, 9.35
[143] IFAW 1,9; Hunt Havoc LACS 1, 9; RSPCA 1, 9 & 10; notes of 'by invitation' meetings in Taunton, Wrexham and York. (On CD Rom).

None of the areas contained any towns and the hunt kennels were located in one of the parishes/communities in each area.[144] Interviews were conducted in 17 parishes in total. In three cases entire hunt countries were covered in the survey. By contrast, in Leicestershire, where the villages have larger populations, a portion of the hunt country was covered.

4.30   Although all the study areas were rural, they differed in a number of respects. For example, the West Cumbria area is very remote, while the Leicestershire area is relatively close to urban centres. Hunting is a significant part of the local economy in the Devon and Somerset study area, but much less so in the others.[145]

4.31   As part of the research, MORI carried out face-to-face surveys of about 150 households in each of the study areas.[146] These were followed up by in-depth interviews with a selected number of respondents.[147] This information was supplemented by telephone interviews with Chairs of parish/community councils and by examining the relevant returns from a survey of hunts carried out by the Countryside Alliance.[148]

Findings

4.32   It is important to bear in mind in considering the research findings that the research was carried out in four areas only and that it was deliberately designed to focus on areas in which organised hunting actively takes place. The study areas were not typical of rural districts as a whole, which include many large villages and market towns. As we have just noted, one of the areas - Devon and Somerset - is known to have a particularly high involvement in hunting. Deadline 2000 expressed strong concerns at the research seminar and in subsequent submissions that the research "was always likely to conclude that most people who agreed to be interviewed were opposed to the abolition of hunting due to the areas selected",[149] which they suggested were strongly pro-hunting. We are not persuaded that the research was biased in the way suggested. On the contrary, the response rate to the survey (77% agreed to be interviewed) was high and was commended as such by the independent scrutineer, Professor Keith Hoggart, and the comparisons with the 1991 Census results for the parishes concerned showed no obvious bias. Only one of the areas (Exmoor) was chosen because of its strong associations with hunting. All the others, like the majority of rural land in England and Wales, were located in areas hunted over by registered packs, but there were no grounds for supposing them to be either typical or atypical of other rural areas. In a number of respects, such as the high levels of in-migration, they would seem to be typical of many rural parishes, although there was a higher proportion of people engaged in agricultural occupations than might have been expected.

---

[144] Milbourne et al, 2.1–2, 3
[145] Ibid
[146] Ibid, 2.4
[147] Ibid, 2.87
[148] Ibid, 2.10, 2.11
[149] Research seminar: Social and Cultural Aspects, 8 May 2000, Session One. LACS 2, un-numbered

4.33   Allowing for some inevitable over-simplification, we think that it is worth highlighting the general picture which emerges:

- there was a high degree of awareness of organised hunting

- there were higher levels of support for hunting (and opposition to a ban on hunting) than previous surveys have suggested

- support tended to be based not so much on importance to the individual - although this was true for hunt participants and some farmers - but a belief that hunting had greater significance for the community as a whole and for others living there

- hunt-based social activities play a significant part in the social life of these communities, but are not as significant as those of the local pub or church

- support for hunting, and a belief in its importance to individuals and to the local community, was particularly strong in the Devon and Somerset study area

- a significant minority was opposed to hunting and would welcome its abolition.

We discuss these findings in greater detail in the following paragraphs.

Support for hunting

4.34   One of the key messages which emerges is that, in these study areas at least, people are more supportive of hunting than previous surveys in rural areas have suggested. Overall, about half of respondents were in favour of hunting with dogs, with the remainder almost equally divided between those who were opposed to it and those who were neither for or against. Support was strongest in the Devon and Somerset study area, where around two-thirds of respondents favoured hunting, and weakest in the Leicestershire study area where just over a third were in favour.[150] Even amongst those who had not seen a hunt or who had not hunted in the last twelve months, there were more people in favour of hunting than against it.[151]

4.35   Broadly speaking, support was highest in all areas amongst men, older people, those who had lived in the area for a long time, people working in rural occupations and those in lower social class bands.[152] But even amongst incoming residents, workers in

---

[150] Milbourne et al, 5.8

[151] Ibid, 5.9. This compares with a survey of 750 households in five case study areas of the English and Welsh countryside in 1999, which found that just under a third of respondents supported hunting wild animals. The highest level of support was 40% in a group of rural parishes in West Devon, followed by 36% in Hampshire villages, 27% in Norfolk, 25% in Cheshire and 19% in Powys.

[152] Milbourne et al, 5.10, 5.11

non-rural occupations and those in higher social classes more people were in favour of hunting than opposed to it.[153]

4.36   Similarly, the research revealed that nearly 60% of respondents in the four study areas were opposed to a ban on hunting. This is a much higher figure than that reported following a MORI poll undertaken in September 1999. In the latter survey only 25% of those polled in rural areas expressed any opposition to a ban on hunting.[154]

4.37   The two main reasons put forward for supporting hunting were its perceived role in controlling pests and its traditional role in the countryside.[155] The former was mentioned by about two-fifths of supporters, and the latter by a third. Interestingly, only some 15% of supporters mentioned its economic importance, with a similar proportion mentioning social and recreational benefits.[156]

4.38   These findings about people's attitudes to hunting are interesting in their own right. But they also provide an important backdrop and context for the assessment of the significance of hunting, especially organised hunting, to the social and cultural life of the countryside. They indicate that people in the areas concerned were, for a variety of reasons, generally supportive of hunting and therefore viewed hunting and its activities in that light.

The importance of hunting at individual and community levels

4.39   Another message which emerges from the research - and which ties in with the findings on the level of support for hunting - is that people tended to accord a higher significance, at the community level, to hunting and hunt-related activities than they did at a personal level. For example, although only a quarter of respondents in the four areas felt that hunting played an important part in their day-to-day lives, almost two-thirds felt that it played an important part of life in their local area. Even in West Cumbria, where only one in ten respondents considered hunting to be important in their daily lives, over half of all respondents thought that hunting played an important role at a community level.[157]

4.40   The reasons put forward for thinking hunting important at a community level differed in certain respects from those advanced in support of hunting in general. Contribution to local employment was mentioned most often - by a quarter of all respondents. The other reasons mentioned most often were hunting's position as a traditional part of rural life, its social role and its part in pest control.[158]

---

[153] Ibid, 5.10
[154] Ibid, 5.31
[155] Ibid, 5.12, 5.13
[156] Ibid, 5.14
[157] Ibid, 5.17, 5.19
[158] Ibid, 5.20

Hunting's contribution to social and cultural life

4.41   As is perhaps already clear from this discussion, hunting's contribution to social and cultural life was not the main factor underlining support for hunting. Nevertheless, it is clear that organised hunting plays an important role in the social life of these communities.   Nearly a third of respondents had attended at least one social event organised by the hunt in the last 12 months, with the figure reaching just over half in the Devon and Somerset study area.[159] But hunting's importance is less significant - even in the Devon and Somerset study area - than that of the local pub or church. In the West Cumbria, Powys and Leicestershire study areas pub-organised activities had been attended by more than twice as many respondents as those organised by the hunt, the same being true for church events in the first two areas.[160] The importance of pub-organised events was accentuated if one measures frequency of attendance. A third of respondents said they had attended pub-organised events at least once a month, compared with half that number in the case of church and hunt events.[161] More generally, it was clear that there was a wide range of other activities taking place, organised by different groups,[162] and other individual pursuits such as walking, gardening and going out for the evening.[163] It is plain, therefore, that any claim, even in respect of strongly rural areas where support for hunting is high, that hunting is the main source of social activity is exaggerated. In other rural communities, particularly larger villages and market towns, it is likely to be even less significant.

4.42   The finding that hunt-based social activities were not the main reason why hunting was perceived as important at a community level tended to be borne out in follow-up interviews.   Only a fifth of interviewees thought that these activities represented the hub of the local community.[164] Nearly half thought that any community function was confined to particular groups such as farmers and hunt participants.[165] About a third thought that these activities contributed either little or nothing to the local community.[166]

Devon and Somerset study area

4.43   On all measures, support for hunting and a belief in its importance to individuals and the community were substantially greater for residents and interviewees in the Devon and Somerset study area than was the case in the other three areas. For example, a half of all respondents in the Devon and Somerset study area thought that hunting was very important or fairly important to their daily lives.[167] This compares with one in five in the

---

[159] Ibid, 4.20
[160] Ibid, 4.22
[161] Ibid, 4.24
[162] Ibid, 4.25, 4.26
[163] Ibid, 4.27
[164] Ibid, 4.28
[165] Ibid, 4.29
[166] Ibid, 4.30
[167] Ibid, 5.17

Powys study area, which had the next highest rating.[168] These findings are not really surprising, given that it is generally recognised that this particular area is the heartland of hunting in England and Wales. But they do bear out the fact that, even amongst rural areas, Devon and Somerset, particularly the Exmoor area, is something of a special case.

Opposition to hunting

4.44   The research findings do not really support the claim that is sometimes made that, even in rural areas with a strong hunting tradition, there is much greater opposition to hunting than is generally supposed.

4.45   As we have already noted, only 25% of all respondents were opposed to hunting, the highest figure being in Leicestershire. But even there the numbers were lower than those who favoured it.[169] Those who opposed hunting with dogs tended to do so because they thought that it was cruel and unnecessary and because they considered that there were better and more humane ways of controlling foxes and other pests. A much smaller proportion of respondents justified their opposition to hunting in relation to the practice of hunting with 8% of opponents considering hunt participants to be either arrogant or elitist. Thus, nuisance and social divisiveness, whilst not apparently of great importance, were mentioned by some of those who opposed hunting. These views tended to emerge more strongly in the follow-up interviews[170]. For some people (approximately 10% of those interviewed) hunting represented an inconvenience to their everyday lives, with several examples provided of dangerous driving and roads being blocked by hunt followers. Others (around 16% of interviewees) pointed to the arrogant behaviour of some followers; the damage caused to fields and verges; gates being left open or damage caused to dry stone walls and fences; problems caused if hounds reach more densely settled areas; and the offence that 'messy kills' or incidents can cause to passers-by. We discuss these issues in Chapter 9 of our report.

4.46   About a fifth of those residents who held mixed views or an anti-hunting viewpoint tended not to discuss their opinions with others, either because of what they perceived as the local support for hunting or because it was not sufficiently significant as a local issue to warrant discussion.[171]

Discussion

4.47   It was put to us that the Countryside Agency's report, State of the Countryside 2000, confirmed that hunting plays little role in rural life.[172] The report[173] lists a wide

---

[168] Ibid, 5.17

[169] Ibid, Table 13

[170] It should be recalled that the follow-up interviews were not with a representative sample of residents and that therefore the percentage figures need to be viewed in that light. They are included to indicate that these opinions were not confined to one or two respondents but represented a significant body of minority opinion within the study areas.

[171] Ibid, 6.11

[172] Research Seminar: Social and Cultural Aspects, Session One 8 May 2000

[173] *The State of the Countryside 2000.* Countryside Agency

range of social activities in rural communities but hunting is not included, even though the report lists activities supported from between nearly 60% of the rural communities (Women's Institute and Mothers' Union) down to 3% to 4% (swimming club). It is clear, however, that the differences result entirely from the fact that the Countryside Agency's report and the study by Dr. Milbourne and his colleagues had very different purposes. In particular, the Countryside Agency's report was concerned with facilities, rather than activities, in a particular parish. It is interesting to note that angling does not figure in the Countryside Agency data either, despite its being a significant leisure activity in the countryside.

4.48   The research findings largely mirror our own perceptions of the complexity - even, perhaps, the contradictory and paradoxical nature - of views on hunting and its importance to individuals and local communities. An obvious example from the research is the finding which we have already noted that, while nearly two-thirds of respondents thought that hunting played an important part in the life of the local area, only a quarter thought it important to their own day-to-day lives. The complexity of views is not particularly surprising. Hunting takes many forms; there are different traditions in different areas; the topography, geography and farming activities can vary greatly; and rural areas are not uniformly "rural" - some are extremely remote, while others have strong urban influences. People too are influenced by their backgrounds, the views of their families and neighbours and their perception of community interests. What will be important to one person will be of no importance at all to his or her neighbour.

4.49   There are good reasons, therefore, to be cautious in extrapolating from any particular set of findings. It also needs to be borne in mind that this particular piece of research deliberately set out to study the social and cultural role of hunting in areas of the countryside in which organised, visible hunting takes place. The findings are, at most, representative of different types of hunting areas. They are not necessarily representative of all hunting areas or of rural areas more generally. As the researchers pointed out too, their work was carried out at a time when the debate about hunting is to the fore and when other rural issues are causing great concern.[174]

4.50   Our feeling from this research, the evidence presented to us and other research findings is that hunting plays a central social role in the lives of many hunt participants and supporters. Many feel too that there is a culture associated with hunting that would be lost to the equestrian industry and to the countryside in general in the event of a ban. In particular, they feel that there is a set of social mores and body of knowledge and understanding associated with hunting which has ramifications extending beyond the hunting field, linked with the proper care of horses, the countryside and other riders and users of the countryside.

4.51   While it is hard to over-estimate the importance of hunting to the lives of those people who are very actively involved in hunting, it is important to recognise that they comprise a relatively small proportion of residents in rural areas and that the effects of a ban on hunting would be felt most acutely by those living in the more isolated rural areas.

---

[174] Milbourne et al, 6.1

Here, population densities are lower and there is less interface with towns and cities as a source of alternative activities. In the less isolated areas, and where the population is more socially diverse, a ban would not have the same impact.

Conclusions

4.52   Rural communities are diverse. Many, especially those near urban centres, have experienced substantial changes in recent years as agriculture has declined in importance, communications have improved and people have moved in from towns. The part played by hunting in the social and cultural life of rural communities varies greatly, depending on factors such as their proximity to urban centres and the type of hunting taking place.

4.53   The social activities organised by the hunts form an important feature of the social life of those communities in which hunting is actively pursued.   For a significant minority, notably hunt participants and farmers in more isolated rural communities, the hunts play a dominant role.   The loss of these activities, if that were the outcome of a ban on hunting, would be keenly felt.   For those who take part, hunting is itself partly a social event, particularly during the winter months when alternative activities are scarce.   For others, the social activities organised by the hunts are significant, but less so than those organised by other groups, in particular the pub and the church.   Even those who would not feel greatly, at a personal level, the loss of the hunts' social activities consider that it would have a detrimental effect on the social life of others and on community life in general.   A number would also feel that it would mark the end of an important, living cultural tradition.   The precise balance between these different responses would vary from region to region and area to area.   Generally, however, the impact would be felt most strongly in the more isolated rural areas.   In areas of greater population density where there are more alternative activities available, and where the population is more socially diverse, a ban would make less of a social impact.

4.54   It is clear that, especially for participants in more isolated rural communities, hunting acts as a significant cohesive force, encouraging a system of mutual support.   Farmers and other landowners - many of whom feel increasingly isolated - are both the linchpins and the main beneficiaries of the system.   Many of them also value hunting as an expression of a traditional, rural way of life and would strongly resent what they would see as an unnecessary and ill-informed interference with it.   As a result it would increase their sense of alienation.

4.55   For another group, the hunt itself seems divisive, intrusive and disruptive.

4.56   Because the organisation of point-to-points relies heavily on voluntary labour supplied by hunt followers and supporters, there could be difficulties in running these events.   Pony clubs also often depend heavily on hunt followers and supporters.   To a lesser extent these too could be affected by a ban.   These activities should be able to continue provided alternative forms of organisation develop.

CHAPTER 5

POPULATION MANAGEMENT AND CONTROL

5.1   Our terms of reference required us to consider the impact of hunting, and of a ban on hunting, on "agriculture and pest control [and] the management and conservation of wildlife".   Chapter 6 discusses in greater detail the animal welfare issues that are associated with hunting and other methods of control.   Chapter 7 addresses issues to do with the effect of hunting on the management and conservation of habitat and other wildlife.   In this chapter we examine:

- the reasons which are put forward by farmers, foresters, game managers and others for managing the fox, deer, hare and mink populations

- the methods that are used and their effectiveness

- the impact of hunting, and the effect of a ban, on the management of these populations

5.2   Our examination of these issues was helped by the research which we commissioned from two teams led by Professor David Macdonald and by Professor Stephen Harris. Both research reports[175] [176] contain a wealth of information summarising evidence drawn from other recent research and surveys as well as other evidence submitted to us. In the following paragraphs we try to summarise the key points and to set out our own conclusions.

5.3   Before turning to a discussion of each of the quarry species, it is worth noting some of the cautionary points that need to be borne in mind in considering the management of animal populations, especially those which may be regarded as pests:

- the population of a particular species is naturally limited by the availability of critical resources such as food and breeding sites or by other factors such as predation and the weather[177]

---

[175] *Management and Control of Populations of Foxes, Deer, Hares, and Mink in England and Wales, and the Impact of Hunting with Dogs.* Macdonald, D.W.[1] Tattersall, F.H.[1],Johnson, P.J.[1],Carbone, C.[1], Reynolds, J.C.[2], Langbein, J.[3], Rushton, S.P.[4] and Shirley, M.D.F.[4] [1] Wildlife Conservation Research Unit, Dept. of Zoology, South Parks Rd., Oxford, OX1 3PS; [2] The Game Conservancy Trust, Fordingbridge, Hampshire SP6 1EF; [3]Wildlife Research Consultant, "Greenleas", Chapel Cleeve, Minehead, Somerset TA24 6HY;[4] Centre for Land Use and Water Resources Research, University of Newcastle Upon Tyne, Porter Building, Newcastle Upon Tyne NE1 7RU

[176] *Management of the Population of Foxes, Deer, Hares and Mink and the Impact of Hunting with Dogs.* Piran White[1],Philip Baker[2],Geraldine Newton Cross[1], James Smart[1], Rebecca Moberly[1], Graeme McLaren[3],Rachel Ansell[2], and Stephen Harris[2] [1]Environment Department, University of York, Heslington, York YO1 5DD, [2]School of Biological Sciences, University of Bristol, Woodland Road, Bristol BS8 1UG,[3]Myerscough College, Bilsborrow, Preston, Lancashire PR3 ORY.

[177]Macdonald et al, 1.3.2

- as a population approaches the maximum dictated by these factors, some form of self-regulation normally sets in. This can take the form, for example, of smaller litter sizes or the postponement of sexual maturity[178]

- there is no natural population "equilibrium level": it will depend on the prevailing combination of influences, including human intervention. It will also constantly alter as influencing factors change[179]

- the reasons for undertaking population management (which may be non-lethal or lethal) are many and varied. They include pest control, sport, food and conservation[180]

- these reasons may also be conflicting. For example, the brown hare can be viewed at the same time as a pest, a game animal and the subject of conservation action[181]

- human intervention in order to manage an animal population can take many forms, ranging from culling to non-lethal methods such as fencing or contraception[182]

- measuring the long-term impact of culling on a population is not straightforward

- culling does not necessarily produce a proportional decrease in abundance or damage: for example, other animals may move into vacant territory[183] or birth rates may increase in response to lower population density; and damage may be caused by particular individuals.[184] It is therefore important to distinguish between attempted and achieved population control, and to bear in mind that a reduction in population does not necessarily translate into a pro rata reduction in a perceived problem

- culling needs to be carefully targeted if it is to achieve maximum impact.

Foxes

Population

5.4   The pre-breeding fox population of England and Wales is thought to total some 217,000, but this estimate has a low reliability. The population almost trebles by the

---

[178] Ibid, 1.3.2; 1.3.2.a.b
[179] Ibid, 1.3.2
[180] Ibid, 1.3.1
[181] Ibid, 2.4
[182] Ibid, 1.3.1
[183] Ibid, 1.3.4.a; 1.3.4.b
[184] Ibid, 2.2.1.b

early summer.[185] Local densities are highly variable, with historically low populations in East Anglia, although numbers now seem to be increasing there. Foxes live in pairs or groups of up to about 5 adult animals, generally comprising one adult male and several females. Usually only one or two females in each group breed. Cubs are born from March to May in litters of four or five.[186]

5.5 Unfortunately, there is very little information about the numbers of foxes which are deliberately killed each year and the methods used. Since the population approximately trebles after the breeding season, and on the basis that the pre-breeding population is roughly stable or increasing slightly, this means that about 400,000 foxes die each year.

5.6 There is no reliable information about how many die by different means. However, there is circumstantial evidence, from surveys of farmers, that deliberate culling is a substantial factor in this mortality.

5.7 There is also a corresponding lack of information about the proportion of foxes which are killed by the different culling methods. Generally, systematic records are those kept by the MFHA packs. However, a study of three contrasting areas does provide some information about the different culling practices in those areas.[187]

5.8 The study showed that, for upland Wales, the east Midlands and west Norfolk, respectively, 35%, 15% and 3% of foxes culled were killed by methods involving the foxhounds, whereas 10%, 3% and 7% involved digging-out with terriers outside the context of the hunt. The proportions for those shot with a rifle (including spot lamping) were 21%, 53% and 64%, and for shotguns (when foxes were driven, usually by hounds, onto standing guns) were 25%, 9% and 4%. Snares accounted for 3%, 13% and 9%. Just over half the foxes killed were in their second year.

5.9 In summary, in the upland area of Wales, terriers or hounds were involved in some way in the killing of 70% of the fox tally, but 27% and 14% in the east Midlands and west Norfolk.

Reasons for population management

5.10 Many farmers and landowners undertake fox control but there are regional variations in the numbers doing so.[188] The only large-scale study which took account of culling by both the hunt and the individual farmer estimated that foxes were culled on an average of 88% of farms across mid Wales, the east Midlands and west Norfolk.[189] Although foxes are widely perceived as a pest, two studies suggested that rabbits, rather than foxes, were viewed as a more significant problem.[190] [191]

---

[185] Ibid,5.2.7.a
[186] Ibid, 10.1.4
[187] Heydon and Reynolds, Table 11. 2000A
[188] White et al,1.4.1.3
[189] Macdonald et al, 3.2.6.B.1
[190] White et al,4.1.4

5.11   The majority of farmers and landowners who do control foxes give several reasons for doing so. Of these, reducing fox abundance is the most frequently mentioned, generally to reduce predation on livestock and game. Foxes are also considered a pest because they are thought to transmit disease. There are considerable regional differences in the reasons for control.[192] [193] In general, more farmers in Wales cite protection of livestock (sheep) as a reason for culling foxes. In East Anglia foxes, where arable farming predominates, are perceived as less of a problem for livestock, but more of a problem for game, reflected in the large numbers of gamekeepers in the region.[194] [195] Surveys indicate that farmers in the Midlands often cite sport as a reason for killing foxes.[196] [197] Many farmers aim to contribute to regional control of fox populations. On farms larger than 200ha, an individual farmer's recent experiences of fox predation were surprisingly unrelated to their control measures, and there was evidence that farmers saw control as a preventative measure.[198]

Predation on lambs

5.12   The main concern centres on fox predation of lambs, especially in upland sheep-rearing areas where intensive husbandry is difficult and where a lower proportion of lambs (40% in mid-Wales) are born indoors.[199] There is evidence that predation levels are generally higher in upland areas than in lowland areas.[200] This probably reflects in part the tendency for more lambs to be born indoors in lowland areas.[201] It may also reflect the relative health, condition and behaviour of ewes. It is not easy, however, to establish with any certainty how serious a problem fox predation represents. Predation is not usually witnessed; it is not always possible to distinguish between the killing of healthy lambs and scavenging dead or dying ones; and other predators, including domestic dogs, also kill lambs.[202]

5.13   In a study carried out by the Game Conservancy Trust in 1995-1997 the total reported pre-weaning losses which were attributed to foxes among all 522,422 lambs (indoor and outdoor) in mid-Wales was 3,134 lambs, amounting to 0.6%.[203] As a proportion of outdoor lambs, the figure would be 1%. At a typical market price in 1996 of £31.50 per lamb the total regional loss of income would have been just under £100,000. Of course, the effect of the loss on an individual farmer will vary, depending on his or her circumstances.

---

[191] Macdonald et al, 2.2.1.b
[192] White et al, 1.4.1.5
[193] Macdonald et al, 2.2.1.f
[194] White et al, 1.4.1.5
[195] Macdonald et al, 2.2.1.b
[196] White et al, 1.4.1.5
[197] Macdonald et al, 2.2.1.f
[198] Ibid, 2.2.1.C
[199] Ibid, 2.2.1.C
[200] Ibid,1.4.2.1.1
[201] Ibid,1.4.2.1.1
[202] Macdonald et al, 2.2.1.c.i
[203] Ibid, 2.2.1.c.i

5.14   The best estimate seems to be that a low percentage (less than 2%) of otherwise viable lambs are killed by foxes in England and Wales.[204] However, levels of predation (or perceived predation) can be highly variable between farms and between different areas.[205]

5.15   It is clear that only a small proportion of foxes kill lambs; otherwise, lamb losses would be much higher. It is widely believed by shepherds that certain foxes are more likely to take lambs, including vixens with cubs and old or injured animals. It is also argued that, once a fox starts taking lambs, it is likely to continue doing so.

Predation on poultry and piglets

5.16   Predation by foxes on poultry is potentially catastrophic because foxes can indulge in surplus killing.[206] However, the vast majority of poultry are reared in secure indoor units and are not at risk.[207] Predation is therefore almost entirely confined to the growing number of smaller, free-range holdings, where losses in large commercial flocks have been estimated to be about 2% a year[208]; losses in small (<200) flocks can be much greater. The NFU informed us that, whereas 86% of eggs came from intensive units in 1995, by 1999 this had fallen to 75% in favour of free range, perchery and other more extensive systems.[209] The extent of losses varies regionally. Foxes can also cause loss of piglets, through predation and disturbance to sows; there has been no systematic study of this problem, but it is almost certainly growing, as numbers of outdoor units are increasing. The NFU report that some pig farmers with extensive outdoor systems report cases of pre-weaning deaths of over 25% directly attributable to foxes.[210]

Predation on game

5.17   It is clear that foxes kill a substantial number of game birds, both wild and hand-reared.[211] [212] Hand-reared pheasants are particularly vulnerable when they are released from their rearing pens.[213] In the absence of fox control a substantial number of birds would be lost before the start of the shooting season. Wild pheasants, on the other hand, are particularly vulnerable during the breeding period. While there are other factors that affect pheasant populations, it is probably the case that foxes are the most significant predator affecting pheasant shooting.[214] Foxes can also have an impact on partridge populations.[215] [216]

---

[204] Ibid, 2.2.1.c.i
[205] White et al, 1.4.2.1.1
[206] Ibid,1.4.2.1.c
[207] Ibid,1.4.2.1.2
[208] Ibid, 1.4.2.1.2
[209] NFU of England and Wales 2, un-numbered
[210] Ibid, un-numbered
[211] Macdonald et al, 2.2.2.b; 2.2.2.C
[212] White et al, 1.4.2.2.1
[213] Ibid,1.4.2.2.1
[214] Ibid,1.4.2.2.1
[215] Ibid, 1.4.2.2.2
[216] Macdonald et al, 2.2.2.b

5.18　It is thought that foxes are significant predators of grouse on commercial grouse moors in England and Wales.[217]

5.19　The impact of foxes on hare populations is also uncertain.[218]　Some studies suggest that the extent of predation has a substantial effect, while other studies are equivocal.[219] [220] The impact may also vary locally.

Predation on other ground-nesting birds

5.20　Many ground-nesting birds are potentially vulnerable to fox predation, particularly species such as terns which nest in colonies.[221]　This has proved a problem, especially on coastal bird reserves.[222]　Local conditions can, however, have a dramatic effect on rates of predation and other factors can affect the vulnerability of ground-nesting species.[223]

Transmission of disease

5.21　Foxes are potentially able to catch and transmit a number of parasitic infections, viral and bacterial diseases to companion animals, domestic stock and hunting dogs. However, although farmers often cite disease control as a motive for killing foxes, there is no clear evidence that foxes have been a significant contributory factor in any disease in this country.[224]

Culling for sport/pleasure

5.22　While the main motivation for culling foxes will often be for one or more of the reasons already mentioned, it is clear that for some people it is the pleasure gained from, for example, hunting, shooting or terrierwork.

Methods used

5.23　The following paragraphs describe the main methods used in attempts to manage the fox population.　As we have already noted, no reliable information exists about their use at a national level, although it is clear that there are marked regional variations.

---

[217] White et al,1.4.2.2.3
[218] Ibid,1.4.2.2.4
[219] Ibid,1.4.2.2.4
[220] Macdonald et al,2.2.2d
[221] White et al,1.4.2.3
[222] Macdonald et al, 2.2.3
[223] White et al, 1.4.2.3
[224] Ibid,1.4.2.4.5

Lamping with a rifle

5.24 This method typically involves the use of a high-powered spot lamp at night, mounted on a vehicle. The fox is caught in the beam and shot with a rifle.[225] Shotguns may also be used. Sometimes a 'squeaker' is employed to mimic a rabbit in order to bring the fox nearer. Efficient lamping requires good vehicular access. Its usefulness can therefore be limited in areas with rough terrain and steep slopes. It also requires terrain that allows safe shooting. Another limiting factor is the extent of vegetative cover. Lamping is most effective in autumn when fox densities are high, cover is reduced and the inexperience of young foxes makes them a relatively easy target.[226]

Shooting by day

5.25 This involves groups or individuals shooting foxes, sometimes in driven shoots where beaters drive foxes from daytime rest to a line of waiting shotguns. It is common too for foxes to be shot at their earths, especially during the cubbing season. Terriers are often used to flush or locate foxes, so that they can be shot, and to kill cubs. Methods involving shooting probably account for over half the foxes killed by gamekeepers.

Hunting with hounds

5.26 We described in some detail the different forms of foxhunting in Chapter 2 of our report. The main types are hunting on horseback and on foot and the Welsh gunpacks, which use hounds to flush out foxes to waiting guns. MFHA-registered hunts account for some 14,000-15,000 foxes each year, although about a third of these are dug out. Upland foot and gun packs may account for 7,000-10,000 foxes; some foot packs may take a high proportion of their cull (about 60%) using terriers.

Digging-out/Terrierwork

5.27 As we mentioned in paragraphs 2.23 to 2.25, this method is widely used by foxhunts, gamekeepers and small groups or individuals. It involves using terriers to locate the fox underground so that it can be dug out and shot.[227] (As we have just noted, terriers are also sometimes used to bolt the fox so that it can be shot or pursued by dogs). Terrierwork seems to be particularly prevalent in Wales and other upland areas, either in association with organised foxhunting or by others.[228] Including digging-out by the registered packs, over a third of the cull of foxes in mid-Wales is the result of terrierwork.[229] Although terriers are widely used by gamekeepers, overall they appear to account for only a small proportion of foxes killed by them[230] but the extent to which they are used to bolt foxes which are then shot is unknown.

---

[225] A calibre .222 or larger is recommended in order to minimise wounding

[226] White et al, 2.1.1.1.1

[227] Macdonald et al, 3.2.2.c

[228] Ibid,5.2.4,a; 5.2.5

[229] *Fox (vulpes vulpes) management in three contrasting regions of Britain in relation to agricultural and sporting interests.* Journal of Zoology 251. Heydon and Reynolds [*date?*]

[230] Macdonald et al, 5.2.6.b; 3.2.2.ci

Lamping with lurchers

5.28   This method of killing foxes involves the use of lurchers to chase and kill foxes which have been caught in the beam of a spotlamp (see paragraph 5.24 above). It is popular in certain areas but, because it is often carried out illegally, there are no reliable estimates of the numbers of foxes killed.[231] [232] [233]

Snares

5.29   Fox snares consist of a heavy wire loop set across an area where a fox is likely to pass, with the free end anchored. The loop is designed to hold the fox by the neck until it can be killed humanely.[234]   A legal snare must have a 'stop' in order to avoid strangulation. Snares are still widely used by gamekeepers,[235] although there appears to have been a shift away from this method in favour of lamping with a rifle. The use of snares is unpopular in sheep-rearing country during the lambing season because of the risk of lambs being caught [236] and is not advisable near footpaths because of dogs. About half of the captures made by snares are of non-target species, but these are generally released alive.[237]

5.30   The Wildlife and Countryside Act 1981 prohibits the use of self-locking snares and the setting of snares in circumstances where they are likely to kill or injure protected species. BASC advises against setting snares where there are signs of badger; near footpaths, rights of way or in areas used regularly for exercising domestic animals; or where livestock are grazing or along fences of fields used for livestock grazing.[238]

Trapping

5.31   Fox traps typically comprise mesh cages that catch the fox alive until it can be killed humanely.[239]   Live-capture trapping is not widely used in rural areas since experience shows that it has limited success.[240]

Poisoning and gassing

5.32   Some instances of poisoning foxes still occur, although this practice is illegal. Gassing is also illegal in practice since there is no approved product which may

---

[231] Ibid,3.2.2a
[232] Ibid, 5.2.6
[233] White et al, 2.1.1.1.3
[234] Ibid,2.1.1.1.2
[235] Macdonald et al, 5.2.6.b
[236] Ibid,3.2.4
[237] Ibid, 6.5.1
[238] *Fox Snaring. A Code of Practice.* BASC. 1994. *Snaring foxes: guidance for the snare user.* The Game Conservancy Trust. 1998
[239] White et al, 2.1.1.1,2
[240] Macdonald et al, 3.2.5

be used. Foxes are sometimes killed, however, by using a hosepipe to direct exhaust fumes into an earth.

Non-lethal methods

5.33   Potential non-lethal methods of controlling foxes fall into three main categories:

- the use of contraceptives and abortifacients

- the use of conditioned taste aversion, repellents or diversionary feeding

- the use of methods such as fencing in order to protect livestock.[241]

5.34   The evidence we have received indicates that the first two of these methods are still essentially experimental and subject to a substantial number of practical difficulties. These include the problem of ensuring that a sufficiently high proportion of the target population is reached.[242]

5.35   The use of physical barriers such as fencing, especially electric fencing, can be effective in small areas but is not practicable on a wider scale.[243] [244]

Effectiveness of the different methods

5.36   As we have already noted, there is a lack of firm information about the extent to which the different methods of control are used. However, the research which we have commissioned from the two research teams reaches very similar conclusions about the effectiveness of the different methods:

- killing with dogs, in its various forms, accounts for a substantial proportion of the numbers of foxes killed

- shooting, however, has a much greater capacity to reduce fox populations

- the overall contribution of traditional foxhunting, within the overall total of control techniques involving dogs, is almost certainly insignificant in terms of the management of the fox population as a whole

- but there are clear regional variations in the importance of the different culling methods, and hunting by the registered and unregistered packs may have an effect in some locations, especially in sheep-rearing upland areas

---

[241] Ibid,3.6
[242] Ibid,3.6.1.a.iv
[243] Ibid,3.6.1.a.i
[244] White et al, 2.1.1.2.1

- population modelling indicates that the main impact on population stems from culling adults and sub-adults, rather than cubs

- culling cubs has no significant effect on the longer-term population unless it reaches very high levels

- culling foxes does not necessarily have a <u>pro rata</u> effect on the problem or perceived problem.

Impact of a ban on hunting

5.37   Although the present impact of the registered packs on managing the fox population may be minor, other than in upland areas such as mid-Wales, it is much harder to predict the effect of a ban. Not everyone accepts that it is necessary to manage the fox population: some argue that it would be satisfactory to rely on natural self-regulation. It is clear, however, that the great majority of land managers do consider it necessary. Given that farmers and others presently do not have to pay the hunts for their efforts in seeking to control the numbers of foxes, there must be a risk that, faced with the prospect of paying for fox control, they would be more willing to allow culling by those who lack expertise.   Moreover, there is evidence that farmers consistently over-estimate the numbers of foxes killed by hunts.[245] This could therefore lead, in the absence of a ban, to their killing more than are actually killed by the hunts. It is clear, too, that some farmers and landowners presently tolerate foxes because of their own support for hunting. If hunting was banned, and the numbers of foxes increased, it is likely that there would be less tolerance of foxes. Finally, there is the issue of the extent to which those who presently engage in non-registered or illegal hunting would comply with a ban.

5.38   It seems probable that a ban on hunting would lead to some increase in shooting and snaring, in response to actual or perceived increases in fox numbers. We discuss in the next chapter their relative acceptability in terms of animal welfare. It is worth noting, however, that lamping has its limitations. It can be time-consuming, is not always suited to the terrain and night shooting can give rise to concern on the part of those living in the area.

5.39   Other means of fox control, in particular shooting, seem capable of killing at least as many foxes as are killed by hunting, except in mid-Wales and some other upland areas. In mid-Wales, methods involving dogs are currently effective in maintaining the population below carrying capacity and cost very little. In the event of a ban, shooting would be the most viable alternative but even this would be difficult because of the terrain.[246] Much would depend, in upland areas, on whether it was still permissible to use dogs to flush foxes to guns.

---

[245] Macdonald et al, 5.2.5, White et al, 2.4.2.4
[246] Macdonald et al, 5.2.7.b., 7.2.1.a

<u>Conclusions</u>

5.40   In most areas of England and Wales farmers, landowners and gamekeepers consider that it is necessary to manage fox populations in view of the damage which foxes can cause to farming and game management interests.

5.41   Methods involving guns probably account for the greater part of those foxes which are deliberately killed, but there are marked regional variations.

5.42   In lowland areas hunting by the registered packs makes only a minor contribution to the management of the fox population, and terrierwork, especially by gamekeepers, may be more important.   In these areas, in the event of a ban, other means of control have the potential to replace the hunts' role in culling foxes.

5.43   In upland areas, where the fox population causes more damage to sheep-rearing and game management interests, and where there is a greater perceived need for control, fewer alternatives are available to the use of dogs, either to flush out to guns or for digging-out.

Deer

<u>Population</u>

5.44   Six species of deer occur in the wild in England and Wales. Of these, only two, roe and red, are indigenous. The remaining species, fallow, sika, muntjac and Chinese water deer, were deliberately introduced for hunting or as wildlife curiosities.[247] Of the six species, only one - red deer - is hunted with dogs by registered packs, although there are a small number of unregistered packs hunting roe deer, and fallow deer were hunted in the New Forest as recently as 1997.[248] In the following paragraphs we concentrate on red deer, since it is this species which is primarily involved.

5.45   Red deer populations are localised in England and Wales. Their numbers increased rapidly in the 1970s and 1980s. There are estimated to be some 12,500 wild red deer in England and Wales, some 10,000 of which are found in the south west of England, with 4,000-6,000 within the staghunting countries, mainly on Exmoor, the Quantocks and in mid-Devon.[249] [250] It is estimated that about 1,000 deer need to be killed each year in the areas covered by the three hunts in order to maintain a stable population.

---

[247] White et al, Section B.1.1

[248] Macdonald et al, 3.3.1

[249] Ibid,1.1

[250] In contrast, there are thought to be some 300,000 wild red deer in Scotland

5.46 Red deer are found in a great diversity of habitats, but the great majority of those in the south west of England frequent wooded valleys and surrounding farmland. They are versatile feeders, eating mainly grass but also browsing on tree shoots, shrubs, sedges, rushes and heather.[251]

5.47 Red deer are social animals but males and females are segregated for much of the year. Herds tend to be larger on open moorland, with groups of up to 40 not uncommon on Exmoor and the Quantocks. Mating occurs between September and October, with births from late May to early June. Calves (nearly always one) are weaned at 6-10 months. Sexual maturity depends on habitat quality, reflected in the varying proportion of hinds which conceive as yearlings. Mortality is highest in calves under 10 months old.[252]

Reasons for population management

5.48 In contrast to foxes and hares, there is virtually unanimous agreement that red deer populations - at least those of any size - need to be managed, mainly because of the damage which they cause to agricultural, forestry and conservation interests, coupled with the fact that populations are currently increasing.[253] We will therefore describe only briefly the main reasons why population management is considered necessary before turning to the effectiveness of the different available methods.

Damage to agriculture

5.49 While there is not great concern about agricultural damage by red deer on a national scale, it is clear that it can be locally significant, especially in the south west of England.[254] The main types of damage are to:

- cereal and other arable crops such as oilseed rape, especially once the ears have formed and the scope for compensatory growth is limited [255] [256]

- field crops such as peas and beans, through rolling or trampling[257]

- root crops, particularly when they are standing over winter[258]

- grassland through grazing and trampling[259]

---

[251] Macdonald et al, 10.2.3
[252] Ibid,10.2.4
[253] Ibid,2.3
[254] White et al,1.2
[255] Ibid,1.2
[256] Macdonald et al, 5.2.1.a.i
[257] White et al,1.2
[258] Ibid,1.2
[259] Macdonald et al, 2.3.1.a.ii; 2.3.1.c

- farm woodlands, through browsing on buds, foliage or shoots[260]

- walls, fences, hedges and banks.[261] [262]

5.50   In the Quantocks, three-quarters of landholders (most being farmers) considered that red deer caused significant damage on their land.[263]   Median annual losses due to deer were estimated at around £500 per holding, but estimating the cost of damage is difficult and such estimates are known to be frequently inaccurate.[264]

Damage to forestry

5.51   The damage which red deer (and other deer species) cause to commercial forests and other woodland is the most important reason for controlling their numbers.[265]   The main causes of damage are by:

- browsing the shoots, particularly the leading shoots, of young trees[266] [267] [268]

- bark stripping - either to eat or as the result of "fraying" or "thrashing" (rubbing antlers to remove their velvet cover or to mark territory) [269] [270] [271]

- browsing the forest floor and preventing regeneration.[272]

Damage to conservation interests

5.52   Deer grazing and browsing can, in some circumstances, be beneficial to conservation interests[273] but the rapid increase in deer numbers has led to problems.[274] [275]   As already noted, it can inhibit natural woodland regeneration: in particular, it can have the effect of removing the "middle" layer in woodland, with knock-on effects for other animals and predators.[276]   It can also prevent or impede coppice regrowth, which can adversely affect the habitat for many other species, including some butterflies.

---

[260] Ibid,2.3.1.c
[261] Ibid,1.2
[262] White et al, 2.3.1.c
[263] Macdonald et al, 2.3.1.b
[264] Ibid, 2.3.1.c.i
[265] Ibid,2.3.2.b
[266] Ibid,2.3.2.b
[267] White et al,1.3
[268] British Deer Society 1, un-numbered
[269] Ibid, un-numbered
[270] White et al, 1.3
[271] Macdonald et al, 2.3.2.b
[272] British Deer Society 1, un-numbered
[273] Macdonald et al, 2.3.3
[274] Ibid, 2.2.3.a
[275] White et al, 1.4.1.a
[276] Ibid, 1.4.1.a

Stalking and sale of venison

5.53   The income to be gained from letting stalking (for recreation) rights and the sale of venison are also reasons why red deer numbers are managed.[277]

Road traffic accidents

5.54   There is concern too about the number of road traffic accidents involving deer of all kinds. It was recently estimated that some 40,000 deer-related road traffic accidents occur each year in the UK, a few of which result in the deaths of the people involved.[278]

Methods used

5.55   There are only two methods used to cull red deer: shooting and hunting with dogs. There are also a number of non-lethal methods used to prevent damage by deer.

Hunting with hounds

5.56   We described in Chapter 2 the way in which red deer are hunted by the three registered packs in the south west of England.

Shooting/stalking

5.57   Shooting by stalking with a rifle or large bore shotgun is the most common method used throughout England and Wales, as well as in Scotland and in Northern Ireland. Smooth bore guns may be used legally only as slaughtering instruments (as used by the hunts) or for humane dispatch of severely injured deer or if shown to be necessary for the protection of cultivated land, pasture or enclosed woodland.[279]

5.58   Rifle culls tend to be taken either from an elevated platform, which helps to ensure a safe backdrop, or by stalking at ground level. Many deer stalkers use a dog to help them find a deer or to track or retrieve a deer which has been shot and injured, fatally or otherwise.[280]

Non-lethal methods

5.59   The main non-lethal methods used for preventing damage by red deer are:

- fencing - permanent or temporary fencing is used to exclude deer from forest plantations, agricultural fields, conservation areas and motorways [281] [282]

---

[277] Macdonald et al, 2.3.4.b
[278] White et al,1.5
[279] Macdonald et al, 3.3.2.c
[280] Ibid, 3.3.2b
[281] Ibid,5.4.6
[282] White et al, 2.2.2 et al

- tree shelters and guards - "growing tubes" are used to protect young trees, especially in small plantations [283] [284]

- habitat modification and diversionary feeding - for example, planting early-maturing grass to divert deer from nearby agricultural crops.[285]

5.60   Live capture of wild deer is illegal in England and Wales (but not in Scotland) except under special licence.[286]   No existing chemical repellent has yet proved to be effective.[287] [288]   Fertility control by immuno-contraception is effective in principle but it is difficult to apply in practice and there are doubts about potential side effects and impact on other animals.[289] [290]

Effectiveness of the different methods

5.61   As in the case of foxes, the two research reports which we commissioned reached very similar conclusions about the effectiveness of the different methods of controlling red deer.

Hunting with dogs

5.62   As we have noted earlier, about 1,000 deer need to be culled each year in the area covered by the three staghunts. The packs have hunted and killed about 160 deer each season over the last 5 years. (They also deal with around 80 additional casualties each year but these animals would probably have died anyway).[291] This contributes only 15% of the total cull required to prevent further population increases within the hunt countries and contributes, therefore, considerably less to regional control.[292]   Practical considerations such as the available number of days for hunting, and its inherent inefficiency - kills are made only about half the days on which hunting takes place[293] - make it unlikely that hunting's contribution to the overall cull could increase substantially. Another difficulty with relying on hunting as a population management strategy is that it is not sufficiently biased towards culling hinds and calves to achieve the desired reduction in overall numbers.[294]

5.63   It is also commonly argued that a secondary contribution made by the hunts to deer management is in dispersing groups of red deer which may be causing particular

---

[283] Ibid, 2.2.3
[284] Macdonald et al, 5.4.6 et al
[285] White et al, 2.2.5
[286] Ibid, 2.2.1
[287] Ibid, 5.4.6.b
[288] Macdonald et al, 2.2.4
[289] Ibid, 5.4.6.b
[290] White et al,2.2.6
[291] White et al, 2.3
[292] Macdonald et al, 5.4.5.a
[293] Macdonald et al, 5.4.1
[294] Ibid, 5.4.3

problems to a farmer or landowner.[295] However, census work and observation of deer suggest that any dispersal effect is only very temporary, although this may be affected by the frequency of disturbance and the extent of nearby cover.[296][297]

Shooting

5.64 As already noted, shooting/stalking is by far the most important method used to reduce red deer numbers in England and Wales, as in the rest of Europe,[298] and accounts for the great majority of deer killed in the staghunting area.

Non-lethal methods

5.65 It is reported that, while fencing can be effective (at a considerable cost) in excluding deer from relatively small areas, it is unsatisfactory as a means of excluding them from large areas (>200 ha) over long periods of time.[299] Individual tree protection is generally cheaper than fencing on areas less than 2-5 ha. Total exclusion of deer can also have a negative effect on the richness of plant, insect, bird and animal life and can discourage enjoyment of the countryside.[300]

5.66 In short, while methods such as fencing and tree guards are a useful part of an overall deer management strategy, they cannot obviate the need, in the south west of England - and, for that matter, in other areas - to carry out substantial culling in order to control population numbers.[301]

<u>Impact of a ban on hunting</u>

5.67 We noted in paragraph 5.62 that, in terms of the numbers of deer killed, hunting makes only a relatively small contribution to deer management in the south west of England.

5.68 It is sometimes argued that, because of the nature of the terrain in this area and its use by walkers and others, it would not be possible safely to rely solely on stalking as a means of culling deer there. However, we have seen no convincing reason why stalking could not operate efficiently in this area. And the numbers of deer killed by the hunts could, in our view, be made up fairly easily by licensed deer stalkers in the area.[302] As evidence given to us by BASC points out, both the Deer Initiative and the BDS/BASC Code of Practice state that 'culling must be carried out safely, legally and humanely'. A system of voluntary qualifications has been introduced through Deer Management Qualifications Ltd. These qualifications – The Deer Stalking Certificate Levels 1 and 2 -

---

[295] Ibid, 3.2.2
[296] Ibid, 5.2.2
[297] Macdonald et al, 5.4.1
[298] Macdonald et al, 3.3.2.b
[299] White et al, 5.4.1
[300] Ibid, 3.26
[301] Ibid, 3.26
[302] Macdonald et al, 7.3.1.a

enable deerstalkers to demonstrate that they have the necessary theoretical knowledge and practical skill.[303]

5.69   However, one of the main arguments that the hunts advance in favour of hunting is that, because of the support which it undoubtedly enjoys from many farmers and landowners in the area, there is a much greater tolerance of deer than would otherwise be the case. It is said that, in the event of a ban on hunting, this "community of interest" would break down, resulting in a substantial reduction, or even extermination, of the red deer population through legal and illegal shooting. This would also lead, it is said, to many more deer being injured and to the deer becoming wary of people, thus reducing their attraction to visitors and others.

5.70   It is very difficult to predict accurately what individual landowners would do in the event of a ban.[304] [305] The majority of land is owned by private farmers and some undoubtedly would seek to reduce the numbers on their land. The National Trust owns 10% of Exmoor National Park and retains shooting rights. We note that the ban on National Trust land has led to disagreements between the Trust and its tenants on appropriate management strategies, as is apparent from evidence supplied to us by the Holnicote Estate Farm Tenants' Association.[306]

5.71   Much would depend on the extent to which the "community of interest" which the hunts presently foster in managing the deer population could be replaced by an effective deer management strategy. The Exmoor Society, which told us that it holds no view on whether or not deer hunting should continue, argues strongly that a ban on hunting would require an "overall culling management system".[307] It suggests that the abolition of a key part of the current voluntary system would be so drastic "that it is simply unacceptable to 'hope' that a culling control system equally environmentally friendly (to the deer's existence) will just evolve; rather, it will have to be put in place." This view is supported by the British Deer Society, which concludes that "in the absence of any form of controlling body with responsibility for co-ordinating the management of the red deer, deer numbers will decline as landowners follow their own agenda".[308] The BDS suggests the formation of a Deer Commission for England. The Government, through the Forestry Commission, already sponsors the Deer Initiative, and a Welsh Deer Initiative is also being developed. The Deer Initiative is a partnership between government agencies and non-governmental organisations, including MAFF, DETR, RSPCA, English Nature, CLA and BASC, seeking to encourage good deer management through local deer management groups.[309] An Exmoor and District Deer Management Society already exists. The Society suggests that the community of interest would be seriously compromised by a ban on hunting. South West Deer Protection, an anti-hunting group, argues that existing deer management groups on Exmoor and the Quantocks are not likely to be successful. It

---

[303] BASC 1, 7.2.1

[304] Macdonald et al, 7.3.1.b

[305] White et al, 5.4

[306] Holnicote Estate Farm Tenants' Association 1, un-numbered

[307] The Exmoor Society 1, 1.14

[308] British Deer Society 1, un-numbered

[309] BASC 1, 7.1.1

urges the need for stronger controls, including a mandatory carcass tagging scheme for wild deer, a Deer Commission and deer wardens.

5.72   It seems probable that, in the event of a ban, the overall numbers of deer in the hunted area might decline somewhat but whether this would be to the extent that would lead to calls for action, such as a ban on shooting, cannot easily be foreseen.[310]

5.73   A possible decline in red deer in the staghunting countries means that farmers and foresters are unlikely to suffer from increased damage because of a ban. Visibility, which is important to the amenity value of deer, is not simply related to abundance, but also to the proportion of the time they spend hidden in cover.[311]

5.74   The redistribution of red deer within their ranges is another potentially important change which might arise from a greater reliance on stalking; this might lead to changes in browsing and grazing pressures and reduce the visibility of the deer in some areas.[312]

Conclusions

5.75   It is generally accepted that red deer numbers in Devon and Somerset need to be controlled. Hunting with dogs presently accounts for about 15% of the annual cull needed to maintain the population at its present level. However, because of the widespread support which it enjoys, and consequent tolerance by farmers of deer, hunting at present makes a significant contribution to management of the deer population in this area. In the event of a ban, some overall reduction in total deer numbers might occur unless an effective deer management strategy was implemented, which was capable of promoting the present collective interest in the management of deer and harnessing such interest into sound conservation management.

Hares

Population

5.76   There are two species of hare in Britain: the brown hare and the mountain hare. Brown hares are widespread throughout lowland Britain but their distribution is very patchy. They are scarce in much of Wales and the west country but abundant in many parts of East Anglia. This seems to reflect regional difference in habitat and farming activities. Mountain hares are almost entirely found in Scotland.[313] Since hunting or coursing of hares in England and Wales is almost exclusively confined to brown hares, the following paragraphs deal entirely with this species.[314]

---

[310] Macdonald et al., 7.3.1.b.

[311] Ibid, 7.3.1.b.

[312] Ibid, 7.3.1.b.

[313] Ibid, 10.3.1

[314] Ibid, 3.4.1a and b

5.77 In the early 1990s there were thought to be about 630,250 hares in England and Wales and a further 187,250 in Scotland.[315] Game bag records indicate a significant decline in numbers in Britain during the 1960s and 1970s, probably due, at least in part, to modern arable farming methods, particularly agricultural intensification and changing farming practices which have reduced the diversity of food available to hares year round. The hare is now included as a UK Biodiversity Action Plan Species on the short list. However, hares are still locally common, and records from game bags and hunting records (from beagling) indicate that, nationally, numbers have been stable since 1983. The second national hare survey in the late 1990s estimated a national population of 752,608, but it is not clear whether this represents a decline.[316] Hare populations can fluctuate considerably from year to year.

5.78 Hares breed from February through to October and occasionally in winter. Litters of up to three leverets are left individually in scrapes; are tended by the female only; and are usually weaned at about three weeks old.[317]

5.79 There is a rapid turnover in population. Apart from natural mortality, through disease and poor nutrition, death results from numerous other causes, including predation by foxes, agricultural machinery and road casualties.[318]

Reasons for population management

5.80 As we have already noted, hares are simultaneously regarded as a pest by some farmers and foresters, as game and as a subject for conservation.[319] This complicates - and leads to conflict in - the management of their population.

Damage to agriculture and forestry

5.81 Hares eat crops such as oilseed rape and turnip, and particularly grasses and cereals. In addition, hares can eat high value market garden crops, and will often kill newly-planted young trees and shrubs. Some of this damage can be of economic significance to individual growers.[320] In livestock areas hares are not numerous and are rarely considered a pest. In arable areas high numbers of hares on winter corn are considered damaging by most cereal farmers and regular winter culls by shooting are undertaken where this occurs.[321]

Shooting

5.82 In some parts of England, especially East Anglia, hare numbers are maintained at high levels for organised shooting.

---

[315] Macdonald et al, 10.3.2
[316] White et al, 1.1.1
[317] Macdonald et al, 10.3.4
[318] Ibid, 10.3.4
[319] Ibid, 2.4
[320] Ibid, 2.4.1.
[321] Ibid, 2.4.1

Deterring poaching

5.83   Conversely, landowners may shoot hares in order to deter poaching and coursing. There is evidence that gangs of poachers are a particular problem in parts of Lincolnshire and East Anglia.

Coursing

5.84   In areas where coursing by the registered coursing clubs takes place high numbers of hares are encouraged and action is sometimes taken to re-populate hares by importing them from elsewhere.[322]   We received anecdotal evidence that, in the past at least, this has happened on quite a substantial basis. We discuss this matter further in Chapter 7.

Methods used

Shooting

5.85   Hare shooting is the means most frequently used by farmers in arable areas for pest control.[323]   It is estimated that some 200,000-300,000 hares are shot in Britain each year.   Apart from ad hoc shooting, hare shoots are commonly organised in February. These normally take place over one or two farms. They consist of a series of drives, with participants shooting hares as they are flushed forward or as they try to break through one of the lines of guns.[324] Hundreds of hares may be shot in a day.

Hunting and coursing

5.86   We described in Chapter 2 of our report the hunting of hares by the registered harrier, basset and beagle packs, and hare coursing by the registered coursing clubs and others.

Other methods

5.87   Hares are also snared and netted. Fencing and tree guards are used to protect trees against hares (and other species). Chemical repellents, habitat modification and scarers are not widely used to limit hare damage in Britain.

Effectiveness of the different methods

Shooting

5.88   There is no doubt that shooting is an effective means of reducing hare numbers, especially if carried out in the form of hare shoots. One piece of research estimated that

---

[322] Ibid, 2.4.1
[323] Ibid, 3.4.2
[324] Ibid 3.4.2

hare shoots on four farms reduced hare numbers by an average of 50%.[325] Population modelling suggests, however, that, because of the hare's reproductive potential, even killing a large proportion of adults or sub-adults would not have a long-term effect on hare populations.[326]

Hunting and coursing

5.89   No-one argues that legal hunting or coursing has an appreciable effect on hare numbers. The AMHB and the MBHA told us that, on average, about 5% of hares seen during a day's hunting are killed and that in the 1998/1999 season the packs killed some 1,650 hares.[327]

5.90   Similarly, legal hare coursing has a negligible impact on hare numbers. The average number killed at official hare coursing events are reported as being some 250 a year.[328] As we noted in paragraph 2.56, however, many more hares are killed through other forms of coursing.

Impact of a ban on hunting/coursing

5.91   It is obvious from what we have just said that a ban on legal hunting and coursing would have no direct impact in practice on hare numbers.

5.92   What is more difficult to assess is the extent to which, in the absence of legal hunting and coursing, hare numbers would be adversely affected by:

- reduced tolerance by farmers of damage to agricultural crops

- less interest in encouraging and sustaining suitable habitats (see Chapter 7)

- greater propensity to allow shooting

- an increase in illegal coursing

- deliberate culling of hares to prevent illegal coursing.

5.93   There is no doubt that, in some areas at present, hare numbers are maintained at high levels for shooting and hunting/coursing purposes. It seems likely, in our view, that, in some of those areas at least, the hare population, in the event of a ban, would be lower than it is now.

---

[325] Ibid, 5.5.4
[326] Ibid, 5.5.1
[327] AMHB and MBHA 1, 67
[328] Macdonald et al, 5.5.3

Conclusions

5.94 **There is little or no need to control overall hare numbers and, indeed, they are a Biodiversity Action Plan species. However, the distribution of hares is uneven: they are abundant in some areas, mainly in the east of England, and scarce in much of Wales and the West Country. Hare hunting and coursing are essentially carried out for recreational purposes and have a relatively small direct impact on hare numbers. A ban would therefore have little effect in practice on agriculture or other interests.**

5.95 **Because hare numbers tend to be maintained at high levels in areas where hunting/coursing occurs, the impact of a ban might well be that, in the absence of other changes, the population would decline in those areas. This would partly result from a loss of suitable habitat but also, in a few areas, from the shooting of hares to deter poaching and illegal coursing. However, in comparison with the impact of organised shooting on hare numbers, a ban on hare hunting and coursing would have a negligible effect.**

Mink

Population

5.96   As we noted in paragraph 2.59, mink were not introduced to this country until the 1920s. They were first confirmed breeding in the wild in 1956 in Devon and are now widespread throughout Britain, with relatively high densities in south west England, west Wales and west Scotland.[329]

5.97   Following an initial rapid increase in the population, there is now evidence that mink numbers have reduced substantially in the last ten years. This seems to have coincided with a resurgence in the otter population. The total population of mink in England and Wales is now thought to be some 18,000.

5.98   Mink are usually found near fresh water, but they also favour some coastal habitats. They are opportunistic, generalist predators, eating a wide range of mammals, birds, fish and invertebrates, their diets varying according to habitat and the time of the year.[330] [331]   Common food items are rabbits, water birds and fish.[332]   Mink tend to be most active at night and during twilight hours.

5.99   Because mink have a very varied diet the risk to a particular prey species of extinction is much greater than where a predator specialises on a particular prey. This is because the automatic checks on predator numbers that would normally emerge as the prey species become scarce do not apply.

---

[329] Ibid, 10.4.1
[330] Ibid, 10.4.3
[331] White et al, 1.2 – 1.4
[332] Macdonald et al, 10.4.3

5.100 Mink climb well and their dens may be above ground in scrub or brush piles, or among tree roots, stones, in a hollow tree or in a rabbit burrow. There are several dens within one home range, most being close to water.[333]

5.101 Mink are largely solitary. Mating occurs between January and March. The kits, usually 3-6, are born between the end of April and mid-May. The young are weaned at 5-6 weeks and are cared for by the female only. Mink have no natural predators in Britain and significant mortality is caused by man.[334]

Reasons for population management

Predation on poultry and game birds

5.102 There have been many reported instances of mink killing domestic poultry, ducks and geese, along with ornamental wildfowl and game birds.[335] Although the overall numbers, and financial loss, are relatively small, mink can indulge in surplus killing. The cost of predation on ornamental wildfowl collections and breeding stock can therefore be high in individual cases.

Predation on fish

5.103 Fish, including salmon and trout, make up a substantial proportion of the diets of mink feeding on waters where they are available. Fish farms and fisheries are therefore potentially at risk. Although there have been instances when this has led to problems,[336] there is little evidence that mink have had a significant effect on fish stocks and angling interests.[337][338]

Predation on wild birds

5.104 Birds may make up as much as 30% of the mink's diet and predation is especially high in the summer when fledglings and young water fowl are vulnerable.[339] Mink have been directly linked to a decline in moorhens, coots and little grebes: moorhens and coots often represent as much as 80% of the birds eaten by mink on lowland waterways.[340][341] However, evidence for an impact on coot is more compelling than for that on moorhens, illustrating subtle differences even between similar species. Furthermore, there is evidence that the numbers taken depend on these birds' relative abundance compared with other prey in a particular locality.[342]

---

[333] Ibid, 10.4.1
[334] Ibid, 10.4.4
[335] White et al, 1.2
[336] Ibid, 1.3
[337] Ibid, 1.3
[338] Macdonald et al, 2.5.3
[339] White et al, 1.4.3
[340] Ibid, 1.4.3.1
[341] Ibid,1.4.3.1
[342] Ibid, 1.4.3.1

5.105 Mink can be very troublesome in the case of ground-nesting seabirds, especially in Scotland and on small islands. Their activities, including surplus killing, have been linked to almost complete breeding failure amongst some colonies of terns and gulls, including some rare species.[343]

Predation on wild animals

5.106 While rabbits, where available, are the animal on which mink in Britain prey most frequently, they also eat substantial numbers of water voles. Mink have been held to be responsible for a major decline in water vole numbers: the population is thought to have fallen by some 80% in the last 10 years or so[344]. The evidence seems to be, however, that water vole populations were already in a general state of decline before mink became widespread, but that mink predation has had an especially severe effect on their already depleted numbers, leading to a risk of local extermination.[345] [346] Water voles are protected under Schedule 5 to the Wildlife and Countryside Act 1981.

Otters

5.107 Mink were initially held responsible for the decline of otters in the 1960s. Research shows, however, that this decline was, on the contrary, caused by the introduction in 1955 of organochlorine insecticides, dieldrin and aldrin, for use in sheep dip and seed dressings. Mink expanded rapidly as they moved into vacant territory. Mink and otter do compete for food resources but, when alternative prey such as rabbits are available, mink become more generalist predators to avoid competition with the otter.[347] The recent resurgence in the otter population confirms that mink will tend to give way to otters.

Methods used and their effectiveness

Lethal methods

5.108 There are three lethal methods used to control mink:

- trapping

- shooting

- hunting with dogs.

---

[343] Ibid, 1.4.3.2
[344] Macdonald et al, 2.5.3.a
[345] Ibid, 2.5.3.a
[346] White et al, 1.4.2
[347] Ibid, 1.4.1

Trapping

5.109 Trapping is recognised as the main method of controlling mink and is widely used by gamekeepers, water bailiffs, farmers and others.[348] There are no firm data on the numbers of mink killed by trapping but research shows that intensive trapping in an area can remove most of the local population.[349]

5.11 Two types of trap are used: cage or tunnel traps, in which mink are captured alive and then shot, and spring traps, which are designed to break the neck of the mink.[350][351]

5.111 Mink do not appear to be particularly trap-shy and trapping can therefore be a relatively efficient means of control provided that the trap is well placed.[352] Trapping success varies at different times of year, depending on the relative mobility of the sexes. Preventative trapping is most effective when it removes pregnant females in spring and territorial residents in the autumn once dispersal is largely finished.[353][354]

5.112 There does not seem to be any marked difference in the effectiveness of the two kinds of traps. Cage traps have the advantage that they enable non-target animals to be released unharmed. On the other hand, they have to be checked daily.[355][356]

Shooting

5.113 Shooting mink is carried out on an ad hoc basis by farmers and others, often incidentally to other shooting.

Hunting with dogs

5.114 We described in paragraphs 2.59 – 2.61 the way in which mink hunting is carried out by the 20 packs in England and Wales.

5.115 Mink hunts account for some 400-1400 mink a year.[357] Packs catch an average of less than one mink per day's hunting, and the majority of mink found by the hounds evade capture, usually taking refuge in rocks or under trees.[358]

---

[348] Macdonald et al, 3.5.3
[349] Ibid, 5.6.4
[350] Ibid, 3.5.3
[351] White et al, 2.1.2
[352] Ibid, 2.1.2
[353] Ibid, 2.1.2
[354] Macdonald et al, 3.5.3
[355] Ibid, 3.5.3
[356] White et al, 2.1.2
[357] Macdonald et al, 5.6.2
[358] White et al, 2.1.3

Non-lethal methods

5.116 Fencing can be an effective means of preventing mink from causing damage.[359] Other techniques such as chemical repellents, habitat modification and fertility control have not been used.[360]

Impact of a ban on hunting

5.117 The Masters of Minkhounds Association recognises that hunting alone is not a sufficient means of controlling mink populations and that it has to be used alongside other control methods. It is clear that the contribution made by mink hunts to the control of mink populations nationally is insignificant. The numbers killed are far too low to make any impact on population numbers, especially given the high fecundity of mink.[361] Moreover, hunting does not target the pre-breeding population of mink: those mink killed from mid-summer onwards are mainly pre-dispersal juveniles, many of whom would not have become adult territory-holders.[362]

5.119 A mink hunt may be successful in temporarily reducing mink numbers and breeding activity but any reductions may be compensated for quickly by other animals moving in. The hunt may be helpful to the farmer, though, in providing a free service and may be able to confirm the presence of mink, or locate it, even if they do not succeed in killing it.[363]

5.120 Set against this benefit, however, is the concern that hunting in areas where otters and mink coexist may disturb otters and prevent them from recolonising areas where they are scarce.[364] Hunting may also cause disturbance to other birds and animals, especially during the breeding season, and cause damage to river banks and vegetation.[365]

Conclusions

5.121 **Mink can cause localised damage to poultry, gamebirds, fishing and wildlife interests. Because mink hunts kill relatively small numbers of mink, and because of their high fecundity and ability to disperse, hunting does not have any significant effect on the mink population at a national or regional level. It can, however, lead to temporary reductions in the mink population in specific localities.**

5.122 **Trapping is potentially an effective means of control but it needs to be carried out fairly intensively from January to April every year to have a lasting impact. It is therefore relatively costly. Hunting can be helpful in providing a free service to farmers and others that identifies where mink are located, enabling them to target trapping efforts more effectively.**

---

[359] Ibid,2.2 and 3.2
[360] Ibid,2.2
[361] Macdonald et al, 5.6.1
[362] Ibid, 5.6.4
[363] MMHA1,5
[364] White et al, 2.1.3 and 5.2
[365] Ibid,5.2

CHAPTER 6

ANIMAL WELFARE

6.1   Our terms of reference required us to consider the impact of hunting, and of a ban on hunting, on animal welfare. We have interpreted this to mean the welfare of the quarry species, that of the dogs and horses involved in hunting and that of other animals which may be incidentally affected by hunting. We also discuss in more detail here the animal welfare issues which are raised by other methods of control, in particular shooting.

Cruelty to animals

6.2   Both sides of the debate agree that the issue of cruelty is a central question in considering hunting.

6.3   Those in favour of hunting with dogs tend to argue that:

- it is as humane as other methods of culling, and more humane than some

- death is very quick and certain: either the quarry is killed or it escapes. Unlike shooting, there is not the risk of leaving a wounded animal which may suffer greatly before it dies

- the chase is a natural aspect of life and death in the case of wild animals

- a quick death at the hands of a predator is preferable to being run over or dying from disease or starvation

- hunting can be selective and target the weak, the old and the sick or those animals that present a particular problem for farmers.

6.4   Those against hunting tend to argue that:

- hunting is more inhumane than other methods since it involves inflicting unnecessary cruelty

- animals suffer unnecessary distress during the chase, which can be artificially prolonged

- animals are not killed quickly and cleanly as is often claimed

- some of the quarry species (i.e. foxes and deer) do not have natural predators in this country and that they are not well equipped to cope with hunting by dogs

- even those animals that escape may be damaged in ways which may mean that they continue to suffer afterwards.

6.5   Much of the debate has taken place to date on the basis of opinions, rather than hard evidence. The only substantial scientific work which has been undertaken so far is in relation to deer. We deal with this at some length below.

6.6   Before turning specifically to the consideration of animal welfare (which has a broader meaning) it may be helpful to reiterate the legal position in respect of cruelty to wild animals.

6.7   Historically, legislation relating to cruelty involving animals applied only indirectly or partially to wild animals. In the Protection of Animals Act 1911, as amended, "animal" was defined as "any domestic or captive animal". It was not until the Wild Mammals (Protection) Act 1996 that legal protection was extended to the generality of non-captive wild animals.

6.8   The 1996 Act makes it an offence if anyone "mutilates, kicks, beats, nails or otherwise impales, stabs, burns, stones, crushes, drowns, drags or asphyxiates any wild mammal with intent to inflict unnecessary suffering". As we noted in paragraph 2.9, there is an exception in respect of "the killing in a reasonably swift and humane manner if the wild mammal had been injured or taken in the course of either lawful shooting, hunting, coursing or pest control activity". There is a further exception in respect of any act done "by means of any snare, trap, dog, or bird lawfully used for the purpose of killing or taking any wild mammal".

Animal welfare

6.9   Animal welfare is a scientific discipline which has developed rapidly in recent years. It is essentially concerned with assessing the ability of an animal to cope with its environment: if an animal is having difficulty in coping with its environment, or is failing to cope, then its welfare may be regarded as poor. This judgement is distinct from any ethical or moral judgements about the way in which the animal is being treated.[366]

6.10   Because it is not possible to ask an animal about its welfare, or to know what is going on inside its head, it is necessary to draw up some indicators which enable one to make a judgement. It is generally agreed that it is better, in judging the welfare of an animal or animals, to use a range of indicators rather than a single approach.[367] [368] The precise nature of these indicators will vary depending on the animal concerned but they will usually comprise a mixture of physiological indicators (such as damage to muscles)

---

[366] Broom 1, *The Welfare of deer, foxes, mink and hares subjected to hunting: a review.* Professor Donald Broom ('Broom')
[367] Broom 1,4
[368] *The effects of hunting with dogs in England and Wales on the welfare of deer, foxes, mink and hare.* Professor Patrick Bateson and Professor Roger Harris. (Report on CD Rom) ('Bateson and Harris'),7.1

and behavioural indicators (such as the way the animal responds to a certain event in comparison with its normal behaviour). Use of these indicators requires a thorough understanding of the physiology, behaviour and ecology of the species concerned.[369] But, because they are only indicators, there is often room for argument, as we note below, about the extent to which a particular finding indicates poor welfare as opposed to, for example, exertion that can be regarded as falling within natural limits.

6.11   We also consider that it is important, in examining the arguments about the welfare of animals subjected to hunting, not to judge them in isolation. In our view, this means not only considering the relative welfare advantages and disadvantages of different forms of culling - assuming that there is a need to kill the animal concerned - but also taking account of what we know, and can reasonably assume, about the extent to which they would be likely to be used in practice in the event of a ban on hunting. We do not believe, however, that it is right to justify hunting in welfare terms by comparing it with illegal means of killing animals.

6.12   Animal welfare is concerned with the welfare of the individual animal, not the management of the wider population. In assessing the impact of hunting on animal welfare we are persuaded that it is necessary to look at it on a relative, rather than an absolute, basis. It should not be compared with only the best, or the worst, of the alternatives. Nor is it right to justify hunting by reference to the welfare implications of illegal methods of control.

6.13   In the event of a ban on hunting, it seems probable that farmers and others would resort more frequently to other methods to kill foxes, deer, hares and perhaps mink. There would be a mixture of motives: pest control; the value of the carcass; and the recreational value to be derived from shooting. It follows that the welfare of animals which are hunted should be compared with the welfare which, on a realistic assessment, would be likely to result from the legal methods used by farmers and others to manage the population of these animals in the event of a ban on hunting.

The welfare of hunted deer

6.14   In the light of the controversy surrounding deer hunting in Exmoor and the Quantocks the National Trust commissioned Professor Patrick Bateson to undertake some research into the welfare of deer hunted by hounds. The report[370] was based on a study of 64 hunted red deer. Bateson and Bradshaw concluded that the hunts cause red deer to experience conditions that lie far outside those that would normally be experienced by the species living in a natural environment. In the light of the report the National Trust decided to ban the hunting of red deer on its land.

6.15   There were subsequently some criticisms of certain aspects of the report and the Countryside Alliance and the Devon & Somerset Staghounds funded further research by Professor Roger Harris and others, known as the Joint Universities Study on Deerhunting.

---

[369] Broom 1,5
[370] *Behavioural and Physiological Effects of Culling Red Deer* (Bateson & Bradshaw 1997)

This sought to replicate, and to extend in some respects, the work carried out by Bateson and Bradshaw. The report,[371] which was published in 1999, broadly confirmed the metabolic measurements undertaken in the earlier study but drew different conclusions about the animal welfare implications. In particular, it concluded that the changes found were similar to those which occurred in horses and humans which had exercised intensively. The report suggested that deer might suffer for only the last 20 minutes or so of a hunt.

The Bateson and Harris Report

6.16   We were very pleased that Professor Bateson and Professor Harris decided to work together in undertaking research for our Committee. Their report reviews the previous work in this area and seeks to set out those matters on which there is general agreement; those matters on which there are some remaining differences of view; and those on which further research would be needed before any firm conclusion could be reached.

6.17   We will not attempt in this chapter to summarise in any detail the scientific material in the Bateson and Harris report. We doubt whether this would be particularly helpful for the general reader of our report, and those who want to study these matters would be better advised in any case to read the Bateson and Harris report. What we have tried to do, in the following paragraphs, is to summarise for the lay reader the general findings and conclusions.

6.18   In both of the earlier studies by Bateson and Bradshaw and by Harris et al., blood and tissue samples were taken from deer which had not been chased and which were killed by rifles. These were compared with samples taken from deer killed by shotgun or pistol at the end of a hunt. These samples were used to carry out a number of tests in order to assess the physiological changes which had taken place.[372]   Field studies were also used by Bateson and Bradshaw to assess behavioural changes in hunted deer.

6.19   Although there are differences among scientists about the interpretation of some of the physiological and behavioural data, there is quite a large measure of agreement about the nature of the challenges presented to the deer during a hunt; the physiological ability of the deer to cope with these challenges; what brings the hunt to a conclusion; and about some of the physiological characteristics of the deer at the end of the hunt. The main differences of opinion centre round the questions whether, and if so at what point, the challenge presented to the deer becomes so severe that it can no longer cope and whether the deer's welfare can be regarded as being seriously compromised.

6.20   We described briefly in Chapter 2 the way in which deer hunting takes place and referred in paragraph 2.40 to the fact that the chase will usually take the form of a series of intermittent flights by the deer as the hounds approach, followed by periods in which it

---

[371] *The Physiological response of red deer (Cervus elaphus) to prolonged exercise undertaken during hunting.* (Joint Universities study on deer hunting).
[372] Bateson and Harris, 5.1

is less active. It is necessary to describe this in a little more detail for the purposes of this chapter. The key point is that the nature of the deer's escape response means that it will always try immediately to put as much distance between itself and the hounds as it feels necessary to do in order for the threat to diminish to an acceptable level.[373] Because the deer is faster than the hounds over a short distance, it will almost invariably succeed in doing this at the first attempt, often establishing a lead of several kilometres over the hounds (roughly equivalent to an hour's hunting) before seeking cover.[374] As the hunt continues, it will normally find it increasingly difficult to effect escape to what it perceives to be a safe distance and, unless it escapes for some reason, there will come a point when it stops, unable or unwilling to continue, and it will then "stand at bay."[375] In terms of escaping the hounds, the mistake the deer makes is to exert itself maximally at each stage: a more "measured" response would greatly increase its chances of outrunning the hounds even over a long distance.[376]

6.21   As we noted in Chapter 2, the average duration of a hunt, in the case of deer that are killed, is three hours and the average distance travelled is over 18 kilometres. The modal speed is 5 kilometres an hour, confirming that, for much of a hunt, the deer is not moving.[377]

6.22   This is, of course, a considerably over-simplified account of what happens in practice. The nature of the chase, including its speed and duration, will vary considerably depending, in particular, on the terrain, the fitness of the animal concerned and the ability of the hounds to follow the scent. But it does describe in outline the course of a typical hunt in which the deer is caught and killed.

6.23   There is some dispute about the extent to which deer are well adapted to a chase of the kind we have just described. Professor Valerius Geist, in particular, has disputed suggestions that, because deer lead generally sedentary lives, they are not capable of responding to a challenge of this nature.[378] Deer have at least some of the physiological attributes to enable them to perform repeated bouts of fast sprinting but Bateson and Harris conclude that the amount of activity involved during hunting falls outside their normal experience and that it is believed to be greater than that which would be experienced during natural predation by wolves in other countries.[379]

6.24   There is general agreement among the scientists that towards, or at the end of a chase of this kind, there is clear evidence of very low levels of carbohydrate (glycogen) in the deer's muscles and that this largely explains why the deer ceases running.[380]

---

[373] Ibid, 4

[374] Ibid, 3,2

[375] Ibid, 3.2

[376] Ibid, 5.2.2

[377] Ibid, 3.2

[378] Professor Valerius Geist 1,10

[379] Bateson and Harris, 7.2.6

[380] Ibid, 3.4

6.25   There is less agreement about some of the other physiological indicators. The research showed that cortisol, often referred to as a stress hormone, increased in hunted deer, but Bateson and Harris conclude that it is not possible on present evidence to say to what extent this was due to the effects of exercise or to psychological stress.[381]

6.26   There was evidence of mild to moderate muscle damage at the end of a hunt.[382] It is not possible to say whether this would have affected the welfare of deer that escaped.[383]   Muscle stiffness would have been a possibility where damage was more extensive.[384]

6.27   There was also some evidence of the break-up of red blood cells. But problems with the collection of samples meant that it was difficult to interpret the findings. There was no evidence, however, of any damage of a kind which would be threatening to the welfare of a deer which escaped.[385]

6.28   The blood temperatures of hunted deer were found to be raised[386] but it is not clear whether the temperature of most hunted animals reached levels that might cause suffering.[387]

6.29   There is dispute about whether the effects of hunting contribute to the death of escaped deer in the following days or weeks by "capture myopathy" or "emotional stress": a condition which has been described in red deer and other species such as antelope. There is, however, no firm evidence on which to reach a conclusion.[388]

Questions raised by the evidence

6.30   As we indicated in paragraph 6.19, the scientific evidence essentially raises two important questions about the welfare implications of hunting deer:

- whether, and if so at what point, the deer ceases being able to cope

- whether, and if so at what point, the deer's welfare can be regarded as being seriously compromised.

6.31   There seems to be a large measure of agreement among the scientists that, at least during the last 20 minutes or so of the hunt, the deer is likely to suffer as glycogen depletion sets in.[389] (Bateson had previously suggested that it was possible that this point was reached after 5km, although this would have depended on the nature of the particular

---

[381] Ibid, 5.2.3
[382] Ibid, 7.2.4
[383] Ibid, 7.2.4
[384] Ibid, 5.2.4
[385] Ibid, 5.2.5
[386] Ibid, 5.2.3
[387] Ibid, 7.2.3
[388] Ibid, 3.5
[389] Ibid, 3.4

hunt).[390] However, the disagreement arises because many of the physiological changes which are observed resemble those found in a human being or horse, especially an endurance horse, involved in a prolonged bout of continuous or intermittent exercise.[391] It is not clear, though, if it is valid to make these comparisons across species.

6.32   It seems to us that, at this point, the argument ceases to turn purely on scientific evidence but, instead, becomes a broader judgement about animal welfare. On the one hand, it is argued that, unlike human beings who can choose to desist from vigorous exercise, the deer has no choice: it is driven by increasing fear of being caught by the hounds.[392] This forces it to run, beyond its normal experience, until it can no longer do so. On the other hand, it is argued that there is no convincing evidence that any suffering involved is greater than is present in any other method of culling deer and that, similarly, there is no firm evidence that deer which escape are seriously or permanently damaged.[393]

6.33   Although there are still substantial areas of disagreement, there is now a better understanding of the physiological changes which occur when a deer is hunted. Most scientists agree that deer are likely to suffer in the final stages of hunting. The available evidence does not enable us to resolve the disagreement about the point at which, during the hunt, the welfare of the deer becomes seriously compromised. There is also a lack of firm information about what happens to deer which escape, although the available research suggests that they are likely to recover.

Comparison between the welfare of stalked deer and hunted deer

6.34   Even if one accepted that hunting deer with dogs involves an appreciable degree of suffering, it would be necessary to compare this with the suffering involved in other culling methods, in particular shooting. This is because virtually everyone accepts that there is a need to cull some of the deer population in Exmoor and the Quantocks.

6.35   An essential piece of information, therefore, is the accuracy of stalkers when shooting deer, since injured animals may escape, leading possibly to a long and painful death. Unfortunately, there seems to be a dearth of reliable information about the accuracy of stalking and the figures which were quoted to us range from less than 2% of deer being wounded and then escaping[394] to 15% or more.[395] There is also the difficulty that the figures may vary between experienced professional stalkers and recreational stalkers.

---

[390] Ibid, 7.2.3
[391] Ibid, 5.2.3
[392] Ibid, 5.2.3
[393] Animal Welfare research seminar, 18 April 2000
[394] Animal Welfare research seminar, 18 April 2000
[395] British Wildlife Management, 2 - un-numbered

6.36   Bateson and Bradshaw[396] attempted to estimate wounding rates by collecting information from stalkers themselves, game dealers and by looking at the records relating to "casualty" deer. They concluded, on the basis of these figures, that about 10% of deer required two or more shots and that a conservative estimate was that about half of the wounded deer escaped detection. In a later study,[397] Bradshaw and Bateson estimated that 2% of shot deer escape wounded.

6.37   As Bateson and Harris point out, comparing the overall suffering of hunted deer with that of wounded stalked deer is very difficult.[398] On the one hand, there is the suffering of all the deer which are hunted, including those that escape. On the other, there is the suffering - for however many hours or days are involved - of a smaller number of shot deer which escape wounded. There are also other possible factors such as the separation of calves and the risk of orphaning.[399] Bateson and Harris conclude that, if the total number of animals that suffer per number culled is taken as the index, the balance of the argument comes down on the side of stalking rather than hunting as the most humane method of culling. They add, however, that the picture is less clear if one takes into account the length and nature of the suffering involved, together with the hunts' role in locating and dispatching "casualty" deer.[400] (In relation to the latter, however, it should be noted that this role is carried out elsewhere in the UK by licensed stalkers, the RSPCA and other groups and individuals).

6.38   It is clear that more work would be required in order to provide further scientific evidence about the welfare of hunted deer and how hunting compares with stalking. Bateson and Harris indicate that this would be needed in the following areas:

- the fate of deer that escape during the hunt

- further investigations of the state of deer during hunting

- the accuracy of stalkers' shooting

- the relative impacts of hunting and stalking in terms of the selection of the deer to be culled and the importance of selective culling to the long-term health of the herd.[401]

6.39   Stalking, if carried out to a high standard and with the availability of a dog or dogs to help find any wounded deer that escape, is in principle the better method of culling deer from an animal welfare perspective. In particular, it obviates the need to chase the deer in the way which occurs in hunting.

[396] '*How often do stalkers wound Red deer*? Deer 11: 180-181Bateson and Bradshaw, 1999,
[397] '*Welfare implications of culling red deer* (Cervus elaphus)'. Animal Welfare9: 3-24 Bradshaw and Bateson 2000
[398] Bateson and Harris 3.6
[399] Ibid, 7.4
[400] Ibid, 3.6
[401] Ibid, 9

6.40   A great deal depends, however, on the skill and care taken by the stalker. It is unfortunate that there is no reliable information on wounding rates, even in Scotland where stalking is carried out extensively. In the event of a ban on hunting, there is a risk that a greater number of deer than at present would be shot by less skilful shooters, in which case wounding rates would increase. Consideration should be given to requiring all stalkers to prove their competence by demonstrating that they had undertaken appropriate training.

The welfare of hunted foxes

6.41   The three main aspects of foxhunting which give rise to concerns about welfare are:

- the chase

- the "kill" by the hounds above ground

- digging-out/terrierwork.

6.42   Unfortunately, there is very little by way of scientific evidence to help us in establishing the facts on these issues. There have been no direct studies, of the kind that we have just described in relation to deer, of the welfare of hunted foxes.[402] [403] There are data on physiological responses of foxes to various stresses (including being chased with dogs in an enclosure) but their interpretation and relevance to hunting and other forms of control are not straightforward. It has been argued that, in view of what is known about the fox's ecology and social systems, the hunted fox, whether being pursued by hounds or being dug out, is bound to experience fear and distress[404] but others dispute this, arguing that this simply amounts to anthropomorphism and that there is no evidence to support the assertion.

<u>The chase</u>

6.43   The average length of the chase of a fox above ground has been estimated at 16-31 minutes, although it can be considerably longer.[405] It is not clear whether, as is usually the case in relation to deer, foxes are caught when they tire or whether they are simply overhauled by the faster hounds. Sometimes they make a mistake, for example by doubling back into the pack.[406]

6.44   Some work has been done on measuring physiological changes when captive foxes are chased by a dog, but it is not known whether the results have any relevance to

---

[402] Broom 1, 16
[403] Bateson and Harris, 8
[404] Broom 1, 14
[405] Bateson and Harris, 8.1
[406] Thomas and Allen 1, 1,3

the chase of a wild fox by hounds.[407] This is because the captive chases were not very similar to real fox hunts and, as with the studies on deer, it is not clear whether the observed changes were due to exercise or to mental stress. However, there is evidence from farmed foxes that fear and anxiety are experienced by foxes in response to stressful stimuli: physiological changes were observed which were not accounted for by exercise alone.[408] There is no firm evidence about whether those that escape are seriously or permanently damaged in any way.[409]

<u>The kill by the hounds above ground</u>

6.45   There has been a good deal of dispute about the way in which the "kill" above ground occurs. Those engaged in foxhunting have tended to argue that death is instantaneous or virtually instantaneous and that in the vast majority of cases it is caused by the leading hound grabbing the fox at the base of the neck, or on the back behind the shoulder, and shaking it, causing the dislocation of the cervical vertebrae[410]This view was endorsed by the Phelps Report[411]. Opponents of hunting have tended to argue instead that the fox is savaged to death or literally torn apart.[412]

6.46   Because the fox's carcass is usually "broken up" by the hounds it is bound to be difficult to obtain conclusive evidence on this matter. But the post mortem evidence which we have seen does at least suggest that - as we had tended to conclude from video footage - it is an over-simplification to say that foxes are almost invariably killed by the leading hound grabbing the fox's neck. Two post mortems carried out for us by the Department of Clinical Veterinary Science at the University of Bristol showed very few injuries to the head and neck area and indicated that death was caused by massive injuries to other vital organs.[413]

6.47   Two post mortem reports do not, of course, amount to a statistically valid sample, but similar findings were reported by a veterinary surgeon, on the basis of three post mortems which he had carried out.[414] On the other hand, evidence from some other veterinary surgeons tended to confirm that the cause of death was neck dislocation or fracture.[415] Of course, in a number of these cases there were also injuries to other parts of the body, consistent with a fox having been "broken up" by the hounds after death.

6.48   Arguably, the precise cause of death is irrelevant. What is more critical is how quickly insensibility and death result and how much suffering, physical or mental, the fox

---

[407] Bateson and Harris, 8.1

[408] Macdonald et al, 6.2.1.a

[409] Bateson and Harris, 8.1.4

[410] CA2, 8.22 and 8.2.3

[411] Phelps, 4.8.2 i (Report of a Review of Hunting with Hounds, Mr Richard Phelps, Professor W.R.Allan and Professor S R Harrop)

[412] IFAW1,24

[413] University of Bristol, Department of Clinical Veterinary Science, 'Report on post mortem findings in hunted foxes'. On CD Rom

[414] Mr Ian Jones, un-numbered document

[415] Baskerville 1; Dampney 1; Thomas and Allen 1,1,3

experiences. Here, again, there is lack of firm scientific evidence to help us. There seems little doubt, however, that in the vast majority of cases the time to insensibility and death is no more than a few seconds, bearing in mind the great disparity between the size and weight of the fox and the hounds.

6.49   The evidence which we have seen suggests that, in the case of the killing of a fox by hounds above ground, death is not always effected by a single bite to the neck or shoulders by the leading hound resulting in the dislocation of the cervical vertebrae. In a proportion of cases it results from massive injuries to the chest and vital organs, although insensibility and death will normally follow within a matter of seconds once the fox is caught. There is a lack of firm scientific evidence about the effect on the welfare of a fox of being closely pursued, caught and killed above ground by hounds. We are satisfied, nevertheless, that this experience seriously compromises the welfare of the fox.

Digging-out/terrierwork

6.50   There are two main areas of concern about digging-out/terrierwork from the perspective of the welfare of the fox: the possible distress experienced by the fox as the terriermen dig down - which may take a substantial time - and the possible distress, or even physical injuries, caused by the terrier.

6.51   Once again, there is no firm evidence about the former.[416] But it seems reasonable to assume that a situation in which the fox is prevented from escaping by the terrier will have adverse welfare implications. As to the latter, the role of the terrier is to hold the fox at bay by barking at it. As Macdonald et al point out, there is no firm evidence about the frequency with which fights occur or on the severity of the injuries.[417] We are aware that terrierwork is better regulated than it used to be and we accept that some of the reports of fights and injuries pre-date those changes. It seems clear, nevertheless, that fights do sometimes occur during digging-out or bolting and we have no doubt that this is more frequent in unofficial terrierwork than in that linked with the registered packs. One of the four foxes post mortemed for us by the University of Bristol, which had been dug out, had suffered injuries to its face, head, neck and eye.

6.52   Although there is no firm scientific evidence, we are satisfied that the activity of digging out and shooting a fox involves a serious compromise of its welfare, bearing in mind the often protracted nature of the process and the fact that the fox is prevented from escaping.

---

[416] Bateson and Harris, 8.1.3
[417] Macdonald et al, 6.2.1.c

Comparison with other methods of culling foxes

6.53   We were frequently told that farmers and others consider that they need a range of methods in order to control the fox population.[418] This reinforces the need to make a comparison between the welfare implications of hunting and those of other methods of killing foxes. The only other methods which are legal in England in Wales are snaring, live trapping and shooting. Although there is not a great deal of scientific evidence, it seems clear that all of these methods raise welfare issues.[419]

6.54   Serious concerns have been voiced about the welfare implications of snaring. Indeed, the UK is one of a minority of countries in Europe which permits snaring. The concerns include the stress of being restrained and the dangers of starvation, dehydration and hyperthermia or hypothermia.[420] There is also the additional stress which the animal may experience at the point at which a human being approaches it and dispatches it. Although experience suggests that snares with a 'stop' carry less risk, even in the case of legal snares, where the stop is required, there is still the possibility of strangulation or serious injury. There is the important point, too, that other animals are commonly caught in the snares set for foxes, with similar implications for their welfare.[421]

6.55   Trapping raises similar concerns, although the fox is not held directly as in the case of the snare, and there is not the danger of strangulation.

6.56   In the case of shooting, it seems to be generally agreed that lamping with a high powered rifle, if carried out properly and in appropriate circumstances, is the most humane way of killing a fox.[422] But as we noted in paragraph 5.24, there are a number of situations in which lamping is not practicable or safe. In particular, because of the need for vehicular access, it is not usually suitable in more remote, upland areas. The use of shotguns, especially in daylight, involves welfare implications. We received a good deal of evidence arguing that it was not easy to shoot foxes and that a fair number were wounded. We suspect that this is correct, given that foxes are relatively small animals.[423] There is also the welfare issue of what happens to orphaned cubs when the vixen is shot during the breeding season.[424] Terriers are used at present by gamekeepers and others to dispatch cubs which have been orphaned in this way.

6.57   On the other hand, shooting does not involve the welfare implications which we have noted in relation to the chase or digging-out.

6.58   It is likely that, in the event of a ban on hunting, many farmers and landowners would resort to a greater degree than at present to other methods to

---

[418] National Gamekeepers' Organisation 1 & 2 –un-numbered; National Farmers' Union of England and Wales 1 & 2- un-numbered
[419] Broom 1, 14–16
[420] Macdonald et al, 6.4.1
[421] Ibid, 6.5.1
[422] Ibid, 6.3.1.a
[423] Bateson and Harris, 8.1.5
[424] Macdonald et al, 6.3

control the numbers of foxes. We cannot say if this would lead to more, or fewer, foxes being killed than at present.

6.59   None of the legal methods of fox control is without difficulty from an animal welfare perspective. Both snaring and shooting can have serious adverse welfare implications.

6.60   Our tentative conclusion is that lamping using rifles, if carried out properly and in appropriate circumstances, has fewer adverse welfare implications than hunting, including digging-out. However, in areas where lamping is not feasible or safe, there would be a greater use of other methods. We are less confident that the use of shotguns, particularly in daylight, is preferable to hunting from a welfare perspective. We consider that the use of snaring is a particular cause for concern.

6.61   In practice, it is likely that some mixture of all of these methods would be used. In the event of a ban on hunting, it is possible that the welfare of foxes in upland areas could be affected adversely, unless dogs could be used, at least to flush foxes from cover.

The welfare of the hunted and coursed hare

6.62   Similarly, in the case of hares, there is little direct information about the welfare during hunting or coursing or how this compares with other legal methods that are used, in particular shooting and trapping.

6.63   In the case of hunting, chases generally last from about half an hour to a hour and a half.[425] For a good part of the time, however, the hare may not be aware that it is being pursued.[426] It seems likely that, if the hare is caught by the pack, insensibility and death follow very swiftly.

6.64   We arranged post mortems on the carcasses of twelve hares which had been killed during organised coursing events. These were carried out by the Department of Clinical Veterinary Medicine at the University of Cambridge.[427] There were difficulties, however, in determining the cause of death in some cases because the neck of the hare is almost invariably broken by the "picker-up" as soon as the hare is retrieved from the dogs. The findings were that the cause of death in one case was probably fatal injuries caused by the dogs. In six other cases it was not clear whether the actions of the dogs, or the picker-up, had led to the hare's death. In the remaining five cases the picker-up was judged to have been the cause of death.

6.65   The only previous study of this kind was carried out in 1977-1979 by the Universities Federation for Animal Welfare. Of 53 hares killed, 43 had neck injuries, 18

---

[425] AMHB 1,8
[426] AMHB 1,8
[427] University of Cambridge, Department of Clinical Veterinary Medicine: Post Mortem Reports on 12 hares killed at Coursing Meetings in March 2000. (Report on CD Rom)

of which were inflicted by the "picker up". No clean breaks were believed to have been caused by dogs (where tooth marks were evident). The UFAW team's assessment was that all chest injuries would have been quickly fatal.[428]

6.66   As far as shooting hares is concerned, we received anecdotal evidence of high wounding rates on organised shoots which would undoubtedly lead to poor welfare. We note that the report of the House of Lords Select Committee which was examining a Coursing Bill in 1976 concluded that "the total physical suffering caused by coursing matches is negligible compared with the suffering of hares wounded by shooting".[429] Dogs are sometimes used to dispatch hares that are wounded by shooting.

6.67   There is a lack of firm scientific evidence about the effect on the welfare of a hare of being closely pursued, caught and killed by hounds during hunting. We are satisfied, nevertheless, that although death and insensibility will normally follow within a matter of seconds, this experience seriously compromises the welfare of the hare.

6.68   We are similarly satisfied that being pursued, caught and killed by dogs during coursing seriously compromises the welfare of the hare. It is clear, moreover, that, if the dog or dogs catch the hare, they do not always kill it quickly. There can also sometimes be a significant delay, in "driven" coursing, before the "picker up" reaches the hare and dispatches it (if it is not already dead). In the case of "walked up" coursing, the delay is likely to be even longer.

6.69   In the event of a ban on hunting and coursing hares, it seems likely that a few more would be shot than at present. There are concerns about the welfare implications of shooting hares because of wounding rates.

The welfare of hunted mink

6.70   In the case of mink too there have been no scientific studies of the welfare implications of hunting and little is known about the welfare implications of other lethal methods of control. There is concern, however, about the welfare implications if traps are placed under water since mink, as aquatic mammals, would take longer to drown.[430] Traps can also catch other species.

6.71   There is a lack of firm scientific evidence about the welfare implications of hunting mink. There seems reason to suppose, however, that being closely pursued, caught and killed by hounds, or being dug out or bolted, seriously compromises the welfare of the mink. The kill, by the hounds or by shooting, is normally quick once the mink is caught. In the absence of hunting, more mink would probably be killed by shooting and, mainly, trapping. These methods involve welfare implications but we do not have sufficient evidence to conclude how they compare with those raised by hunting.

---

[428] Macdonald et al, 6.2.3.b.ii
[429] NCC 1,14
[430] Bateson and Harris, 8.2.2

The welfare of other animals incidentally affected by hunting

6.72   There are two concerns here:

- the welfare of any wildlife which may be incidentally affected by hunting

- the welfare of farm animals and pets.

6.73   There is no firm evidence about the former. We mention in the next chapter the particular concerns which have been expressed about the impact of fox and mink hunting on badgers and otters respectively. More generally, it seems reasonable to assume that other wildlife will be disturbed, if only temporarily, by the hunt. We see no reason to suppose, however, that, in the ordinary course of events, this will result in any serious concerns on welfare grounds.

6.74   We discuss in Chapter 9 the concerns which have been expressed to us about the attacks by hounds on pets and the distress caused to farm animals. Although we do not know how frequently these incidents occur, attacks on pets clearly do cause unnecessary suffering to the animals concerned and distress to their owners.

6.75   There is some evidence that hunting incidentally affects the welfare of wildlife. In particular, we have been informed about the stopping-up of badger setts and a few isolated cases of disturbance to otter – both of which are protected species - and wildfowl during mink hunting. The frequency of such incidents is disputed.

6.76   The welfare of pets which are attacked by hounds is clearly compromised, and their owners often suffer great distress.

The welfare of the hounds and the horses

6.77   We received evidence expressing concern about the welfare of the hounds and the horses involved in hunting.[431] These tended to focus on:

- injuries or death of hounds caused, in particular, by trespass on roads and railway lines

- the common practice of putting hounds down after some six or seven years' hunting when they are judged to have come to the end of their working lives

---

[431] Association of British Dogs and Cats Homes 1, un-numbered, British Equine Veterinary Association 1, un-numbered, British Horse Industry Confederation 1, 21, Cotswold Support Groups For the Abolition of Hunting 1, Part 1, West Sussex Wildlife Protection Group 1, un-numbered, Mr Dave Wetton 1, un-numbered, International League for the Protection of Horses 1, 2a, IFAW 1, 104-6, The Kennel Club 1, un-numbered, League Against Cruel Sports 1, 51-53 National Canine Defence League 1, un-numbered, RSPCA 1, 34, Wessex Wildlife 1, 6.4

- the possibility that thousands of hounds might have to be put down if hunting was banned

- injuries to terriers in the course of terrierwork

- injuries to horses during hunting

- the possibility that horses too might have to be put down, in the event of a ban, or that their welfare would be compromised in other ways.

Injuries or death of hounds

6.78   There have been a number of reported incidents in which hounds have strayed onto roads and railway lines and have been killed or injured as a result. A well-publicised example was the death of seven hounds in the New Forest in which were electrocuted crossing a live rail.[432]

Putting hounds down

6.79   It is a common, but not universal, practice for hounds belonging to the registered packs to be put down after some six or seven years' hunting, when they are considered to have reached the end of their working lives. The Countryside Alliance estimated that the MFHA packs put down about 3,000 hounds a year in this way.[433] The Countryside Alliance and the MFHA explained to us that this was necessary in most cases because hounds were not domesticated animals; and that it would be unfair to subject them to the more constrained and solitary life of a pet dog.[434] In some cases, however, especially with hounds belonging to the Fell Packs, the hounds retire to live with the families who "walked" them as puppies and who have often continued to look after them during the summer breaks.

6.80   The anti-hunting organisations tend to argue that it is unnecessary to put hounds down in this way. They also argue that hunts breed too many dogs and are too ready to put them down if they are not thought suitable for some reason.[435]

6.81   Whether hounds can be successfully re-homed is clearly an important issue when considering the impact of a ban on hunting. The hunts argue that the majority of the present 20,000 or so hounds would have to be put down.[436] The Countryside Alliance told us that where re-homing had been tried it had failed because the hounds would not settle and invariably returned to their hunt kennels.[437] Opponents of hunting contend, however, that many of the hounds could be re-homed; that some could be retrained for

---

[432] IFAW 1, 118
[433] CA, 'Details of number of hounds involved in hunting'
[434] CA 1, 73; MFHA 1, 10
[435] IFAW 1, 118
[436] CA 1, 73
[437] CA, 'Details of number of hounds involved in hunting'

drag hunting; and that hunts could anticipate a ban by reducing numbers by natural means.[438] The National Canine Defence League's view was that, while they did not accept that hounds could not be rehomed, in practice this could be successfully arranged in only a very few cases.[439]

Injuries to terriers

6.82   We discussed in paragraph 6.51 the question whether fights occur between terriers and foxes underground in the course of digging-out/terrierwork or bolting (eg from rockholes). As we indicated, there is no firm information on this, although we are satisfied that fights do occur from time to time and that these would involve some compromise of the welfare of the terrier.

Injuries to horses

6.83   Concern was expressed to us that horses may be injured during hunting.[440] This is undoubtedly true but we have seen no evidence that hunting involves appreciably greater risk of injury than other vigorous equestrian activities. Some evidence has raised the issue of the retirement of racehorses and the welfare implications of a ban on hunting. At present, many flat-bred horses transfer to hunting, point- to-pointing or National Hunt racing once their flat careers are over. We do not have evidence of the scale of such transfers. In the event of a ban on hunting, it is possible that more retired race horses would be destroyed.

6.84   We have received evidence of injuries to terriers during terrierwork. This clearly involves some compromise of the terrier's welfare when it occurs.

6.85   We have received no evidence that hunting, in general, raises greater concerns about the welfare of the horses and dogs involved than other activities such as horse racing or greyhound racing, except for small number of deaths or injuries to hounds which result from straying on roads or railways lines. There are other concerns about the hunts' practice in putting down hounds which are considered too old to hunt and about the numbers of hounds which might be put down in the event of a ban. Similarly, there are concerns over the fate of surplus horses if hunting were to be banned, and of retired racehorses. Strictly speaking, these matters do not raise animal welfare concerns provided that the hounds and horses are destroyed humanely. Rather, they raise ethical issues, which are outside our terms of reference. But any need to put down hounds or horses, in the event of a ban, could be minimised if there was a suitable lead-in time before it was implemented.

---

[438] RSPCA 1, 42
[439] National Canine Defence League 1, un-numbered
[440] IFAW 1, 118

CHAPTER 7

MANAGEMENT AND CONSERVATION OF HABITAT AND OTHER WILDLIFE

7.1   In this chapter we examine the extent to which hunting has a positive or negative impact on the management and conservation of habitat and other wildlife.

7.2   Foxes, deer and mink can all raise difficulties from a conservation perspective. As we noted in chapter 5, foxes prey on game and ground-nesting birds. Deer damage woodland habitats. Mink eat a wide variety of birds and small animals. To the extent that hunting contributes to controlling the numbers of these species - and that these difficulties could increase in the event of a ban on hunting - hunting has a potential benefit in conservation terms. However, we noted that, other than in upland areas, hunting accounts for only a small percentage of foxes killed each year; that it accounts for only about 15% of the numbers of deer that need to be killed in the area hunted over by the three staghound packs; and that the minkhunts kill relatively few mink.

7.3   But we also received a good deal of evidence from the Countryside Alliance and the hunts highlighting the important role which, they argue, hunting has traditionally played in conserving habitat, not only for the benefit of certain quarry species but also for other wildlife and plants. It is said that, if hunting was banned, many farmers and landowners would no longer have an incentive to conserve these habitats and that many of them would be lost. The arguments mainly centre on the hunts' role in creating and managing habitat for foxhunting and hare hunting and coursing. Mink, as we have already noted, are not a conservation species and there is no need to create or manage habitat specifically for deer.

7.4   We have been handicapped in our assessment of these wider benefits by the lack of information from independent sources about the relative importance of hunting in comparison with the many other factors that influence habitat and landscape management. In particular, we received very little evidence on these issues from the wide range of statutory and non-statutory organisations concerned with wildlife and landscape protection.

Habitat conservation in the interests of foxhunting

7.5   There is no doubt that, historically, the landscape of many parts of lowland England, especially the Midlands, has been strongly influenced by the desire to establish and conserve good foxhunting country. As the Countryside Alliance pointed out, this has taken the form, in particular, of planting, managing and conserving woodland, hedges and other forms of cover in which foxes generally live.[441]

7.6   The efforts made to increase agricultural production, following the Second World War, had a dramatic effect on the English countryside. The acreage of arable land

---

[441] CA1,11.4

increased at the expense of grassland, reducing biodiversity and creating less habitat for wildlife. It is estimated that half of England's hedgerows were removed to accommodate bigger machinery and provide more land for cultivation. In the years 1990-1993, alone 2,240 miles of hedgerow were lost each year. Hedge and ditch maintenance machinery led to less traditional, and indiscriminate, forms of hedge maintenance, reducing the density of hedges and their wildlife value. Recent surveys by the Institute of Terrestrial Ecology show that as much hedgerow is now being planted as is being lost,[442] but new hedgerow does not have the same conservation value as old hedgerow. Many areas of grazing and scrub were also improved for agriculture during the post-war period. These changes led to marked declines in the numbers of birds, animals and plants. Alongside the loss of particular habitat and features, farming methods changed, especially in the 1970s and 1980s. The trend away from mixed farming towards specialisation reduced farmland biodiversity. In grassland areas the shift from hay to silage production adversely affected wildlife and so did the loss of winter stubbles due to the prominence given to winter cereals on arable farms. In both types of farming the environment has been made poorer by the increased use of fertilisers and pesticides.

7.7   Few would argue that hunting is important enough to mitigate many of these effects. For example, we received no evidence to suggest that significant numbers of hunting farmers have been prepared to maintain large areas of winter stubble for spring cropping to benefit mounted followers. Nor are we aware that the trend to silage production has been resisted by those seeking to maintain hare numbers. However, there is some evidence that certain features, particularly woods and hedges, were preserved for foxhunting by farmers and landowners who wished to maintain habitat. At a time of intensification of agriculture, hunting farmers showed less tendency to remove hedgerows and other non-productive habitat. For example, Macdonald noted in a survey of over 800 farmers that, during the 1970s, those farmers who were enthusiastic foxhunters removed less hedgerow than farmers who shot or who were interested in neither activity.[443]

7.8   However, more recently, with a move away from over-production and a shift towards a package of agri-environment schemes, which place more emphasis on environmental management of the countryside and protection and creation of habitat, the differences between hunting and non-hunting farmers have lessened. The 1998 survey of farmers' behaviour over the last decade showed no significant difference in the length of hedgerow removed by hunting farmers and non-hunting farmers. There were differences, however, in their management of other non-productive habitats, with hunting farmers more likely to encourage shelterbelts, ponds and parkland trees.[444]

7.9   The evidence we received from the Countryside Alliance and hunts illustrated the ways in which hunts themselves are engaged in conserving habitats which are suitable for foxhunting but which also have a wider nature conservation benefit. In addition, there is evidence of committed conservation practice from specific hunts and landholdings, such

[442] IFAW 1,86
[443] Macdonald et al, 7.2.2.b
[444] Macdonald and Johnson 2000

as Ashford Valley Hunt and Wight Conservation. This information draws on material being collated by the Game Conservancy Trust, the Standing Conference on Countryside Sports and some of the hunts.

7.10   Woodland management and the management of field boundaries are the two main activities undertaken.

Woodland management

7.11   Because foxes like to lie up in ground cover, lowland hunts sometimes coppice small areas in rotation, producing small clearings which provide favourable habitat for plants and for many birds and butterflies. Similarly, gorse may be managed by cutting or burning back. Woodland rides may be created to provide access for foxhunting for horses and hounds. These act as wildlife corridors between areas of habitat for light-demanding species, such as butterflies, whilst maintaining aerial walkways between trees for arboreal species, such as dormice. Coppicing and ride maintenance are widely advocated by woodland conservation organisations and statutory agencies for their benefits to wildlife.

7.12   These beneficial activities may be undertaken directly by hunts themselves on land which they own or on behalf of other landowners. Alternatively, farmers and landowners may undertake these activities because of their interest in hunting. A number of studies have attempted to gauge the direct role of hunts. A British Field Sports Society survey of 158 lowland fox hunts in 1995 recorded that 98 of the hunts undertook covert laying and management and 10 had planted new coverts.[445] A total of 5,700 hectares of woodland were managed in this way, often through the use of volunteer labour.[446] In England, the MAFF census of agricultural holdings for 1999 recorded 255,000 hectares of woodland.[447] Thus, on the basis of the 1995 survey figures, hunts would appear to contribute to the management of just 2.2% of the woodland area on farms.

7.13   However, evidence provided by the Game Conservancy Trust suggests a considerably higher area of woodland managed by hunts.[448] Unfortunately, this fresh research initiative is not yet complete and so the data presented by the Game Conservancy are from 31 of 185 hunts. Of these, 28 (90%) have given locations of woodland they say they manage, amounting to a total of 15,723 hectares of woodland (an average of 562 hectares per hunt). The Game Conservancy Trust calculate a total of 157,477 hectares of huntable woodland within the 28 hunt country boundaries.[449] On the basis of these figures, the hunts appear to be managing 10% of the woodland available to them in their hunt countries.

---

[445] CA 1,11.8

[446] *Countryside Sports: Their Economic, Social and Conservation Significance.* Review and Survey by Cobham Resource Consultants. Published by Standing Conference on Countryside Sports, 1997

[447] MAFF Statistical Press Release, 1999

[448] Game Conservancy Trust 1, 3.2

[449] Ibid, 3.4

7.14   We are not clear why there is this considerable difference between the 1995 survey figures and the more recent information collected by the Game Conservancy Trust. We note, however, that the latter intends to carry out visits in due course to check the position on the ground.

7.15   All this work carried out by the hunts should be seen in the context of habitat management taking place as a whole in Britain.   As land use policy in Britain has recognised the importance of habitat management, and an increasing proportion of agricultural support is offered in the form of land management grants rather than output subsidies, so more positive habitat management is taking place.

7.16   Hunts and their supporters' clubs clearly do carry out important conservation work. For example, some of the woodlands which they manage are "ancient woodlands" and therefore of high conservation value.   However, a much greater amount of conservation work and land management is carried out by other landholders and dedicated conservation bodies.

Hedgerow Management

7.17   The data collected by the Game Conservancy Trust also show that many hunts say that they are actively involved in maintaining hedgerows in order to provide good jumps. Hedge laying by hand, though labour-intensive, avoids hedges becoming "gappy" and fragmented and produces a much better habitat for small animals such as voles and dormice. A number of hunts run hedge-laying societies and hold annual competitions. Hunts also contribute to the management of bridleways and maintenance of fences, dry stone walls and gates.[450]

Conservation in the interests of hunting and coursing hares

7.18   In the case of hare hunting and coursing it is more difficult to disentangle the conservation efforts made in the interests of hunting and coursing from the game management (such as predator control) undertaken in the interests of shooting hare and other game such as partridges and pheasants.

7.19   The hare is the only one of the four quarry species considered to be of conservation importance. As we noted in paragraph 5.77, the brown hare is now the subject of a UK Biodiversity Action Plan, which aims to double spring numbers by 2010.

7.20   In their evidence to us the Countryside Alliance drew attention to research carried out by the Game Conservancy Trust (which the Trust also sent to us separately) between 1988 and 1990 which looked at the effect of hare coursing on hare populations on two estates where hare coursing took place.[451] The Game Conservancy Trust found that, on

---

[450] Hobson 1,2
[451] CA1, 11.15

these estates, hare numbers were maintained at relatively high densities and that the direct mortality associated with hare coursing was very low.[452]

7.21   The Game Conservancy Trust found, in addition, that coursing estates had made or retained habitats which benefited hares, for example areas of grass instead of cereal and root crops; that they had prohibited organised shooting; and that they had taken active steps to protect hares from predation and poaching.[453][454]

7.22   Related research studied the impact of beagling on hare populations. It found, similarly, that beagling made very little impact on hare numbers.

7.23   The evidence submitted to us indicated that the hunts and coursing clubs presently contribute to hare conservation by:

- joining with other organisations to publicise the problems caused to hares (and to birds and other animals) by modern agricultural practices such as the methods used to cut silage or hay

- taking part in county Biodiversity Actions Plans

- encouraging the planting of game cover crops, which also benefit farmland birds

- collecting information regularly about hare numbers. For example, the rules of the AMBH provide that all Masters of Hounds may be required to complete a "Hare Survey Form" giving details of hares seen on each day's hunting. The data are collated by the Game Conservancy Trust and assist in monitoring the health of the hare population.[455] As the Game Conservancy Trust confirm, these records provide a better indication of changes in winter populations than do game bag records.[456]

The negative impact of hunting on conservation

7.24   On the other side of the coin, we also need to take into account the negative impact that hunting can sometimes have on conservation interests. These include:

- some disturbance of the area being hunted and to the habitat and vulnerable wildlife there

- disturbance of otters and other riparian animals and birds by mink hunts during the summer breeding season

---

[452] Game Conservancy Trust, 2.4 hare coursing
[453] CA1,11.5
[454] Game Conservancy Trust, 2.4 hare coursing
[455] CA1,11.19 and 11.20
[456] Game Conservancy Trust, 1.5.8

- interference with badger setts when stopping-up and digging-out during foxhunting

- transportation of hares for coursing, which might not survive or which might spread disease.

7.25 Hunting mink with hounds is argued to have a detrimental effect on wildlife conservation because of the disturbance caused when the hounds and the whips investigate potential lying-up spots or dig out mink that have gone to ground. Mink hunts tend to operate from April to September, which includes the breeding season for birds and a time when many species are vulnerable to disturbance.[457] There are no quantitative data regarding this issue, but a small survey by Dorset Wildlife Trust of academics and researchers working with otters showed that they were of the opinion that mink hunting would pose a significant risk to otters, although few had come across examples of such disturbance. Several conservation bodies, including the National Trust, do not allow mink hunting on their land when otters are present.[458] The Environment Agency discourages mink hunting where otters and other wildlife may be disturbed.[459] The Otters and Rivers Project (OARP), a network of 24 Wildlife Trust staff working across England and Wales on otter, river and wetland conservation, after collecting evidence from a variety of sources, concluded in their evidence that mink hunting may, in some cases, damage riverine habitat and disturb riverine species at particularly sensitive times of year. They added that it may have a direct impact on otters, both in terms of disturbance and in preventing otters from re-colonising and establishing in sensitive areas.[460]

7.26 We received evidence from several badger protection groups around the country, which reported incidents of prosecutions and other evidence of people entering terriers and digging out badger setts.[461] All claimed that legal forms of hunting with dogs facilitated this illegal activity, since participants could claim that they were in pursuit of a fox and had erroneously pursued a badger. Badger protection groups also claimed cases of the hard stopping of setts by hunts when stopping up, so causing badgers to become trapped in their setts. It is difficult to quantify the extent to which this is practised throughout England and Wales, since no aggregate records have been submitted. The RSPCA obtained 271 convictions for badger offences from 1986 to 1997.[462] [463] The League Against Cruel Sports states that its records show that, between 1986 and 1994, 18 members of official working terrier clubs and 11 officials or employees of registered fox hunts were committed of badger digging or other offences under badger protection legislation.[464] Whilst, it is unknown how many of these relate specifically to sett

---

[457] The Wildlife Trusts 1, un-numbered

[458] National Trust 5.3

[459] *Mink*. Environment Agency (1995)

[460] The Wildlife Trusts 2, un-numbered

[461] National Federation of Badger Groups 1, Glamorgan Badger Group 1, West Sussex Badger Protection Group 1

[462] Badger Watch and Rescue, Dyfed 1, un-numbered

[463] Ibid, Appendix 3, *Legal and Illegal 'Sports': The Facts*. Campaign for the Protection of Hunted Animals

[464] LACS 1, Appendix 10, point 33

disturbance from digging-out, there is sufficient evidence to suggest that illegal practice is taking place, whether inadvertently or otherwise.

7.27   We received a certain amount of evidence about the live capture of hares, by driving them into long nets and boxing them, for movement from one area of the country to another for purposes of re-stocking. This is carried out for the benefit of hunting and coursing, but is also seen by the registered hare associations as being helpful in transferring hares from areas where their numbers might constitute a nuisance value to areas where successful introduction would contribute to biodiversity. Both the AMHB and the NCC emphasise that freshly-transported hares should not be hunted or coursed. The NCC state that hares should be imported onto an estate in February/March to be coursed 6 months later at the beginning of the next season.[465] The AMHB recommends that, ideally, if fresh hares are introduced into a "country", the hunt should be directed away from the specific area as much as possible for 2-3 seasons to allow the population to establish itself.[466] The AMHB also recommends that any reintroduction of hares into an area should be in accordance with the local Biodiversity Action Plan, and the International Union for Conservation of Nature's Guidelines for Reintroduction, 1998, which state the conditions that need to be satisfied before attempting to reintroduce a species.[467]

7.28   The actual number of hares transported is not possible to gauge accurately, partly because it may often be carried out quietly so as not to attract the attention of poachers.[468] Some estimates put the number transported for coursing at several thousand per year.[469] The NCC states that the estate at Altcar, where the Waterloo Cup is held, was re-stocked successfully in 1987 and that seven out of 24 clubs have also transported hares in recent years.[470] The AMHB state that the local hunts say they reintroduced hares onto Exmoor five or six years ago and that there is now a healthy and balanced population.[471]

7.29   We received no firm evidence about the welfare implications of transporting hares, although some anecdotal evidence suggested that it might be a cause for concern in relation to the spreading of disease. Nor did we receive any clear evidence that hares had been transported shortly before hunting or coursing events. Doubts have been expressed, however, about whether re-stocking has other than a temporary effect on local hare populations.[472]

7.30   There is also an indirect relationship between hunting and pasture management. If a ban on hunting were to lead to a significant reduction in the number of horses kept, then there might also be a related reduction in the amount of grazing pasture and hay meadows maintained on land holdings.

---

[465] CA oral evidence, 10 April 2000. Session 2
[466] AMHB - telephone conversation
[467] AMHB - telephone conversation; Hare Hunting Association (HHA) 2,10
[468] AMHB - telephone conversation
[469] Harris et al, 2.1.2
[470] CA oral evidence, 10 April 2000. Session 2
[471] HHA 2,10
[472] Harris et al, 2.1.2

Assessment of the influence of hunting on the conservation of habitat and wildlife

7.31   We mentioned earlier the difficulty in distinguishing, in the case of the hare, from conservation specifically for hunting or coursing from conservation for wider game management.   But the difficulties go wider than this.   For example, the Game Management Project revealed that game considerations were a strong motivating factor in influencing woodland planting and management practices.[473]   Farmers and landowners who released pheasants for shooting were twice as likely to have planted new woodland as those who did not release pheasants.

7.32   It is difficult to distinguish the effect that hunting has had on influencing land management practices from the broader impact of game management for shooting.   Foxhunting has undoubtedly had a beneficial influence in lowland parts of England in conserving and promoting habitat which has helped biodiversity, although any effect has been in specific localities.   In the case of hare hunting and coursing, it seems clear that those interested in these activities have helped to maintain habitats which are favourable to the hare and to a number of other species.

7.33   We now turn to the more critical assessment of what the impact would be, from a conservation point of view, of a ban on hunting.

The conservation effects of a ban

7.34   Some of those who support hunting have argued that, in the event of a ban, there could be an adverse impact on conservation of hedgerows and thickets.[474]   It is necessary, however, to look at the various influences which bear today on farmers' and landowners' practices in managing their land.

7.35   It is possible that a ban on hunting would remove the incentive for certain landholders to manage parts of their land in a way that provides suitable habitat for their quarry species but which is also beneficial for other fauna and flora.   However, the removal of this incentive would not necessarily lead to the destruction or abandonment of such areas in all cases.   The extent to which landholders would change their patterns of management, in the event of a ban, would depend upon the presence of other influences which bear on their land management practices.

Baseline environmental regulations

7.36   Agricultural and rural land use are subject to a number of controls to protect the environment.   For example, there are significant restrictions on woodland clearance through the Forestry Commission's felling licence system.   Some woodland trees are also

---

[473] *Game Management in England.* Cox G, Watkins C and Winter M. Cheltenham: Countryside Press.1966
[474] CA1,12.2

subject to Tree Preservation Orders. Woodlands designated as SSSIs are afforded a high degree of protection, although SSSI status does not in itself ensure that best management practices will be undertaken. The planting of new woodlands is also subject to some controls. Important hedgerows enjoy a degree of protection under the Hedgerow Regulations 1997. Farms entered into agri-environment schemes are likely to be restricted, through scheme conditions, in the extent to which they can remove hedges or trees. There are also a number of regulations relating to environmental pollution which are less relevant to this inquiry.

Policy and markets

7.37   It is undoubtedly the case that farmers' actions are strongly influenced by the signals received through the market and from policy measures. For example, hunting did not prevent many of the post-war trends towards intensification of production which took place in response to market/policy signals. Increased acreages of winter wheat and of silage are two examples of changes that have brought financial benefits to farmers but have not benefited either the natural environment or hunting. Attempts to limit expansion of production, as part of the reform of the Common Agricultural Policy, include the use of set-aside and the identification of areas eligible for arable aid. These, alongside quotas and stocking density rules in the dairy and livestock sector, act as important constraints on farmers' land management actions.

Agri-environment schemes

7.38   These schemes, run by MAFF in England, exert a growing influence on the way in which agricultural land is managed. The current schemes are: Arable Stewardship, Countryside Access, Countryside Stewardship, Environmentally Sensitive Areas, Farm Woodland Premium, Habitat, Moorland, Nitrate Sensitive Areas and Organic Farming. As an indication of the take-up of these schemes, we note that the Countryside Stewardship Scheme had nearly 150,000 hectares by the end of 1999; over a million hectares were designated in the Environmentally Sensitive Areas Scheme; and by the end of 1998 nearly 50,000 hectares had been approved for planting under the Farm Woodland Premium Scheme.[475] [476] To set these figures in context, we note that England has an agricultural area of 9.6 million hectares rough grazing and 0.2 million hectares of farm woodland.[477]

7.39   In Wales, with the exception of the Organic Aid Scheme which remains separate, all agri-environment schemes have now been subsumed within a single scheme, Tir Gofal, run by the Countryside Council for Wales. Farmers throughout the Principality are eligible to apply to Tir Gofal.

---

[475] MAFF AUK 99
[476] IFAW 1,86
[477] MAFF Statistical Press Release on 1999 June Census for England

<u>Farmers' attitudes and objectives</u>

7.40   In an attempt to evaluate the importance of hunting as an incentive to farmers to engage in positive conservation activities, we sent a questionnaire to Farming and Wildlife Advisory Group conservation advisers in England. They were asked to put in rank order a set of nine factors that, in their experience, motivate farmers to undertake conservation activity in their own particular county. The advisers were asked to undertake the exercise for each of seven key aspects of conservation activity.[478]   20 advisers responded. The results show that personal interest, appropriate advice and encouragement and the incentives offered by agri-environment schemes are seen by FWAG advisers as the most important factors likely to motivate farmers to undertake conservation activities. Hunting is seen to be of relatively low importance except in the case of woodland management, where it is ranked fourth in importance, and woodland planting (fifth). In both cases, game management is considered to be of greater importance. However, in some counties hunting was seen as the second or third most important factor encouraging farmers to manage woodland for conservation or plant new woods.

7.41   It is important to recognise that these are the views of a small number of people. However, FWAG advisers are uniquely placed to make judgements of this kind. The results certainly seem to indicate that, for woodland management at least, hunting may well continue to have some importance in influencing farmers' actions. This is consistent with the evidence provided by the hunts.

Conclusions

7.42   Hunting has clearly played a very significant role in the past in the formation of the rural landscape and in the creation and management of areas of nature conservation. Nowadays, however, hunting with dogs is likely to form only a relatively minor factor in determining farmers' and landowners' land management practices. It still plays a role, though, in certain localities in respect of woodland planting and management.

7.43   Hunting exerts much less influence than agricultural market and policy trends, the management of game for shooting or incentives under agri-environment schemes. With the possible exception of hare conservation, a ban on hunting with dogs would be unlikely to have a major impact from a conservation perspective. In the case of the hare, on those estates which favour hare coursing or hunting, rather than shooting, a ban might lead farmers and landowners to pay less attention to encouraging hare numbers. The loss of habitat suitable for hares could have serious consequences for a number of birds and other animals.

---

[478] A summary of the responses is on the CD Rom.

CHAPTER 8

DRAG AND BLOODHOUND HUNTING

8.1   Drag and bloodhound hunting have come to assume an important position in the debate about the future of hunting. At one extreme, it has been argued that they provide a ready-made replacement for hunting live quarry and that it would be a simple matter for hunters, followers, hounds and horses to switch from one activity to the other. Indeed, it is often added that those riders who presently dislike hunting would be attracted to drag and bloodhound hunting if they became more widely available. At the other extreme, it has been frequently argued that drag and bloodhound hunting are completely different from hunting live quarry; that they are artificial and hold very little attraction for most of those who presently go hunting; and that very few would take up these sports even if hunting was banned.

8.2   We thought it was important that we should try to reach some view about where the truth lies between these two extremes since it is critical to judgements about the impact of a ban on hunting on such matters as employment and the social and cultural activities which are presently linked with hunting. In order to help us establish the facts, we commissioned research from Royal Agricultural College Enterprise (RACE), which looked at drag and bloodhound hunting and its potential to replace live quarry hunting.[479]

8.3   In this chapter we also discuss briefly the development of drag coursing, which to some extent simulates hare coursing.

Drag and bloodhound hunting

Background

Draghunting

8.4   Draghunting originally developed in this country as a means of testing the speed and ability of hounds by laying a trail over a specified distance. This, in turn, encouraged the practice of following the hounds on horseback.[480]

8.5   During the second half of the nineteenth century draghunting became popular in its own right and was actively encouraged by the army.[481] [482] There are still two surviving "military packs".

8.6   There was a decline in the number of draghunt packs in the early 20th century, with only six packs recorded in 1957.[483] But the numbers have risen gradually to sixteen

---

[479] *Drag and Bloodhound Hunting.* Will Manley, Julia Hallett, Graham Cox, Graham Smith. Royal Agricultural College Enterprise. (On CD Rom) ('RACE')
[480] MDBA1, 4
[481] RACE, 2.2
[482] MDBA1, 4

(including three provisionally registered packs), twelve of which have been formed in the last 30 years.[484]

8.7   The scent used, and the way in which it is laid, have varied over the years and are still subject to experimentation. Historically, it was often the droppings and bed of a fox, flavoured with aniseed. Nowadays, the drag is typically some absorbent material soaked in human or animal urine and aniseed, but chemicals are also used.[485] [486] The drag is usually trailed in a bag by a "dragman" or "line layer", either on foot or on a horse, although one pack has tried attaching the scent to the horse itself.

8.8   The "dragman" or "line layer" will set off about half an hour or so ahead of the hunt and will typically lay a line of two to three miles[487]. The hounds - usually at least 15 foxhounds[488] - will be taken to the area where the line begins. Once they find the scent, they will pursue it with the mounted field following on behind. After a rest of some fifteen minutes or so another line will be laid and the process repeated. Normally, three to five lines are laid in a day. Because there is no long period of casting around for a scent or drawing a covert for live quarry, draghunts do not usually last more than a couple of hours.[489]

8.9   The lines laid will normally be predetermined, taking account of the landowner's wishes, and will usually take in a variety of natural obstacles and purpose-built jumps. The field, however, will not necessarily know the proposed lines.[490] Greater variety over the line is possible in open country.[491]

8.10   Many draghunt packs operate over enclosed grassland but some operate on hill, forest and open commons.[492] The packs have much larger areas registered to them than foxhound/harrier packs, typically covering five or six foxhound countries.[493] The hunts meet, on average, 24 times each season.[494] This compares with about 50 meets for the average foxhound/harrier pack, excluding autumn/cub hunting.

Bloodhound hunting

8.11   The bloodhound is a dog which has been specially bred for its exceptional scenting ability, in particular its ability to hunt the natural scent of a human being.[495]

---

[483] RACE, 2.2
[484] Ibid, 2.2
[485] Ibid, 2.1
[486] MDBA1, 5
[487] Ibid, 5
[488] RACE, 5.1
[489] Ibid, Table 5.2
[490] Ibid, 5.3.3
[491] RACE, 2.1
[492] MDBA1, 5, 6
[493] Ibid, 10
[494] Ibid, 10
[495] Ibid, 5

There are only some 320 hunting bloodhounds in the UK,[496] all of which are bred by the packs themselves.

8.12   The sport was developed in the late 19th Century with the first Bloodhound Trials being held in 1898.[497] There are now thirteen packs in England and Wales, all of which have been formed since 1970.[498]

8.13   In the case of a bloodhound pack the hounds follow the scent of a runner ("the clean boot"). The way in which the event is organised is virtually identical to a draghunt, with the runner setting off ahead of the hunt in order to lay a trail.[499] The hunt, though, is usually slower and less ground is covered.

8.14   Some bloodhound packs hunt mainly on grassland but others, especially in the east of the country, hunt chiefly on arable land.[500]

Similarities and differences

8.15   We found that the research undertaken by RACE helped to draw out some of the differences between drag and bloodhound hunting - which are relevant in considering the extent to which either or both might serve as substitutes, or replacements, for live quarry hunting. As RACE pointed out, the two have tended to be viewed as much the same activity[501] - a view which is reinforced by the fact that the MDBA acts as the governing body for both sports. In particular, it seems clear that there is much greater emphasis in the case of bloodhound hunting on "hound work" (or venery), whilst in the case of the draghunts there tends to be more emphasis on riding and jumping, although several draghunts have few, or even no, jumps.

Extent to which drag and bloodhound hunting might replace live quarry hunting

8.16   Having noted the differences between draghunting and bloodhound hunting, it is nevertheless sensible to consider them jointly, for the most part, in discussing the key issue of whether they would serve as a satisfactory replacement for live quarry hunting. This is because many of the main considerations, such as the availability of suitable land, apply to both sports.

8.17   It is clear from the RACE research that much of the previous discussion of this issue has been based on inadequate analysis of some of the key issues, such as the differences in the respective appeal of the sports and their potential for expansion.

---

[496] Ibid, 1.9
[497] Association of Bloodhound Breeders 2,1
[498] RACE iii, 13
[499] MDBA1, 5
[500] Ibid, 5
[501] RACE, 10.1

Appeal

8.18   We have already noted that it has often been said that drag and bloodhound hunting offer little attraction to present participants in hunting and that relatively few people would switch to them.[502] Some support for this comes from some earlier research in which only 14% of respondents with first-hand experience thought that they would take up draghunting following a ban.[503]

8.19   As part of its research into this issue, RACE looked at the profile of a sample of those who presently take part in the respective activities in order to see whether there were any significant differences. Their main findings were that:

- there was a substantial overlap between the two groups. Most respondents had very wide experience of hunting: very few had experienced only one activity or the other[504]. But, while many followers of the draghunt or bloodhound packs had been out recently with the foxhounds/harriers, the converse was not usually true[505]

- in two areas a higher proportion of those taking part in draghunting or bloodhound hunting was female. It appears that this was related to the fact that these packs were relatively recently established: there was little difference in the area in which the draghunt pack was well established[506]

- draghunting participants tended to be younger.[507]   (According to a 1999 BETA survey, live quarry hunting has a greater percentage of mature riders than other equestrian activities.)[508]

- relatively large numbers of drag and bloodhound hunting participants worked professionally with horses[509]   and they came from households where the average numbers of horses kept was high - over five horses each - and with a greater proportion of ridden, rather than hunting, horses[510]

- there were twice as many farmers amongst the foxhunter and harrier participants as there were in the drag and bloodhound group[511]

- generally speaking, the drag and bloodhound hunting participants hunted on fewer days, but this may be due to the fact that these hunts meet on fewer

---

[502] CA1, 32
[503] RACE, 2.4.3
[504] Ibid, 4.1.5
[505] Ibid, 4.1.5
[506] Ibid, 4.1.1
[507] Ibid, 4.1.2
[508] BETA, 7.03 (NES Chart 22b)
[509] RACE, 4.1.4
[510] Ibid, 4.2.1
[511] Ibid, 4.1.4

occasions and that participants would usually have to travel longer distances.[512]

8.20   Whilst these findings suggest that there are some differences in the profile of those who engage in the different types of hunting, they do not indicate that participants fall into discrete categories.[513]   Indeed, the key finding is perhaps the substantial overlap in participation.

8.21   What also seems clear is that neither drag or bloodhound hunting would serve as a natural replacement activity for those who presently go out hunting on foot, for example those who follow the fell packs or beagles.

8.22   The RACE research suggests that, not surprisingly, there are a number of similarities in the things which people particularly enjoy when they go out foxhunting or drag or bloodhound hunting.   Riding across country - often country to which people could not normally have access - ranks very highly for all these activities.   The opportunity to meet friends is also highly prized, although the pattern of the day allows less time for this in the case of drag or bloodhound hunting[514].   There are also, however, some significant differences:

- watching the hounds work is rated much less important in the case of those who ride to draghounds

- conversely, the latter particularly enjoy challenging jumps

- the unpredictability of the day is particularly important to those who follow the foxhounds, but rated least important to those who go draghunting[515]

- both draghunting and bloodhound hunting seem to offer fewer attractions for car and foot followers.   Those who do watch tend to be friends and relatives, who position themselves at strategic points, usually to watch the jumping.

8.23   We have already noted that drag (and bloodhound) hunts generally last no more than a couple of hours, and there is some evidence that these activities particularly appeal to those who do not want - or have not got the time - to give up a whole day to the sport.

8.24   There is a danger in over-simplifying these findings, since there is considerable variation in each of the activities.   In particular, the balance between hound work and equestrian interests, in the case of drag and bloodhound hunting, will often reflect the wishes of the Master and his or her background.   But what this analysis suggests is that, at least as they are presently organised in this country, draghunting particularly appeals to those who want to take part in some fairly concentrated and testing jumping; bloodhound

---

[512] Ibid, 4.1.5
[513] Ibid, 10.4
[514] Ibid, 7.2
[515] Ibid, 7.2

hunting has greater appeal than draghunting for those with an interest in hound work; and foxhunting particularly appeals to those who like the unpredictability of hunting live quarry and the fact that it is suitable for people of widely different horseriding abilities. As one person put it to us, "one of the joys of foxhunting is its uncertainty and variability."[516]

8.25   We now turn to the more difficult issue of whether it is possible to address satisfactorily any of the features which might discourage people from switching from hunting live quarry to drag or bloodhound hunting.

8.26   It is clear to us that draghunting does not have to be - as it is sometimes portrayed - "fast and furious" jumping, suitable only for would-be steeplechasers. As we have noted, there are already draghunts which have no, or few, jumps and it is common for other hunts to provide alternative, easier, jumps or "byes". Draghunting - and bloodhound hunting - are suitable in principle, therefore, for riders of all abilities, although some terrain will clearly be better suited to different levels of skill. Nonetheless, it is the case that there is a greater emphasis in draghunting on riding, and jumping, expertise.

8.27   Making draghunting or bloodhound hunting less "predictable" is more problematic. In part, this turns on the ability to introduce some of the vagaries (and fascination) associated with hound work in foxhunting. This depends crucially on the ability to simulate satisfactorily the way in which a fox gives off scent and the way that scent subsequently "lies". It seems that there is, in practice, a correlation between the greater strength of the artificial scent in draghunting and the "predictability" of the day. It is fair to say that there is still a great deal of mystery about the manner in which animal scent is produced and how it interacts with land and air temperatures and the prevailing weather conditions[517]. What is clear, though, is that it is not possible to lay a trail artificially which simulates fully the subtlety and complexity of the scent left by a fox as it moves through the countryside. A practical illustration of this is the fact that, when hounds come across the scent of a fox, they can usually tell quickly in which direction it is moving, whereas draghounds cannot do this in the case of the "dragman" or "line layer".[518]

8.28   It is not possible at present, therefore, to simulate fully the hound work which occurs in foxhunting or hare hunting. A consequence of this is that the hounds tend to be more mute.[519] There is less of the "hound music" which hunting enthusiasts have often cited as one of the joys of hunting. There are, however, ways in which the hound work - and therefore the experience of the mounted field and followers - can be made a little more varied. These include:

---

[516] Mr J A Cunningham
[517] RACE, 9.1–9.2
[518] Ibid, 9.2.3
[519] MDBA1, 5

- lifting the line - the drag can be "lifted" to simulate the casting around that occurs when a foxhound pack temporarily loses the scent of a fox

- "a floating line" - as already noted, in more open country it is possible to have greater uncertainty about where the line begins, so that more hound work is required to discover it

- doubling back, running on stone walls etc. - the person laying the drag can mimic some of the actions the foxes sometimes take when being pursued by foxhounds.

8.29   It seems clear, however, from the discussion which took place at our seminar that, while all of these can be tried, and indeed are already practised by some drag and bloodhound hunts, they cannot simulate very closely the subtlety, complexity and unpredictability of the scent left by a live animal quarry. This no doubt explains too why, although attempts have been made here and in other countries to "slow down" drag and bloodhound hunts, they have met with limited success. Drag and bloodhound hunts simply do not have the same "rhythm" as a typical foxhunt. On our visit to a German draghunt, for example, we were told that it had been their aim, for several seasons to reduce the pace of the day but they had not been able to do so.

8.30   The difficulties over scenting and the relative speed and predictability of the day may explain why there has not been a dramatic increase in the popularity of draghunting in Germany. Indeed, we were told at our seminar that the UK, even with its relatively small number of packs, is probably one of the leading countries in the draghunting world.[520]

8.31   We also recognise the force of the argument put to us that, while people may be perfectly happy to "stand around" during a foxhunt as the hounds try to pick up again the scent of the fox, they would not wish to do so if there was no underlying reason: expecting people to wait around simply in order to slow down the pace of the day is not likely to be popular.

8.32   It also needs to be borne in mind, though, that not everyone would welcome introducing a greater amount of unpredictability into the day. Those who are looking for a quick exhilarating ride might not enjoy the longueurs often associated with foxhunting.

Availability of suitable land

8.33   A key issue in assessing the potential of drag and bloodhound hunting is whether there would be sufficient suitable land available. On the face of it, there ought to be ample opportunity, in the event of a ban on hunting, to expand since foxhound packs currently hunt some 61% of the land in England and Wales. Moreover, because of the greater predictability of drag and bloodhound hunting, they can take place in areas which would be unsafe for foxhound or harrier packs, for example near motorways and

---

[520] Seminar, 28 April 2000, Session 1

railways. But the answer is far from clear cut. It turns crucially on the nature of the land required - its type, size, ease of access - and even more critically on whether farmers and landowners would be willing to make it available. Turning first to the type of land required, we have already noted that drag and bloodhound hunting can take place in very different types of countryside. There is no reason in principle why they should be any more restricted in this respect than any of the existing mounted live quarry packs.

8.34   An important limitation, however, is the amount and type of land required for laying lines. Again, on the face of it, this might not appear to be a problem since the lines can be planned in advance and because, unlike in the case of the foxhound packs, they can be laid nearer railways and roads, although there is still the risk that the hounds may go astray by, for example, following the scent of a deer. But there are the following difficulties:

- because the participants have essentially come out to ride over a pre-planned course, they would not be content with the kind of intermittent to-ing and fro-ing that can often occur in a foxhunt where, for example, the riders may go back and forwards between two coverts. Nor would they want to be taken on roads or lanes if this could be avoided. They are also more likely to want to ride over different courses rather than following the same course on a number of occasions each season

- similarly, because the ride is usually continuous, a lot of ground is covered in a short time

- because the scent of the drag or human runner does not have the same qualities as that of a fox, it is not possible to lay lines very close together, to "double back" or to run them across each other (except perhaps at right angles).

8.35   Taken together, these limitations mean that drag and bloodhound hunts tend to need long, fairly straight lines, which will usually mean having to cross land belonging to a number of farmers, all of whom will have to give their consent.

8.36   Another practical difficulty is that, in some areas, the drag and bloodhound hunts rely heavily on foxhound packs to erect and maintain jumps. If this voluntary labour disappeared, the drag and bloodhound hunts might have difficulty in providing sufficient jumps in some areas.

8.37   Ease of access is also an important factor. The lines need to begin and end in places which can be reached by participants and followers.

8.38   We now turn to the question of whether, assuming sufficient suitable land was available, farmers would be willing to allow it to be used for draghunting or bloodhound hunting in the event of a ban. The evidence submitted to us by the MDBA[521] indicated

---

[521] MDBA1, 10

that their members currently have great difficulty in opening up new country. The RACE research surveyed a number of farmers in different areas in an attempt to establish whether there were differences in their attitudes to allowing the various types of hunting on to their land and, if so, why. Although the findings need to be treated with some caution, the research suggested that:

- farmers with arable farms are much more likely to allow access to the foxhounds/harrier packs than to drag or bloodhound packs[522]

- the most frequent single reason farmers give to explain why they do not, or might not, allow access for drag or bloodhound packs was that the packs did not kill foxes[523]

- the answers were not related to farm size or owner/occupier or tenant status.[524]

8.39   A suggestion that has often been made is that farmers would be more willing to allow access to drag or bloodhound packs if they were able to charge.[525] The survey of foxhounds/harrier and drag/bloodhound participants carried out by RACE[526] indicated that the majority agreed that it would be acceptable in principle for farmers to do this, although it is impossible to say how acceptable the participants would actually find this in practice. As far as farmers are concerned, the RACE survey[527] suggests that a substantial proportion of those who do not, or would not, allow drag/bloodhound hunting would reconsider their position if offered a direct payment.

8.40   We are doubtful about the practicability of a payment system. There might be some instances in which it would work satisfactorily. It seems more likely, however, that it would be difficult to devise and operate a system that would apply equitably amongst a substantial number of farmers, the use of whose land might vary considerably; and that any sums which would be large enough from the farmers' point of view would increase considerably the cost to participants.

Costs

8.41   Apart from the additional cost involved if farmers had to be paid, drag hunts would no longer benefit, in the event of a ban on hunting, from being able to kennel their hounds with the local foxhound pack, as several do at present. It is conceivable, therefore, that a ban on hunting might put at risk the viability of a number of existing draghunts.

---

[522] RACE, 6.2.1
[523] Ibid, 6.3.1
[524] Ibid, 6.2.3
[525] RSPCA1, 14
[526] RACE, 7.3.4
[527] Ibid, 8.3

Suitability of horses/riders

8.42   It has been argued that, because of the more testing nature of bloodhound and, especially, draghound hunting, many of the horses currently used for foxhunting would be unsuitable.[528]   Similarly, many of the riders would not be accomplished enough to cope with the amount of jumping usually involved. We think that there is some force in this argument, although, as we have noted, drag and bloodhound hunting can be more varied than is sometimes suggested.

Conclusions

8.43   It is clear, as we have said at the beginning of this chapter, that much of the previous debate about the viability of drag and bloodhound hunting has been motivated more by their apparent usefulness as a means of attacking or defending hunting than by any objective assessment of these sports.   The RACE research, together with other evidence we have received, has been helpful in throwing light on many of these issues. Nevertheless, any conclusions are bound to be tentative since they involve trying to predict what a number of different players - participants and would-be participants, farmers and others - would do in a hypothetical situation. It was put to us, for example, that there would be a reaction against drag and bloodhound hunting in the event of a ban on live quarry hunting.   Indeed, it was said that the publicity given to drag and bloodhound hunting in the context of a ban had already led to some resistance by farmers and others. The circumstances in which a ban was introduced might also affect attitudes. No doubt many farmers' attitudes would harden if there was a bitter campaign against a ban. On the other hand, a period for adaptation might make it easier for foxhound/harrier packs to transform themselves into draghound packs if they chose to do so or for others to take over at least some of the hounds and kennels for this purpose.

8.44   Drag and bloodhound hunting are different from live quarry hunting. In particular, they involve the laying of a man-made trail.   They lack the unpredictability and, consequently, some of the interest associated with a live quarry. The hound work, especially in the case of the draghounds, is less subtle and complex.

8.45   There would be greater incentive, in the event of a ban, to expand the number of drag and bloodhound packs and the level of participation in both sports. Because bloodhounds are in short supply, and are not easy to breed, any growth in the short term would mainly come from using foxhounds for draghunting. The scope for expansion is impossible to predict with any accuracy at present because the existence of hunting as a complementary activity means that there has been little motivation in practice to develop the sports. The popularity of horse riding, however, suggests that greater efforts would be made to develop substitute activities in the event of a ban on hunting. The kinds of opportunities that drag and bloodhound hunting already offer in some areas might be expanded. There is some scope for adjusting the level of skill required in drag and bloodhound hunting to

---

[528] MDBA1, 11–22

riders of different ability levels. There is also possible scope for developing other forms of cross country riding, possibly on a fee-paying basis.

8.46   Some of the evidence we received suggested that there would be considerable reluctance on the part of farmers to make available sufficient, suitable contiguous land and that this could considerably limit the growth of these sports. It is questionable whether the possibility of making payments to farmers would overcome these difficulties. A payment system would not be easy to devise and operate and would be likely to increase significantly participants' costs.

8.47   A few of those who presently take part in live quarry hunting already go drag or bloodhound hunting as well. In the event of a ban, some more would take up one or other of these sports. And, no doubt, if more diverse types of draghunting were developed, some new recruits would come from those who do not presently hunt live quarry. But others would either not give these sports a try or would not persevere with them. In particular, they offer little attraction to non-mounted participants and followers. Evidence from elsewhere, in particular Germany, suggests that draghunting and bloodhound hunting would not change materially or experience a major upsurge in popularity. Instead it would be simply one - and not necessarily the most important - of a number of equestrian activities to which participants in mounted hunting might turn in the event of a ban.

Drag coursing

8.48   Drag coursing is a relatively recent development in this country, although it is popular in Australia (where live hare coursing is banned) and also takes place in some other countries, including Germany and Finland. There are believed to be four clubs currently operating in England and Wales, all based in the West Country, where there are generally fewer hares than in the East of England.

8.49   The sport takes the form of a race between two dogs (generally greyhounds, lurchers or whippets), as part of a knock-out competition. The dogs chase a drag resembling a hare, which is pulled by a cable. (In the example we saw the cable was attached to the wheel of a motor car, which had been jacked-up off the ground: the speed of the engine was increased as necessary by the "driver" in order to keep the drag just far enough ahead of the dogs).

8.50   The dogs race a course of at least 350 yds and the first past the post is the winner. Apart from the obvious fact that no live quarry is involved, the main difference between drag and live coursing is that the former is usually a straight race to the finishing line. Although the drag can bounce from side to side as it hits rougher ground, the action does not simulate the jinking and twisting of a hare. Nor, therefore, does it test the skill and agility of a dog in "turning" a hare. But there seems to be some evidence that some dogs at least find it more interesting than conventional racing on a greyhound track.

144

8.51   Drag coursing is at present fairly rudimentary in this country but it could no doubt be developed considerably, as has clearly happened in some other countries.

Conclusions

8.52   In the event of a ban on live hare coursing, drag coursing might have some appeal, especially to those owners of greyhounds who are essentially interested in racing their dogs. It would have less appeal for those people who particularly enjoy the contest between the hare and the dog.

8.53   It is unlikely that either drag and bloodhound hunting or drag coursing would of themselves mitigate to any substantial extent any adverse effects on the rural economy or the social life of the countryside arising from a ban on hunting.

CHAPTER 9

PRACTICAL ASPECTS OF HUNTING: THE CONCERNS

9.1   Many people represented to us that their main concern about hunting was that it was cruel. We discussed this issue fully in Chapter 6. We were also asked to look at "the practical aspects of different types of hunting with dogs". Accordingly, we examine in this chapter the evidence we received which pointed to concerns about particular aspects of the way in which hunting and coursing are carried out. We also mention various areas which might form the subject of further research, if a ban on hunting was not introduced.

9.2   There are a number of aspects of the way that hunting is carried out which give rise to particular concern.

The practical aspects of hunting

Trespass, disruption and disturbance

9.3   We mentioned in chapter 4 that we had received a fair number of complaints about trespass by hunts. These were usually from farmers or landowners in rural areas who objected to the hunt and/or hunt followers going onto their land. We were told that this happened frequently even where the individual concerned had previously made it clear that they objected to the hunt's presence. We also received complaints from those living in villages and on the edge of towns about the invasion of residential property. These complaints often drew attention to the fact that these events could be frightening or distressing for those involved, especially if pets were put at risk or actually attacked or if a fox was killed in front of them or members of their family.

9.4   We also received a number of complaints about the general disruption and disturbance which hunts can cause to those going about their daily business. A particular problem in some areas seems to be the blocking of roads and lanes, as well as access to people's property, by followers' vehicles.   Trespass on roads and railway lines also occurs: there have been a number of well-documented cases in which hounds have been killed or injured and considerable disruption and inconvenience has been caused to travellers.

9.5   The sense of grievance which was felt was compounded in some cases by what was said to be an arrogant, high-handed and unsympathetic response from some of the hunts.   We were also told that those who complained were sometimes threatened physically, had their property damaged or were warned that their businesses might suffer if they continued to cause difficulties. Another criticism was that there was no easy means of seeking redress and that it was difficult to identify with whom responsibility lay. There was a lack of confidence in the hunts' procedures for dealing with complaints.

9.6   We must also record that we received evidence that hunt followers and supporters are themselves sometimes subjected to abuse, intimidation, threats and physical violence by those opposed to hunting. We deplore behaviour of this kind, from whichever quarter it comes.

9.7   We must emphasise that we have no reliable means of assessing the validity and extent of the various complaints. We have no doubt that incidents of trespass do occur, not least because (as we have witnessed) it is difficult to keep control of hounds when they are in hot pursuit of their quarry. We also recognise that some of these incidents can arouse strong feelings. But we also accept that serious incidents of trespass and disruption are probably not numerous in relation to the number of days' hunting which take place each year. We are also aware that there have been a few convictions for attacks on hunt supporters and hunt opponents.

9.8   There are too many cases of trespass, disruption and disturbance. These are most common where hunts operate too close to residential areas and interfere with the movement of traffic on roads. We do not want to exaggerate these problems but they can cause distress to the individuals and families involved. To some extent hunts could avoid these problems themselves, by being more selective about the areas in which they hunt. This would be likely to lead to fewer hunts. Steps that might be taken, in the absence of a ban, include: restricting hunting in certain parts of hunts' countries; reducing or amalgamating the number of hunts; requiring permission to be obtained in writing on a regular basis from farmers and landowners; penalising trespass, or repeated trespass, over land where permission has not been given; and improving means of seeking and obtaining redress.

Openness

9.9   The concerns which some people have about hunting are undoubtedly exacerbated by a sense that it is not really open to public scrutiny. The hunts have taken some steps in recent years to make themselves more accountable. It is nevertheless the case that many of their activities take place on private land and that, as a matter of practice, events like the killing of the fox or the deer are usually witnessed by only a few people. It is unfortunate, too, that some of those who do try to observe hunting behave in such a way as to make themselves very unwelcome. This serves only to increase any defensiveness on the part of hunts.

9.10   In the absence of a ban, organised hunting should be conducted on a more open basis than at present in order to provide greater reassurance that approved procedures are being followed. One possible option would be the appointment of individuals as independent monitors who would have the freedom to take photographs and video evidence. Their task would be to observe organised hunting and to take up with the hunt, and others as necessary, any concerns that they might have about the way in which it is being conducted. They might also serve as a channel for complaints by others. It would no doubt be helpful if monitors were appointed by a reputable, independent body.

Autumn/cub hunting

9.11   We described in paragraph 2.29 the practice of autumn/cub hunting of foxes. The MFHA and the Countryside Alliance, in their evidence to us, argued that autumn/cub hunting serves a number of useful purposes. They pointed out that a survey of hunts carried out in January 2000 showed that some 40% of the foxes killed by the registered packs were killed during autumn/cub hunting and that it takes place at a time when the fox population is at its highest and most concentrated.[529]

9.12   It is also argued by the hunts concerned that autumn/cub hunting is useful in dispersing the fox population, thus reducing their concentration in any one area.[530]

9.13   The third purpose served by autumn/cub hunting, in the view of the MFHA and the Countryside Alliance, is that it serves as a very useful means of introducing young hounds to hunting. Autumn/cub hunting takes place in a comparatively confined area and with fewer riders and other followers around to distract them.[531]

9.14   It does not seem to us, from the evidence we received, that these arguments are wholly persuasive. As we noted in paragraph 5.36, there is little evidence that, in spite of the numbers killed, this activity is particularly effective in reducing fox populations or that dispersal has the benefits which the MFHA claim. It is clear too that it is not necessary to practise autumn/cub hunting in order to train young hounds. A number of packs, including the Fell Packs and the Welsh gun packs, use other methods.

9.15   Those who object to autumn/cub hunting also point to the practice of "holding-up" i.e. the steps taken to prevent the escape of foxes from the wood or coppice. We are aware of the concern which some people feel about this practice and, more generally, about the principle of using young foxes (whether fully grown or not) to train young, inexperienced hounds.

9.16   In the absence of a ban, consideration could be given to a number of options for responding to the concerns about autumn/cub hunting. These options include: prohibiting the practice entirely; introducing a closed season for hunting foxes, so that hunting would start at a later date than it does at present; permitting it only in those areas where it was clearly necessary as a means of controlling fox numbers; and prohibiting the practice of "holding up".

Digging-out and bolting/Terrierwork

9.17   Digging out and bolting foxes with the use of terriers was a topic which also aroused strong feelings on both sides of the debate. On the one hand, it was argued, especially by hunts, farmers in upland sheep-rearing areas and gamekeepers, that digging-out or bolting (see paragraphs 2.23 to 2.25) was very important in controlling the

---

[529] CA2, 8.5.1.
[530] CA1, 13.28 MFHA, 10.2
[531] MFHA1,10.2; CA2, 8.5.4

number of foxes.[532] It was pointed out that, in some areas, well over half of the foxes killed by hunts resulted from digging-out and that it was the only legal means of killing foxes underground.[533] Moreover, as we noted in paragraph 5.27, it seems likely that an even larger number are killed as the result of terrierwork by other groups and individuals. There is also the issue that terriers may be used to dispatch orphaned cubs.

9.18   On the other hand, many opponents of hunting clearly felt that it was wholly unacceptable that a fox, having gone to ground, whether in a natural or artificial earth, should be dug-out or bolted.   Their concerns were exacerbated by reports of injuries received by foxes and terriers fighting underground.

9.19   Another point which needs to be borne in mind is that the fact that digging out foxes is a legal activity makes it more difficult to take action to combat badger-baiting since those who appear to be intent on the latter can argue that they are planning to dig out foxes.

9.20   Digging-out and bolting foxes is a complex issue because of the perceived needs in different parts of England and Wales.   In the absence of a ban, serious consideration could be given as to whether this practice should be allowed to continue and, if so, under what conditions.   Possible options would be to ban it altogether; confine it to those areas where it is considered necessary as a means of controlling fox numbers or in the interests of animal welfare; make the practice subject to the general legislation on cruelty by removing the present exemptions for hunting; or improve monitoring by the hunts and by any independent monitors.

Stopping-up

9.21   Another practice which gives rise to particular concern is that of stopping up foxes' earths, badger setts and other possible refuges before a foxhunt begins (see paragraph 2.20).   As we noted in Chapter 7, we received a good deal of evidence about this activity, especially from badger watch groups.[534]   They argue that there are still far too many instances in which hunts and others are illegally stopping-up badger setts by using hard material or soil cut back from the sett itself.

9.22   The Countryside Alliance argued that there was no evidence of any malpractice.[535]   Whilst we accept that there is a lack of firm evidence linking malpractice to the hunts, we do not think we can disregard entirely the written and oral evidence we received from badger protection groups and their supporters on this issue.

9.23   We recognise that badgers are now more numerous than at the time when they were first given legal protection.   We also recognise that, if hunts were not permitted to stop up badger setts, foxes would be more likely to go to ground there and would have to

---

[532] NFU1,6; FWP1, 1.10.11 and 13.2
[533] CA2, 3.8.5
[534] National Federation of Badger Groups 1, 5.1; Nottinghamshire Badger Group
[535] CA2, 8.6.1

be left. Similarly, we recognise that if the same prohibition applied to foxes' earths many more foxes would escape unscathed. However, consideration could be given to both of these issues in the absence of a ban.

9.24 There have been many suggestions put to us that, at times, hunts and others contravene the law relating to the stopping-up of badger setts. One option, in the absence of a ban on hunting, would be to remove the present exemption for hunts. In the case of stopping-up of foxes' earths, there are a number of possible options which could be considered in the absence of a ban. These include: prohibiting the practice entirely; confining it to those areas where it is considered necessary in the interests of controlling fox numbers; or otherwise limiting the circumstances in which it may be done or the way in which it can be carried out.

Use of artificial earths

9.25 It is clear that it used to be common practice, especially in the case of hunts in lowland England, to provide artificial earths for foxes, particularly when planting new coppices or coverts. We received no firm evidence that this is still being done but we were told that some existing earths were still being "re-furbished" and even that foxes were being encouraged to use them by, for example, providing food.[536]

9.26 The Countryside Alliance told us that, given that the purpose of hunting in many areas was to preserve a sustainable and healthy fox population, they did not consider that the practice of providing artificial earths was objectionable if the particular locality did not already offer suitable habitat. They argued that this balance between preservation and control was seen in other contexts such as game shooting and fishing.[537] It was also put to us that artificial earths could be useful in helping to ensure that foxes' earths were in suitable places: for example, away from chicken runs. We consider, however, that it is hard to reconcile any use of artificial earths by the hunts with the argument that foxes are a pest and that their numbers need to be controlled through hunting.

9.27 The active use of artificial earths, with a view to hunting, is inconsistent with the stated objective of controlling fox numbers through hunting. In the absence of a ban, hunts could be required, or encouraged, to end this practice.

Deliberately interfering with the quarry's flight

9.28 Deliberately interfering with the flight of the quarry takes place in a number of situations, for example:

- preventing the flight of young and adult foxes during autumn/cub hunting (see paragraph 9.15 above)

---

[536] IFAW1,ii; CA1,13.41
[537] CA2, 3.13.3

- attempting to prevent the quarry from going onto land where the hunt does not have permission to go

- trying to keep the quarry - and therefore the hounds - away from areas such as roads and railway lines

- attempting (on the part of hunt saboteurs) to rescue the quarry or to help it make its escape.

9.29.   The research which we commissioned on the welfare of hunted deer indicated that close contact with human beings, including attempts at interfering with its flight, had a noticeable effect on the deer.[538]   Such interference, whether in relation to deer or other animals, also seems to sit uncomfortably with the notion that hunts usually embrace of hunting an animal in its "wild and natural state".

9.30   There is concern about deliberate direct interference by people with the quarry's flight. In the absence of a ban, action could be taken to amend, where necessary, the rules of the relevant associations and to ensure that such interference does not take place unless it is in the interests of the safety of the people or animals involved. In particular, provision could be made to ensure that there was no interference with the flight in order to prolong the chase, prevent the quarry escaping or to prevent it entering land where the hunt did not have permission to go.

A closed season for hares

9.31   We noted in paragraphs 2.48 and 2.54 that there is no legally-prescribed closed season for hunting and coursing hares but that the rules of the relevant associations forbid hunting after the end of March and coursing after 10 March.

9.32   We also noted in paragraph 5.78 that hares breed from February onwards - and, indeed, we understand that hares sometimes produce leverets in January.[539]   In our view there is a case for having a legally-prescribed closed season for killing hares. This ought, logically, to apply to all forms of killing, including shooting.

9.33   There is understandable concern that the seasons for hare coursing and hunting are too long in relation to the hare's breeding season. In the absence of a ban on hunting, an option would be to introduce a closed season. Consideration would also need to be given to whether a closed season should apply to shooting.

Hunting hinds with calves

9.34   Concern was expressed to us about the practice of hunting hinds with calves. It was argued that, at the start of the season, hinds may have a totally dependent calf at foot; that calves have great difficult in keeping up with a chase; and that eventually the hind is

---

[538] Bateson and Harris 7.2.2.
[539] Macdonald et al, 10.3.4.

forced to abandon it.[540] The MDHA argued, on the other hand, that by November last year's calves are able to thrive without their mother and said that any hind with a late-born calf would not be hunted.[541] We simply record that, whatever the precise degree of dependence, a number of people clearly find it distressing to see a hind and calf being chased and to observe the apparent dilemma of the hind about whether to stay with the calf or to pick up speed and leave it behind.

9.35   Hunting hinds with a calf gives rise to understandable concern. It puts the hind in a position of having to choose between saving itself and staying with the calf. We are not able to say how often this situation occurs but action could be taken to end this practice in the absence of a ban.

Legislative action

9.36   All these concerns about these practical aspects of hunting would be resolved, in principle, by a ban on hunting, subject to any exemptions or exceptions which were considered necessary.

9.37   We have indicated that, in the absence of a ban, consideration could be given to amending the Protection of Badgers Act 1992 and to introducing a closed season for hares - which would presumably have to be done through legislation.

9.38   Some of the other practices which we have discussed, such as deliberate interference with a quarry's flight, would not seem to be particularly amenable to legislative action but might best be considered, in the absence of a ban, in the context of changes to the hunts' rules or through some form of public regulation or licensing. We discuss this issue below. One other possible legislative approach would be to remove the present exemptions for hunting in the Wild Mammals (Protection) Act 1996. This would give an important signal that hunting should be subject to the same standards as apply to other organisations and individuals. And it would give a clearer opportunity to test views about cruelty in the courts. In practice, though, it might have only a limited effect, since the principal offence in that Act bites only on certain activities, namely, "mutilating, kicking, beating, nailing or otherwise impaling, stabbing, burning, stoning, crushing, drowning, dragging, or asphyxiating with intent to inflict unnecessary suffering". Few of these activities appear to apply to hunting.

9.39   In the event of a ban on hunting, the various concerns would be resolved, in principle, subject to any exemptions or exceptions permitted in the legislation. There would be no need, therefore, to consider separate action. In the absence of a ban, one possible legislative approach would be to remove the present exemptions for hunting in the Wild Mammals (Protection) Act 1996. This would be an important signal and give opponents of hunting a clearer opportunity to test their views about cruelty in the courts. In practice, this might have only a limited effect since the activities penalised by that Act have little relevance to hunting.

---

[540] IFAW1,27
[541] MDHA1,4

Hunting practised outside the registered hunts and coursing clubs

9.40   As we have noted at various points in our report, a great deal of hunting takes place which is not regulated in any way by the rules of the various hunting and coursing associations. Some of this involves trespass and, as we mentioned in paragraph 2.57, it is sometimes associated with threats and intimidation to farmers and landowners. We suspect too that a number of those taking part in such activities do so for base motives and have little regard for animal welfare. Finally, because they take place in rural areas, they are difficult to police.

9.41   We have suggested possible changes which could be considered in the absence of a ban. These ought to apply, where they are relevant, to other forms of hunting as well as to regulated hunting. Some of those changes - in particular, those relating to autumn/cub hunting and the use of artificial earths - are almost entirely directed at hunting by the registered hunts and coursing clubs and are therefore matters which could largely be implemented by amendments to their rules. But the possible changes relating to interference with badger setts and a closed season for hares could not be implemented satisfactorily by this means. Consideration would no doubt have to be given, as we have suggested, to amending the existing legislation. The appropriate means of implementing any changes in respect of digging-out and bolting/terrierwork would depend on the nature of the changes being made.

9.42   If action is taken to address any of the concerns about the way hunting is carried out, it would be important to consider whether, and if so how, it could be applied to hunting undertaken by those operating outside the registered hunts and coursing clubs.

Licensing and regulation

9.43   Our discussion of the possible means of regulating digging-out and bolting/terrierwork and the stopping-up of foxes' earths brings us to the question whether, in the absence of a ban on hunting, some form of public licensing or regulation of hunting might be considered.

9.44   We noted in paragraph 2.9 that there is no body of legislation in England and Wales which is specifically concerned with hunting. Appendix 8 to our report summarises such provisions as do exist and which, as will be seen, are scattered in various Acts, few of which are of recent origin. Nor is hunting controlled through any public licensing or regulatory system. There is, of course, a system of self-regulation through the rules of the various Masters' associations, the main provisions of which are summarised in Appendix 6. This is being strengthened by the establishment of the Independent Supervisory Authority for Hunting, whose role we describe in that appendix. We have not been able to study the existing arrangements closely, although we became aware of some lack of confidence in the procedures for dealing with complaints.

9.46   There is a lot to be said for an effective self-regulation system since it avoids having to set up such a system at public expense. However, the system applies only to hunting which takes place under the auspices of the various associations. It does not impinge on the activities of the unregistered packs and coursing clubs. Nor, of course, does it cover the activities of all the individuals who go out hunting singly, or in small groups, with their dogs.

9.47   The fact that such control as exists over hunting is largely through self-regulation contrasts markedly with the position in a number of countries where licensing or similar systems are common, often covering all forms of hunting, not just hunting with dogs. The latter is the case in, for example, Germany, France and the Nordic countries.

9.48   We think it is perhaps surprising that, without a greater measure of regulation, hunts should be able to go into the countryside with the responsibility for a pack of hounds that are often not under close control, and which can have a marked effect on the lives of other people.

9.49   We consider that it might be productive, in the absence of a ban, to explore the possibility of introducing some form of licensing system, possibly on the lines of those which exist to regulate hunting in some other countries. Because this takes us rather a long way from our original terms of reference we have not considered this issue in any depth. But we could envisage a system in which licences would be issued only to recognised hunts or to individuals, such as gamekeepers, who satisfied certain requirements. For example, an applicant might have to satisfy the relevant authority that he or she was a suitable person; that they did not have convictions for offences involving cruelty to animals; and that they had the requisite training and knowledge. In the case of terrier work, another requirement might be membership of the National Working Terrier Federation and adherence to its code of conduct.

9.50   An important aspect of a licensing system, in the context of the complaints which we received about various aspects of hunting, is that, in the absence of a ban, it could enable action to be taken where hunts or individuals had acted improperly. For example, it would be open to the licensing authority to withdraw a hunt's or an individual's licence, or to attach conditions to it, in the context of a breach.

9.51   A system of this kind would also assist, in the absence of a ban, in tackling illegal hunting. In particular, it would make it easier to deal with those intent on illegal coursing, or on badger baiting, since they would require a licence to hunt.

9.52   The fact that hunting (of all kinds) is not subject to some form of licensing contrasts markedly with the position in a number of other countries.

9.53   The existing self-regulation operated by the various hunts and coursing associations has been adapted over the years to deal with emerging concerns and evidence of damage to animal welfare. It will be strengthened by the establishment of the Independent Supervisory Authority for Hunting. None of this regulatory

activity applies, however, to hunting carried out by those outside this regulatory framework. It is a reasonable assumption that any adverse impact on animal welfare is greater in the case of the latter than it is with hunting under the auspices of the various self-regulatory bodies. In the absence of a ban, consideration could be given to strengthening the supervision of these forms of hunting. It is for consideration whether, in that event, there would be advantage in establishing some form of licensing system to control all forms of hunting with dogs.

Further Research

9.54   We have noted, in earlier chapters, a number of issues on which there appears to be a lack of firm information. A good many of these would probably lend themselves to further work, and could be considered as possible research studies, if a ban on hunting was not introduced. A number of them would be of considerable relevance even if there was not a ban.

9.55   The following are the main topics which we think might benefit from being pursued in this way:

Foxes

- the numbers of foxes that are killed by different forms of human intervention in different areas and, the impact of this mortality on their populations and on the damage they cause

- elucidation of the interaction between natural mortality and culling

- the incidence, and effect, of fox predation on lambs and the consequences of attempted fox control on these losses

- the role of dispersal in fox populations

- the comparative welfare implications of different methods of killing foxes

Deer

- the fate of deer that escape during hunting

- wounding rates in stalking/shooting deer

Hares

- wounding rates in hare shooting

<u>Mink</u>

- effects of disturbance caused by mink hunting

9.56 Consideration could be given, in the absence of a ban on hunting, to commissioning research on a number of topics.

CHAPTER 10

IMPLEMENTING A BAN

10.1   The Committee's terms of reference required us to consider "how any ban might be implemented". We stressed in paragraph 1.4 that we had not been asked to consider whether hunting should be banned. We also stressed that nothing in our report should be construed as indicating that we had formed any view on whether there should be a ban.

10.2   We need to enter two more caveats in this chapter. The first is that we did not see it as our task to <u>recommend</u> how a ban should be implemented but, instead, to identify the main issues which we think would need to be considered by anyone contemplating legislation. The second is that none of us has a legal background, although we have been assisted in considering these matters by Mr Michael Fordham, whom we appointed as our Counsel.

10.3   There are a number of aspects in considering how a ban might be implemented:

- its compatibility with the European Convention on Human Rights

- its scope and form

- the timetable for implementation

- how it might be enforced

- whether controls on other types of hunting might also be necessary or desirable in consequence in order to prevent unsatisfactory practices

- whether other measures might be required to manage the populations of the animals concerned

- whether steps might need to be taken to encourage other activities (in particular, drag or bloodhound hunting) to replace hunting with dogs or to preserve sporting, social or cultural activities associated with hunting

- whether any measures might be needed to deal with the financial, economic, employment or other consequences of a ban.

10.4   As part of our consideration of some of these matters we arranged a seminar, in preparation for which we asked the Countryside Alliance and Deadline 2000 to submit papers. The seminar, which was also attended by a representative of the Association of Chief Police Officers, focused on the legal, rather than enforcement, issues involved in implementing a ban. The papers, and the seminar discussion, have been helpful in enabling us to address the various matters which need to be considered.[542]

---

[542] The papers, and the transcript of the seminar, are on the CD Rom

Compatibility with the European Convention on Human Rights (ECHR)

10.5   A fundamental argument put to us by the Countryside Alliance was that a ban on hunting would be incompatible with the ECHR. This matter was considered at some length in the papers prepared by the Countryside Alliance and Deadline 2000 and was also discussed fully at the seminar itself. The papers helpfully included Opinions by distinguished Counsel on both sides. Counsel's Opinion, relied on by Deadline 2000 specifically addressed a draft Bill which had been prepared, whilst Counsel for the Countryside Alliance had considered the matter in principle.

10.6   Counsel for the Countryside Alliance (Edward Fitzgerald QC) concluded that, in his opinion, there was "a serious argument that the proposed ban on hunting with dogs will violate [both] Article 1 of Protocol I and Article 8". Counsel for IFAW (David Pannick QC, Richard Drabble QC and Rabinder Singh), relied on by Deadline 2000, concluded that, in their opinion, "a ban on hunting wild mammals with dogs would be compatible with the Convention".

10.7   The Convention rights will become part of national law from 2 October 2000, when the key provisions of the Human Rights Act 1998 come into force. Under the Act the higher courts will be able to make a declaration of incompatibility with the Convention in relation to an Act passed by Parliament.

10.8   It was clear to the Committee from the submissions and Opinions on both sides that the main argument centred on two Articles in the Convention: Article 8, which deals with respect for private life, and Article 1 of Protocol I, which deals with the right to peaceful enjoyment of property. (Although there has also been some discussion in this context of Articles 5 (right to liberty and security), 6 (right to a fair trial), 11 (freedom of assembly and association) and 14 (prohibition of discrimination), it does not appear that a strong case could be mounted for arguing that a Bill to ban hunting would infringe any of these articles.)

Article 8

10.9   Article 8 provides as follows:

"1. Everyone has the right to respect for his private and family life, his home and correspondence.

2. There shall be no interference by a public authority with the exercise of this right except such as is in accordance with the law and is necessary in a democratic society in the interests of national security, public safety or the economic well-being of the country, for the prevention of disorder or crime, for the protection of health or morals, or for the protection of the rights and freedoms of others."

10.10 There are two main issues: whether hunting with dogs can be regarded as coming within the concept of "private life" and, if it does, whether interference is justified on the grounds set out in Article 8 (2). On the first issue, both sides agree that "private life" may encompass certain aspects of social interaction with others. But they disagree on whether a ban on hunting with dogs would constitute an interference with this right. The Countryside Alliance contend that it is an activity which is strongly identified with the ethos of a local community. They also point out that it takes place, at least in part, on private land. Deadline 2000, on the other hand, argue that the nature of the activity, even when it takes place on private land, is essentially public in character. The Fitzgerald Opinion concluded that a ban would "probably constitute an interference with Article 8 rights", albeit not "one of the more intimate or core aspects of private life". The Pannick Opinion concluded that "we do not consider that hunting with dogs falls within the concept of private life at all".

10.11 If it were the case that private life is interfered with, the issue of a legitimate objective (i.e. the protection of morals) seemed to the Committee to be crucial. That question seemed to the Committee to turn on two key factors: first, whether hunting with dogs is viewed as inherently or necessarily causing unnecessary suffering; second, whether, if it was so seen by members of the public or Parliament, this could constitute sufficient "moral" grounds in the absence of objective, scientific evidence.

10.12 Both sides agree that, if Article 8 (1) is engaged, the key tests are whether the interference has a legitimate basis (i.e. whether interference is necessary "for the protection of morals"), whether there is "a pressing social need" for the interference and whether it is proportionate. In reaching a judgement on the former, the European Court of Human Rights would allow a State a "wide margin of appreciation" - on the basis that States are better able to judge what is appropriate in their particular circumstances. Similarly, the domestic court would be likely, we understand, to afford Parliament "a discretionary area of judgement". The Countryside Alliance argue, however, that it would not be sufficient simply to assert that hunting with dogs is immoral: there would need to be objective evidence that hunting involves unnecessary suffering, including by reference to that involved in other methods. They also point out that this argument is particularly relevant to the draft Bill prepared by Deadline 2000 since the latter would penalise hunting per se, without any need to prove unnecessary suffering. Deadline 2000, on the other hand, argue that the test would be met in the light of the fact that Parliament would have decided on a free vote, after an inquiry and much public debate, that hunting is morally wrong and cruel. The question of a permissible approach to "moral" grounds was also addressed in supplementary representations: a closing submission by the Countryside Alliance and a further opinion for IFAW, relied on by Deadline 2000.[543]

10.13 The Countryside Alliance also argue that a ban would fail the "proportionality" test. This is in the light of what they regard as the lack of firm scientific evidence in respect of unnecessary suffering and the impact that a ban would have on rural communities and people's lives and livelihoods. Deadline 2000 argue, on the other hand, that their draft Bill meets the test since it does only what is necessary to achieve its

---

[543] These additional papers are also on the CD Rom.

purpose - to ban hunting with dogs - and because it contains suitable exceptions and limitations.

<u>Article 1 of Protocol I</u>

10.14 Article 1 of Protocol I provides as follows:

> "Every natural or legal person is entitled to the peaceful enjoyment of his possessions. No-one shall be deprived of his possessions except in the public interest and subject to the conditions provided for by law and by the general principles of international law.

> The preceding provisions shall not, however, in any way impair the right of a state to enforce such laws as it deems necessary to control the use of property in accordance with the general interest or to secure the payment of taxes or other contributions or penalties."

10.15 Both sides agree that Article 1 of Protocol I is engaged, in the sense that a ban on hunting, though it would not actually deprive someone of the use of land or the animals involved, would constitute a control on their use (according to Deadline 2000) or an interference with the substance of ownership (according to the Countryside Alliance). The issue then turns on whether this is justified in accordance with "the general interest" and whether a fair balance is struck between the general public interest and the interference with the fundamental rights of individuals.

10.16 Both sides also agree that the "general interest" test is interpreted by the European Court with considerable latitude to national authorities. The approach to which we were referred is to ask whether Parliament's judgement as to what was in the public interest is "manifestly without reasonable foundation". The Countryside Alliance, however, question whether this "general interest" test is satisfactorily met. They also argue that, even if the Court held that it was met, there is a strong likelihood that a "fair balance" would require economic compensation for owners of packs and for landowners. Deadline 2000, on the other hand, argue that the Bill meets the "general interest" test since it is concerned with the protection of morals and the prevention of cruelty and that it is proportionate to these aims. They also take the view that any losses to landowners would be speculative - other activities such as shooting and humane trapping would be unaffected - and that, in any event, no form of compensation scheme would be required.

Conclusions

10.17 Legislation to ban hunting might be open to challenge under Article 1 Protocol I (property rights) and, possibly, Article 8 (respect for private life) of the European Convention on Human Rights. We are not qualified to express an opinion on whether any challenge along these lines would succeed. Key questions would be whether the undoubted interference with property, and possibly with private life, was justified under Convention principles, bearing in mind the nature

of the interference and the latitude enjoyed by the national authorities. An important consideration would be whether legislators could point to unnecessary suffering or some other reference point beyond mere disapproval, to reflect the general interest (or, to the extent necessary, the protection of morals and pressing social need). A relevant issue would be the form of the Bill: one which required proof of unnecessary suffering, or some similar test, would be less open to argument than one which banned hunting per se.

Scope and form

10.18 As our report shows, hunting with dogs of foxes, deer, hares and mink raises different issues according to the species involved and the way in which hunting takes place. Hare coursing is different again. Some previous attempts at legislation in this area have focused on one activity, for example foxhunting or hare coursing. Others, for example the Bill introduced by Mr Michael Foster MP in 1997, have sought to implement a wider ban on hunting with dogs. The draft Bill prepared by Deadline 2000, which we mentioned in paragraph 10.5, takes the latter approach, proposing a ban on the intentional hunting of a wild mammal with a dog. As we note below, however, it also contains a number of exceptions in relation to certain activities involving certain species. Anyone introducing legislation would therefore need to decide at the outset how broad the scope of the Bill should be, in particular to which species it should apply and which activities involving dogs it should cover.

Defining the offences

10.19 Any offences created need to be described sufficiently clearly so that those who might be affected by the legislation, and those who have to enforce it, know which activities constitute an offence and which do not.

10.20 There have been two broad approaches, in the context of Bills concerned with hunting, to formulating the main offence:

- defining as precisely and as exhaustively as possible the activities which are to be prohibited

- relying on a common understanding of what is meant by expressions such as 'hunting with dogs', backed up by any necessary exemptions or clarifications.

10.21 A main difficulty with the first approach is that the result may be to exclude inadvertently acts which the legislation was intended to cover. A main difficulty with the second, broader approach is that it may simply not be clear enough what is intended to be caught, resulting in uncertainty all round.

10.22 The approach adopted in recent Bills has varied. The Bill originally introduced by Mr Foster contained a definition of hunting but it was removed, at the Government's suggestion, during the Standing Committee consideration of the Bill in the House of

Commons. The Protection of Wild Mammals (Scotland) Bill, recently introduced in the Scottish Parliament, does not contain a definition. Nor does the draft Bill which we mentioned in paragraph 10.5. In their evidence to us, Deadline 2000 said that they favoured a simple offence of intentional hunting, coupled with any necessary exemptions, on the lines of the draft Bill.[544] They also pointed out that the terms 'hunt' and 'hunting' already feature in existing legislation. The Countryside Alliance, on the other hand, argued that the absence of a definition would be unsatisfactory, since it would lead to confusion and uncertainty.[545]

10.23 There have been different approaches too in respect of the mental element of the principal offence. The Foster Bill, as originally introduced, penalised any person who "uses, causes or permits any dog to hunt any wild animal". In the Bill as amended by the Standing Committee, the offence was simply couched in terms of hunting a wild animal with a dog.

10.24 In addition to the form of the main offences, consideration would also have to be given to the need for any secondary offences. The Foster Bill included offences relating to owners and occupiers of land and owners and keepers of dogs. The draft Bill also has an offence relating to the possession of instruments and appliances.

Exemptions

10.25 As we have noted, recent Bills have tended to be cast in terms of a prohibition on the hunting of wild mammals with dogs and that the terms "hunting" and "hunting with dogs" may sometimes have a broader meaning than the activities which we have examined. The main areas in which the case for an exemption would need to be considered are in relation to:

- the hunting of any of the animals concerned for food

- the hunting of animals for the purposes of pest control

- the use of dogs for the purposes of locating or retrieving an animal which has been shot or otherwise injured.

A secondary issue has been whether the exemptions should be framed in respect of the use of a single dog only.

Powers of arrest, search, seizure and entry

10.26 All the recent Bills have contained provisions giving the police powers of arrest, search, seizure and entry. The Countryside Alliance argued that these powers were disproportionate and criticised in particular the provision governing police powers of

---

[544] Seminar, 10 April 2000, Session 3
[545] CA paper for seminar

entry on or over land and buildings.[546] Deadline 2000, on the other hand, pointed to similar provisions in the Wildlife and Countryside Act 1981.[547]

<u>Geographical coverage</u>

10.27 Another issue which would need to be addressed in preparing legislation would be whether it should apply equally to the whole of England and Wales or whether there would be any possibility of geographical variation. As we acknowledged in Chapter 5, there is considerable local variation in the practice of hunting and in attitudes towards it. Perhaps the strongest case, for some variation of this kind applies in respect of foxhunting in upland sheep-rearing areas where, as our report indicates, it would be difficult to use any other method to cull foxes. One possibility, therefore, would be for the legislation to contain a provision which would permit hunting to take place in certain areas under some form of special authorisation.

<u>Conclusions</u>

10.28 Consideration should be given to whether any ban would be manifestly unjust, bearing in mind the activities caught and not caught by it.

10.29 Consideration should be given to whether any ban could be framed sufficiently clearly to enable people to regulate their conduct. A central issue would be whether a Bill would need to have a detailed definition of the prohibited offence and any exceptions or exemptions.

10.30 It would be necessary to consider the form of exceptions that should apply in particular areas, especially sheep-rearing upland areas, and for particular cases, such as the pursuit of injured deer or dealing with orphaned foxes underground or for research purposes. It would be necessary to establish the number and type of dogs that should be permitted for this purpose.

10.31 Unless there was a good reason on objective grounds, we do not think it would be satisfactory to have different legislative provisions in force in different regions of the country.

<u>Timing</u>

10.32 In introducing legislation to ban hunting it would be necessary to decide how quickly it was intended to bring it into force. There are three possible approaches. The first would be to implement a ban quickly by means of an early specified date. The second would be to defer implementation to a later specified date. The third would be to include an order-making power allowing the Home Secretary to bring different provisions into force at different, unspecified dates.

---

[546] CA paper of 9 May 2000
[547] Deadline 2000 paper for seminar, 24

10.33 Not surprisingly, those organisations and individuals who wish to see hunting banned have argued that there would be no need to delay implementation and that a ban should take effect as quickly as practicable once the relevant Bill has been passed. Deadline 2000, in their evidence to us, said that the legislation "should come into force within a fixed, short period from the legislation receiving Royal Assent". They went on to argue that, since the legislation which they were envisaging would not involve the need to establish new machinery or make secondary legislation, it should include a standard provision for commencement two months after Royal Assent.[548]

10.34 On the other hand, we received evidence suggesting that there would be advantage in having a longer period in which hunts and others could prepare for a ban. This could even take the form of a transitional period in which the number of days' hunting by the registered packs would reduce in stages. The Countryside Alliance, though firmly maintaining their opposition to a ban, argued that, in the following areas, the impact could be lessened to a degree by phasing-in:

- disposing of hounds and horses, firearms and ammunition etc

- re-housing those who would lose their jobs and accommodation

- making new arrangements for the control of the quarry species

- preparing new legislation to promote animal welfare

- making alternative arrangements for the collection and disposal of fallen stock

- putting in place compensation arrangements.

10.35 It would be feasible to implement a ban quickly. This would have the advantage of certainty, encouraging those concerned to get on as rapidly as possible with making any necessary adjustments. There are stronger arguments for allowing a reasonable period of adjustment. This would enable more time, for example, to reduce naturally the number of hounds; to develop draghunting and other activities; to put in place new population management strategies; and to mitigate wherever possible any social and economic consequences of a ban.

10.36 A strong objection to a delay in implementing a ban would be that, in the meantime, various practices which opponents of hunting view as particularly objectionable would be allowed to continue. It might be possible to meet some of these objections by taking action in the meantime to ban or curtail some of these activities by considering the options discussed in Chapter 9.

---

[548] Deadline 2000 paper for seminar, 29

How a ban might be enforced

10.37 In principle, the enforcement of legislation can be carried out by a number of different agencies, including the police, local councils or bodies, such as inspectorates, established specifically for the purpose.

10.38 The last two approaches seem to us to be more appropriate in the case of regulating or licensing an activity, rather than simply enforcing a prohibition. Accordingly, we think that, in the case of a ban on hunting, the obvious course would be to look to the police to enforce the legislation in the normal way.

10.39 It was put to us by the Countryside Alliance and others that the police might face certain difficulties in enforcing a ban. The main arguments advanced were that:

- the law would be strongly resented by many people, some of whom would not comply with it

- because the police are reluctant to enforce legislation where there is a lack of public support, they would not seek to give it a high priority

- police resources were, in any case, already heavily stretched, which would also encourage them to give enforcement a low priority

- the police would find it difficult to enforce a ban because many of the activities take place in fairly remote areas and, with the exception of hunting by the registered packs, many of the activities would not be very visible.[549]

10.40 We recognise that enforcing legislation of this kind would pose difficulties for the police and the prosecuting authorities. We also recognise, however, that similar difficulties are experienced in other areas of the law. It would be for Parliament to weigh up these arguments, amongst others, in considering whether a ban should be introduced and the form it should take.

10.41 Legislation implementing a ban might well pose some enforcement difficulties for the police. These matters should be considered by Parliament when examining a Bill.

<u>Whether controls on other hunting activities might be necessary/desirable</u>

10.42 In considering the present impact of hunting with dogs, and of a ban on hunting, we have necessarily had to spend some time looking at other forms of control, in particular shooting. We have not had an opportunity to consider these matters in great depth. But we think that there are a number of possible improvements which might be considered, in the event of a ban on hunting.

---

[549] CA, paper for the seminar, 1.32.1

Stalking/shooting

10.43   We noted in Chapters 5 and 6 the importance of stalking/shooting in the culling of red deer and the uncertainty about wounding rates. We also noted that, in the event of a ban on hunting, there is a risk that a greater number of deer would be shot by less skilful shooters, leading to increased wounding rates. We concluded that consideration should be given to requiring all stalkers to prove their competence by undertaking appropriate training. Another issue which could usefully be considered is whether cull records should be kept.

Use of snares

10.44   We noted in Chapter 6 that even those snares that may be used legally to catch foxes raise considerable welfare concerns on a number of grounds. We also noted that it seemed likely that, in the event of a ban on hunting, the use of snares, along with other lethal methods, would be likely to increase. The use of snares was not part of our terms of reference, and we not been able to examine their use in any depth. We conclude, nevertheless, that consideration should be given to the use of snares in general.

Closed seasons

10.45   We have already noted, in paragraph 9.33, that consideration might be given, in the absence of a ban, to introducing a closed season for culling hares and that it would be necessary to consider whether this should apply to shooting as well.

10.46   In the event of a ban on hunting, consideration should be given to the training of stalkers, the use of snares and the possible case for a closed season for culling hares.

Whether other population management measures might be necessary/desirable

10.47   A point that has struck us forcibly, in carrying out our review, is how difficult it has been to acquire reliable information about the population of foxes, deer, hares and mink and about the numbers killed. More fundamentally, we note that, in contrast with the position in many other countries, there is no national, nor even a monitoring scheme for censussing their populations, as a basis for planning their management or conservation. We are sure that it would be helpful if this could be remedied, not only for the mammals with which we are concerned but for other mammals as well.

10.48   As far as the quarry species are concerned, we have noted in Chapter 5 that a ban on hunting would make it necessary to re-think fundamentally the way in which the red deer population is managed in the Devon and Somerset area. It would be important to develop some new system for collective management of the deer there.

10.49 Consideration should be given to the possibility of developing arrangements for monitoring and managing the populations of the four quarry species and other mammals. A ban on hunting would make it necessary to review the existing arrangements for managing deer in the Devon and Somerset area in order to ensure that an effective strategic management system is in place.

Encouraging other/alternative activities

10.50 We discussed at some length in Chapter 8 of our report the extent to which drag or bloodhound hunting might serve as a substitute for live quarry hunting in the event of a ban on the latter. We concluded that fewer people would be likely to switch to these sports than has sometimes been suggested.

10.51 We do not think, however, that there is any specific action which central government should take in this area. The extent to which one or other of these sports would be taken up would be determined, in the end, by how attractive people found them as a recreational activity, compared with other possible ways of spending their time and money. Given the size of the horse-owning community, it would have every incentive to develop these and other equestrian activities.

10.52 We also noted in Chapter 4 that a ban on hunting might lead to some difficulties in respect of the organisation of point-to-point meetings, pony clubs and puppy shows. The first of these activities is of some significance because of its links with National Hunt racing. No doubt, in the event of the introduction of legislation to ban hunting, the various equestrian bodies, including the Jockey Club, would consider what action it would be necessary to take to ensure the future of point-to pointing and what contribution they and others could make to this objective.

10.53 In the event of a ban on hunting, there is no specific action which central government should take to promote other activities such as drag or bloodhound hunting.

<u>Measures to deal with financial, economic and employment aspects</u>

10.54 We discussed in Chapter 3 the ways in which a ban on hunting might impact on individuals, businesses and local communities.

10.55   There are three main groups who would be affected financially by a ban on hunting:

- hunt employees

- the hunts

- farmers and other businesses[550]

10.56   In the case of those employees who would find themselves displaced from their jobs, there would probably no action which central government could do. We think that, for the most part, there is probably no action which central government could take to address these matters since the effects would be very localised and would not, in general, be susceptible to action at a national level. We would therefore expect that local authorities and others, in those areas most directly affected, would consider whether steps could be taken locally to mitigate the effects of a ban. We have already noted, however, that there might be scope for some concerted effort to retrain people who would lose their jobs, possibly in the form of local job-creation schemes.

10.57   In the case of the hunts, the main issue which would arise would be whether some form of compensation should be paid in the event of their having to put down hounds and because the hounds would no longer be required. We noted in Chapter 6 that there is disagreement about whether it would in fact be necessary for all, or even most, of the hounds to be destroyed and that this would depend on the speed in implementing a ban. Leaving that question to one side, we understand that the principle which is generally applied, when considering issues of compensation, is whether the individual concerned is actually deprived of a particular benefit, rather than whether some limitations are placed on its use. It would be a matter for the Government to consider, in the event of a ban and in the light of clearer guidance about its likely effects, whether any compensation should be paid in this particular case.

10.58   As far as farmers and other businesses are concerned, the main area in which central government action might need to be considered as in respect of the 'fallen stock' service presently provided by many hunts. We discussed in paragraphs 3.57 to 3.61 the effects which a ban on hunting would be likely to have on this service and the fact that the ending of this service, in the event of a ban, might have significant impact on individual farmers.

---

[550] We also received evidence from a chartered town planner (Mr Robin Bryer) suggesting that hunt countries are, in effect, planning units and that, as most hunts meet more than 28 times a year, a new hunt would require planning permission. Mr Bryer suggested that every hunt established prior to 1947 has deemed planning consent and a ban would amount to the revocation of planning permission for each and every hunt with compensation implications. We have taken some advice on this issue and we are not persuaded that a hunt country is a separate planning unit. A hunt country will include many separate farms or agricultural units and a planning area is one which is physically and functionally one for the purpose of planning. In addition, as meets are spread over many locations within a country, hunting is very unlikely to take place on the same site more than 28 times a year. Therefore, for a recreational activity of this nature, planning permission would not be required and there would be no compensation implications under planning legislation.

10.59 As well as the disposal of farm animals, the loss of the hunt kennels' fallen stock service would affect the disposal of equine carcasses. The collapse in the trade in horse hair and hides, and the ban on the use of equine meat in commercial pet food, has made the disposal of equine carcasses more expensive, with current charges at a commercial incinerator of £300 or more.

10.60 In the event of a ban on hunting, consideration would need to be given to possible action in respect of the fallen stock service provided by many hunts and to whether there would be a case for compensation if hounds had to be destroyed and hunts had no further use for their kennels.

ORGANISATIONS WHICH SUBMITTED WRITTEN EVIDENCE

First Round

Addison, Ian
Advocates For Animals
Airedale Beagles
Albion Saddlemakers
Allen, D
Amman Valley Fox Control
Animal Concern - Dumbarton
Animal Welfare Information Service
Ashdown Forest Wildlife Protection Group
Ashford Valley Hunt
Association of Bloodhound Breeders
Association of British Dogs and Cats Homes
Association of British Riding Schools
Association of Lurcher Clubs
Association of Masters of Harriers and Beagles - with MBHA
Association of Show and Agricultural Organisations
Atherstone Hunt
Avon Vale Hunt Supporters' Club
Badger Watch and Rescue - Dyfed
Badgworthy Land Company
Badminton Horse Trials
Badminton Trust
Barlow Hunt Supporters' Club
Baskerville, R.E.
Beeby, Frank - Grain and Agricultural Merchant
Bereleigh Estate
Berwyn Foxhounds
Bicester Hunt with Whaddon Chase
Bishop Burton College
Blean Beagles
Boddington, Dr D.G.
Border Hunt
Bournemouth University
Braes of Derwent Hunt
Brighton & Storrington Foot Beagles
British Association for Shooting & Conservation - The West Essex Committee
British Association of Shooting and Conservation
British Bloodstock Agency
British Deer Society
British Equestrian Trade Association

British Equine Veterinary Association
British Falconers' Club
British Horse Industry Confederation
British Horse Racing Board
British Horse Trials Association
British Shooting Sports Council
British Veterinary Association
Broom, Professor
Bryer, Robin
Burghley Horse Trials
Bywell County Fair
C N Spencer Ltd. Timber Merchants
Calcutt & Sons Limited, Winchester
Carnavon Arms
Cattistock Hunt
Central Committee of Fell Packs
Cheltenham Racecourse
Cheshire Hunt
Chippenham Branch of the RSPCA
Churchward, Robert - A Master Speaks
Claro Beagles
Cobham, Ralph
Colne Valley
Conservative Animal Welfare Council
Conservative Anti-Hunt Council
Copes Petrol Station
Coquetdale & Borders Coursing Club
Cordings of Piccadilly
Cotely Harriers
Cotswold Hunt
Cotswold Show & Country Fair
Cotswold Support Group for the Abolition of Hunting
Cottesmore Hunt
Country Landowners Association
Country Life Magazine
Country Sports for the Disabled
Countryman's Weekly
Countryside Alliance
Countryside Alliance - Staghunting and Sustainable Use
Countryside Alliance Australia
Countryside Alliance Education
Countryside Animal Welfare Group
Countryside Council for Wales
Countryside Foundation for Education
Course, R

Craighill Memorial Scholarship 1991 - Hypothetical Consequences of Closing
   Down a Large Pack of Hounds
Craighill Memorial Scholarship 1996/7 - The Relationship Between Hunting and
   Recreational Access
Crowborough Town Council
Cunningham, J A
Cunnington, W.B.
Curre Hunt
Cutcombe Parish Council
Dallas, Melvin
Dava Enterprises
Deer Initiative
Deerhounds Coursing Club Annex 1
Deerhounds Coursing Club Part 1
Denny, D J B
Devon & Somerset Residents' Association for Deer Protection
Devon & Somerset Staghounds' Hunt Club
Devon County Show
Dodson & Horrell
Doncaster Bloodstock Sales Limited
Dugdale, D
Duke Of Beaufort's Hunt
Dulverton East, Dulverton West, Minehead and Exmoor Hunts
Dulverton Town Council
Dulverton West Hunt
Dunstone, Dr Nigel
East Kent Hunt
East of England Agricultural Show
East Surrey & West Surrey Badger Protection Societies
East Sussex County Council
Eddy, R.G.
Edwards, Richard
Endangered Exmoor
Epinet Communications Plc.
Essex and Suffolk Hunt
Essex Ferret Welfare Society
Exeter League Against Cruel Sports
Exford Parish Council
Exmoor and District Deer Management Society
Exmoor National Park Authority
Exmoor Parish Council
Exmoor Society
Farmers' Bloodhounds
Farmers' Union of Wales
Farriers Arms, Gloucestershire
Farriers' Registration Council

Federation de Association de chasseurs de l'UE
Federation of Welsh Packs
Field Magazine, The
For Wildness' Sake
Foresight: The Countryside Alliance's Campaign For Shooting
Forest and District Beagles
Foster, Peter
Four Burrow Hunt
French Association of Hunting Packs
Frenette, Peter
Game Conservancy Trust
Garth & South Berks Foxhounds
Geist, Professor Valerius
George of Stamford, The
Gillingham & Shaftesbury Show
Graftons of Market Harborough
Great Yorkshire Show
Greatwood - Caring for Retired Racehorses
Green Collars - The History of the Tarporley Hunt
Hampshire Country Sports Day
Hampshire Hunt
Hampshire Minkhounds
Harford Foxhounds
Harrop, Professor Stuart
Haydon Hunt
Heart of England Falconry
Heythrop Hunt
Hill, Kevin
Hobson, Desmond
Holnicote Estate Farm Tenants' Association
Honeybrook Farm Animal Foods
Horse and Pony Taxation Committee
Hounds Magazine
Humane Slaughter Association
Hunting Association of Ireland
Hunting Calendar
Hursley Hambledon Hunt
Hurworth Hunt Kennels
Hurworth Hunt Supporters' Club
Hydestile Wildlife Hospital
Inglewood, Lord MEP
Institute of Terrestrial Ecology
International Fund for Animal Welfare
International League for the Protection of Horses
International Masters of Bloodhounds
Irish Council Against Bloodsports

Irish Masters of Bloodhounds
Irish Masters of Foxhounds Association
Island Woollens
J M Castle & Son
JMG Andrews - Chartered Surveyors
J M Osbourne & Co
Johnson Field Sports
Jorrocks Hunt Club
Kennel Club, The
Kreeger, Terry
Lambourn Trainers' Association
Langbein, D J
League Against Cruel Sports
Leave Country Sports Alone
Liberal Democrats Forum for the Countryside
Llanarmon D.C. Foxhounds Society
Lowther Horse Driving Show
M. Jones & Co. Agricultural Engineers
Maclean, Rt Hon David MP
Macmillan, Dr Douglas
Ministry of Agriculture, Fisheries and Food
Mallalieu, Baroness
Malmesbury Trailers
Mammal Society
Market Rasen Race Course
Master of the Celtic Bloodhounds
Masters of Deerhounds Association
Masters Of Draghounds and Bloodhounds Association
Masters of Foxhounds Association
Masters of Foxhounds Association of America
Masters of Minkhounds Association
Melchbourne and Yielden Parish Council
Meon Valley Beagles
Middle Way Group
Midmore, Peter
Miller Mundy, Mark
Miltons Estate
Molland Estate
Molland Parish Council
Morgan, Ian
Morpeth Hunt
Mortimer, Sir John
National Association of Farriers, Blacksmiths and Agricultural Engineers
National Birds of Prey Centre
National Canine Defence League
National Coursing Club

National Farmers' Union
National Farmers' Union South West
National Federation of Badger Group
National Gamekeepers' Association
National Greyhound Racing Club
National Trainers' Federation
National Trust
National Trust Deer Warden
National Vermin Control
National Whippet Coursing Club
National Working Terrier Federation
Natural Animal Feeds
Naturewatch
New Forest Commoners' Defence Association
Newbury & District Agricultural Society
Newcastle & District Beagles
North East Essex Badger Group
North East Hampshire Agricultural Association
North Tyne Hunt
Nottinghamshire Badger Group
Oakely Foot Beagles
Old Berkeley Beagles
Old Berks Point to Point
Old Surrey Burstow & West Kent Hunt
Oliver-Bellasis, Hugh
Opinion of a Retired Government Wildlife Management Adviser
Pellow, Clifford
Pembrokeshire & Carmarthenshire Mink Hounds
Percy Hunt
Perdix Publishing
Peterborough Royal Foxhound Show Society
Phelps, Richard
Plas Machynlleth Foxhounds
Point-to-Point Secretaries' Association
Portman Foxhounds
Preshaw Estate
Produce Studies Group
Pytchley Hunt
Pytchley Hunt Supporters Club
Quantock Staghounds
Quorn Hunt
Racehorse Owners' Association
Radley College Beagles
Rat Hunting
Reaseheath College
Renny, Donna

Rickard, Sean
Ripley Agricultural and Horticultural Association
Royal Artillery Branch, The Pony Club
Royal Society for the Prevention of Cruelty to Animals
S & A Fabrication
Saluki or Gazelle Hound Club
School of Farriery, Hereford
Scruton, Roger - Fox Hunting - The Modern Case
Sherston Wine Company, Wiltshire
SIM Engineering Ltd.
Sir Watkins Williams Wynn's Unit Farming and Widlife Competition
Smith, Malcolm - Article in The Biologist - "Natural Born Killers"
Sotheby's
South Dorset Hunt
South Marsh Coursing Association
South of England Agricultural Society
South Pembrokeshire Foxhounds
South West Deer Protection Group
South West Lancashire Fox Control Society
Southdown & Eridge Hunt
Southern Counties Rosettes
Southill Livery & Riding Centre
Sport Horse Breeding of Great Britain
Sportsman Association of Great Britain and Northern Ireland
Stags Chartered Surveyors
Standing Conference on Countryside Sports
Stormont Strategy
Surrey Union Hunt
Surrey Wildlife Preservation Group
Swaffham Coursing Club
Swann, William
Sylvarbor Consultants
Tattersalls
Taunton Vale Foxhounds
Tavistock Country Show
Thomas, Rhodri AM & Elin Jones AM
Thoroughbred Breeders' Association
Thurlow Estate
Timber Growers' Association - Eastern England Region
Transport and General Workers' Union (Rural and Agricultural)
Tregynan & District Fox Destruction Pack
Trinity Foot Beagles
Tyleri Farmers' Foxhounds
Tynedale Hunt Supporters' Club
Ullswater Foxhounds
Union Of Country Sports Workers

Universities Federation for Animal Welfare
Upper Banwy Fox Control Society
Vale of the White Horse Pony Club
Veterinary Opinion on Hunting With Hounds (LH Thomas & WR Allen)
Wadworth & Co
Warren, Dr Derek R
Warwickshire Pony Club
Wealden Mink Hounds
Weardale and Tees Valley Beagles
Weatherby's Group Limited
Webber, Dominic
Webster, John
Welsh Farmers Fox Control Association
Welsh Hawking Club
Welsh Hounds Association
Welsh Society for the Prevention of Cruelty to Animals
West Glamorgan Badger Group
West of England Bookmakers Association
West Somerset Foxhounds & Minehead Harriers Country Fair
West Sussex Badger Protection Group
West Sussex Wildlife Protection Group
Whetton, Dave
Whippet Coursing Questionnaire
Wight Conservation
Wigtownshire Hunt
Wildaid Trust
Wildlife in Need
Wildlife Network
Wildlife Support & Campaign For Creature Care
Wildlife Trusts
Wilson Group
Wilton Hunt
Windsor Clive International, Wiltshire
Woof Wear - Horse Protection, Cornwall
Worcestershire Hunt Point to Point Club
World Society for the Protection of Animals
Worshipful Company of Farriers
Wright, Matthew
Wye College Beagles
Zetland Hunt Survey

ORGANISATIONS WHICH SUBMITTED WRITTEN EVIDENCE

Second Round

Addison, Ian
Association of Bloodhound Breeders
Association of Lurcher Clubs
Atherstone Hunt
Badger Watch and Rescue Dyfed
Bates, Mick AM
Bicester Hunt with Whaddon Chase
British Equestrian Trade Association
Bryer, Robin
Cambridge & District RSPCA
Central Committee of Fell Packs
Clean Boot Club
Cooper, Caroline
Cotswold Support Group for the Abolition of Hunting
Countryside Alliance
Countryside Alliance - Brian Fanshawe
Deadline 2000
Deer Commission of Scotland
Delaney, David
Denny, D.J.B.
Devon and Somerset Staghounds
Dewar-Finch, Peter
Dorset Badger Group
Dulverton East, Dulverton West, Minehead & Exmoor Hunts
Endangered Exmoor
Essex & Suffolk Hunt
Essex Ferret Welfare Society
Evans Bros Estate Agents
Exmoor and District Deer Management Society
Exmoor Parish Council
Farmers Weekly
Federation of Welsh Packs
For Wildness' Sake
Forest and District Beagles
Forest Enterprise
G.C. Gordon Lennox Estate Company Limited
Galpin, Carol
Garnier, Edward QC MP
Gilling, Tim
Golding, K.B.

Hafren Veterinary Group
Haigh, Katrina
National Trust Deer Warden
Hare Hunting Associations
Hart, Simon
Hayes, Edna
Horton, Dr. J.C.
Hound Trailing Association
Ingram
Johnson, Flora
Kennel Club, The
Lambourn Trainers' Association
League Against Cruel Sports
League Against Cruel Sports - Main Road Madness
Liberal Democrat Forum for the Countryside
Lippit, Gretchen
Markham, Gary
Marriage, Edmund - British Wildlife Management
Masters of Foxhounds Association
Masters of Mink Hounds Association
Matson, Richard
Morgan, Ian
National Gamekeepers' Organisation
National Lurcher and Racing Club
National Trust
National Working Terrier Federation
New Forest Animal Protection Group
National Farmers' Union of England and Wales
North East Essex Badger Group
Northumberland County Show
Paterson, Owen MP
Pinney, Tim
Plynlimmon Foot Pack
Prowse, Miss H.A.
Quantock Staghounds
Ryder, Dr. Richard
South West Deer Protection
Staines, Professor Brian
Surrey Union Hunt
Swann, William
Sylvarbor Consultants
Thom, Liam
Thomas, Dr L.H.
Thurlow Estates
Treggiari, Dr.
Tregynon/Cefn-Coch and District Fox Control Society

UK Chasers and Riders
Union of Country Sports Workers
Vasquez, Luis
Warren, Derek
Watts, J.A.
Wealden Minkhounds
Wessex Wildlife
West Somerset Bridleways Association
West Surrey Badger Group
West Sussex Badger Protection Group
West Sussex Wildlife Protection
West Wales Animal Aid
Westwood, John
Wetton, Dave
White, Denys
Wigtownshire Hunt
Wildlife in Need
Wildlife Trusts
Wise, Douglas
Wright, Matthew
Young Family
Zetland Hunt

ANALYSIS OF WRITTEN EVIDENCE SUBMITTED BY INDIVIDUALS

3.1   We decided at an early stage that we wished to hear from a broad spectrum of opinion, including from as many members of the public as possible. We felt that it was important to try to learn the reasons put forward by people for their very strongly held beliefs.

3.2   We would like to take this opportunity to thank all those who wrote to the Inquiry for their contributions.

First Round Evidence

3.3   Accordingly, on 19 January 2000, we issued a general invitation to interested parties inviting them to submit evidence to the Committee addressing the issues in our terms of reference. Although the closing date for submissions was 21 February, we were concerned that we should hear from as many people as possible and so attempted to be flexible over admitting evidence.

Analysis

3.4   We received a total of 5,945 letters in response to the invitation. Of these 5,669 were from supporters of hunting and 263 from those who wished to see it banned. 13 people did not express a view either way.

Quarry species

3.5   From the correspondence we received it would appear that most people, on both sides of the issue, are focused on foxhunting. 70% of those in favour of hunting and 73% of those opposed to hunting said that it was the form of hunting of prime concern to them. Of the other respondents who mentioned a specific form of hunting, deer hunting was mentioned by 6% of those who supported hunting and 7% of those opposed to hunting; the hunting of hares, in all forms, was mentioned by 2% of those who supported hunting and 20% of those opposed to hunting.

Reasons for supporting hunting

3.6   Most correspondents gave more than one reason. We set out below the main reasons which were given and the frequency with which they were mentioned (as a percentage)

Reason for supporting hunting	Percentage
Economic (direct and indirect)	83
Social	72
Pest control	40
Equestrian	32
Traditional/Cultural	32
Most humane method of control	32
Wildlife and habitat conservation	30
Natural method of control	26
Fallen stock service	21
Civil liberty/Freedom of the individual	21
Cruelty of other methods	17
Destruction of hounds/horses in the Event of a ban	9
Fundraising for charity	2

Reasons for banning hunting

3.7   We received 263 letters from those opposed to hunting.   Again, most correspondents mentioned more than one reason for wanting hunting banned.

Reason	Percentage
Hunt havoc/disruption/trespass	31
Cruelty to quarry species	28
Barbaric	15
Not needed	9
Manifesto promise	7
No reason given	4
Intimidation/arrogance by/of hunters	4
Cruelty to hounds/horses	2

Second Round Evidence

3.8   We received many fewer submissions from individuals in the course of the second round of evidence. In the main we believe this was because individuals felt that they had already voiced their opinions and contributed as fully as they could to the debate.

3.9   Of the 72 items received, 46 were from those opposed to hunting and 25 from supporters of hunting, with 1 person not expressing a view one way or the other.

3.10   22% of the responses from those opposed to hunting said that the reason for writing was as a direct result of press coverage which quoted the Chairman as saying that over 90% of the correspondence received to date had been from people supporting hunting. 13% of the letters from different correspondents were photocopies of the same letter. 6% of correspondents stated that the reason for writing was that their MP had asked them to do so.

Geo-demographic analysis

3.11 We also commissioned a geo-demographic survey of the postcodes of correspondents. Not all correspondents included their postcode. We carried out an analysis on a sample of 4,937 correspondents who were supporters of hunting and a sample of 169 who were opposed to hunting. It is not possible to draw any definite conclusions from the analysis of those opposed to hunting because the sample was too small.

3.12 ACORN (A Classification of Regional Neighbourhoods) is one of the leading consumer classification systems which segments people living in Great Britain into any one of 6 Categories, 17 Groups or 54 Types (plus 1 unclassified in each case).

3.13 The 6 ACORN Categories range from the most established and affluent people (In Category A: "Thriving") through to the people with the greatest hardship (In Category F: "Striving"). The postcode analysis that we carried out showed that the majority of correspondents (70%) who supported hunting were in Category A: Thriving. This compares with 20% of the population as a whole.

3.14 When we look closer at the analysis of correspondents who supported hunting and consider ACORN Types, more than half (52%) of the correspondents fell into just two types: Type 2, "Villages with Wealthy Commuters" and Type 6, "Agricultural Villages, Home Based Workers".

3.15 These percentages can be considered relative to the percentage of people in that Type in the population as a whole. This is shown as an index (base 100). The following table shows the Types with indices greater than 110.

Correspondents who supported hunting

ACORN Type		% of sample	Index
6	Agricultural Villages, Home-Based Workers	21.4	1537
2	Villages with Wealthy Commuters	30.9	1042
7	Holiday Retreats, Older People, Home-Based Workers	2.9	410
27	Rural Areas, Mixed Occupations	12.0	344
3	Mature Affluent Home Owning Areas	4.9	175
1	Wealthy Suburbs, Large Detached Houses	3.5	134

3.16 It is more difficult to draw conclusions from the ACORN analysis of results for those who are opposed to hunting because the total sample was too small. However, it is interesting to note that the distribution across the Types is greater but that the percentages and index numbers are for broadly similar Types as far the correspondents who were supporters of hunting. The following table shows the four Types with the largest Index:

Correspondents opposed to hunting

	ACORN Type	% of sample	Index
6	Agricultural Villages, Home-Based Workers	11.2	808
2	Villages with Wealthy Commuters	13.6	459
8	Home Owning Areas, Well-Off Older Residents	5.3	352
27	Rural Areas, Mixed Occupations	8.9	254

DETAILS OF COMMISSIONED RESEARCH

4.1   Details are given below of the specifications for the main pieces of research commissioned by the Committee of Inquiry. The draft and final research reports relating to these contracts are on the CD Rom accompanying the Committee's report, together with transcripts of the seminar proceedings at which the draft research reports were discussed.

4.2   Intended contracts 1 and 9 were not let.

CONTRACT 2: HUNTING WITH DOGS: EXPENDITURE, AND NUMBERS EMPLOYED, BY HUNTS AND THEIR FOLLOWERS

Research objectives

a) to provide independent verification of the quality and accuracy of the Countryside Alliance data set

b) to estimate the <u>direct</u> expenditure by hunts and their supporters on hunting and hunting-related matters, broken down by main categories

c) to estimate the number of people employed directly by hunts, showing what proportion of their time is directly related to hunting activities, whether there are seasonal variations and in what capacities they are employed

d) to estimate the number of people employed by hunt followers on hunting-related activities, showing what proportion of their time is directly related to hunting activities, whether there are seasonal variations and in what capacities they are employed

e) to estimate the income of hunts, broken down by main categories

f) to draw attention to any marked variations in these figures with respect to different types of hunting/coursing and different locations within England and Wales.

All data for (b) to (f) should be aggregated at both national and regional levels and should be presented alongside comparative figures for the economy as a whole.

CONTRACT 3: THE INDIRECT EFFECTS OF HUNTING WITH DOGS ON THE RURAL ECONOMY AND THE LONGER-TERM EFFECTS OF A BAN

Research objectives:

a) to undertake a critical review of the existing literature relating to employment/expenditure in rural areas <u>indirectly</u> generated by hunting and to the longer-term effects of a ban

b) to suggest, in the light of existing evidence and any further information which can readily be obtained, what is the appropriate multiplier to use in estimating the indirect effect on employment/expenditure in rural areas of hunting with dogs

c) to describe and categorise significant indirect and multiplier effects resulting from the pursuit of hunting with dogs in England and Wales, indicating the types of employment and expenditure most likely to be affected and regional variations

d) to consider the extent to which, and over what timescale, any negative effects of a ban on hunting would be counteracted by other changes which are occurring, or are likely to occur, in the rural economy (for example, in patterns of employment)

e) to indicate the extent to which this would be likely to vary according to sector and locality

f) in the light of the findings from the review, to conduct multiplier analysis based on the data supplied by the Committee's own commissioned research on direct impacts. This should include estimates of employment equivalents from the expenditure figures for hunts and hunt followers. The analysis should distinguish as far as possible between different types of hunting and different areas of England and Wales.

CONTRACT 4: THE EFFECTS OF HUNTING WITH DOGS ON THE SOCIAL AND CULTURAL LIFE OF THE COUNTRYSIDE IN ENGLAND AND WALES

Research objectives:

a) to review existing literature relating to the impact on the social and cultural life of the English and Welsh countryside of hunting with dogs and to the effects of a ban on such hunting. It is not anticipated that this literature will be extensive

b) to provide information, from a number of areas where hunting takes place, which assesses what involvement or contact, if any, individuals in those localities have with hunting or hunting-related activities; what impact hunting or these activities have on their lives

c) the extent and strength of support for, or opposition to, hunting and these activities; the main reasons underlying different views; the likely impact of a ban on hunting; and the social and occupational background of the people concerned

d) to consider the social and cultural role of hunting in representative localities in England and Wales

e) to summarise the findings, distinguishing those matters on which there is general agreement from those which are disputed and distinguishing as far as possible between different types of hunting and different areas of England and Wales

f) to suggest what further research would need to be carried out to clarify areas of dispute and to remedy significant gaps in our understanding of these matters.

CONTRACT 5: MANAGEMENT OF THE POPULATION OF FOXES, DEER, HARES AND MINK AND THE IMPACT OF HUNTING WITH DOGS

Research objectives:

a) to give an account, drawn from existing literature, of the reasons why landowners, farmers and others seek to exercise control over the populations of foxes, deer, hares and mink in the interests of agriculture, forestry, fishing and land management in England and Wales. This should also include control in the interests of conservation of wildlife, habitats and landscape

b) to consider the impact, from these perspectives, of the hunting with dogs of these animals, drawing out such quantitative information as can be provided

c) to consider the likely effects, from these perspectives, of a ban on such hunting

d) to summarise the findings, distinguishing those matters on which there is general agreement from those which are disputed and distinguishing as far as possible between different types of hunting and different areas of England and Wales

e) to suggest what further research would need to be carried out to clarify areas of dispute and to remedy significant gaps in our understanding of these matters.

CONTRACT 6: METHODS OF CONTROLLING FOXES, DEER, HARES AND MINK

Research objectives:

a) to review existing evidence relating to the different methods of controlling foxes, deer, hares and mink, including hunting with dogs, in England and Wales

b) to consider the actual and potential effectiveness, practicability and cost of those methods, quantifying the results wherever possible

c) to discuss issues relating to the acceptability and wider impact of the different methods of control

d) to summarise the findings, distinguishing those matters on which there is general agreement from those which are disputed and distinguishing where necessary between different areas of England and Wales

e) to suggest what further research would need to be carried out to clarify areas of dispute and to remedy significant gaps in our understanding of these matters.

CONTRACT 7: THE EFFECTS OF HUNTING WITH DOGS IN ENGLAND AND WALES ON THE WELFARE OF DEER

Research objectives:

a) to review the existing scientific evidence relating to the effect of hunting with dogs on the welfare of deer

b) to review the existing scientific evidence relating to the ways in which the welfare of deer is affected by other methods of control or as part of their natural life cycle

c) to summarise the main findings, distinguishing those areas about which there is general agreement from those which are disputed

d) to summarise, in layman's language as far as possible, what conclusions can reliably be drawn about the welfare of deer during, or subsequent to, hunting with dogs, in comparison with the effect on their welfare of other methods of control

e) to record any existing scientific evidence relating to the effect on the welfare of foxes, hares and mink of hunting with dogs, in comparison with other methods of control or as part of their natural life cycle

f) to suggest what further research would need to be carried out to clarify areas of dispute and to remedy significant gaps in our understanding of these matters.

CONTRACT 8: DRAG AND BLOODHOUND HUNTING

Research objectives:

a) to review existing evidence relating to the practice of drag or bloodhound hunting (or similar activities) in England and Wales and in other countries

b) to undertake any necessary additional enquiries, in particular in areas of England and Wales where drag or bloodhound hunting takes place, in order to assess the following:

- the attitudes of participants and followers to drag or bloodhound hunting

- the age, social groups and other characteristics of those who participate in, or follow, drag or bloodhound hunting

- whether those concerned were previously, or are presently, involved in hunting animals with dogs

- whether attitudes to drag or bloodhound hunting differ significantly between those who have hunted animals with dogs and those who have not done so

- where people have previously devoted, or are presently devoting, resources to hunting animals with dogs, how these compare with those devoted to drag or bloodhound hunting

- the attitudes of local landowners and farmers to drag or bloodhound hunting and in what circumstances they allow these activities to take place

- the possible scope for making drag or bloodhound hunting more attractive, both to those who currently hunt dogs with animals and those who do not do so

- what effect, if any, drag or bloodhound hunting has on wildlife, the landscape and habitats.

c) to summarise the findings, distinguishing those matters on which there is general agreement from those which are disputed and distinguishing where necessary between different areas of England and Wales.

VISITS UNDERTAKEN BY THE COMMITTEE

5.1   Members of the Committee made a number of visits in order to familiarise themselves with hunting and related activities.

5.2   On each visit members were accompanied by observers from the Countryside Alliance and Deadline 2000. Their role was to advise the Committee as necessary and to provide reassurance that the Committee were seeing activities as they would normally take place.

Date	Club/Hunt/Venue	Attended
FOXHUNTING		
9 February	Border	Lord Burns, Professor Winter
21 February	Thurlow	Lord Soulsby, Dr. Edwards
26 February	Brecon and Talybont	Lord Burns
28 February	Plas Machynlleth	Dr. Edwards, Professor Winter
6 March	Irfon and Towy	Lord Burns, Professor Marsh, Lord Soulsby
14 March	Coniston	Lord Burns, Dr. Edwards, Professor Winter
18 March	Duke of Beaufort's	Lord Burns, Dr. Edwards, Professor Marsh, Professor Winter
22 March	Essex Farmers' and Union	Lord Burns, Professor Marsh
24 March	Blencathra	Professor Marsh

28 March	Blencathra	Lord Soulsby

DEER HUNTING

17 February	Devon & Somerset	Lord Burns, Dr. Edwards, Professor Marsh, Professor Winter,
1 April	Devon and Somerset	Lord Burns, Dr Edwards

HARE HUNTING

19 February	Old Berkeley Beagles	Lord Burns, Professor Winter
23 February	Waveney Harriers	Lord Burns, Professor Winter

HARE COURSING

4 February	East of England	Lord Burns, Dr. Edwards, Lord Soulsby,
11 February	Kimberley & Wymondham	Professor Marsh
14 February	Alresford	Dr Edwards, Professor Winter
22 February	Altcar (Waterloo Cup)	Lord Burns, Lord Soulsby

MINK HUNTING

20 May	Ytene	Dr. Edwards, Professor Marsh, Professor Winter

OTHER VISITS

17 February	League Against Cruel Sports Sanctuary, Baronsdown	Lord Burns
19 March	Draghunting: Staff College and Royal Military Academy Sandhurst	Lord Burns, Dr Edwards, Professor Marsh, Lord Soulsby
1 April	League Against Cruel Sports Sanctuary, Baronsdown	Lord Burns, Dr. Edwards Professor Marsh, Professor Winter
17 April	RSPCA Wildlife Hospital, West Hatch	Lord Burns, Dr Edwards
25 April	Draghunting: near Dusseldorf, Germany	Lord Burns, Dr Edwards
30 April	Drag coursing: Wickwar Park Coursing Club	Dr. Edwards
7 June	Lamping: near Chute, Hampshire	Lord Burns, Lord Soulsby, Professor Marsh

ROLE, RULES AND RECOMMENDATIONS OF THE MASTERS' ASSOCIATIONS AND OTHER ORGANISATIONS

6.1 The various Masters' associations are the governing bodies of all hunts and clubs that wish to be 'recognised'. They have constitutions, rules, codes of conduct and disciplinary powers intended to ensure the proper management of hunting activities. Of particular relevance to this Inquiry are the codes of conduct as they relate to humane treatment of the quarry, and to relations with other users of the countryside whose interests may be affected by hunting with dogs.

The Independent Supervisory Authority for Hunting (ISAH) Ltd

6.2 The Phelps Review of Hunting With Hounds, commissioned by the Countryside Movement and published in 1997, recommended the creation of an independent authority to oversee the activities of its member associations. The purpose was to obviate the need for statutory control of hunting with hounds by providing an effective regime of self-regulation and more transparent accountability. The company, ISAH Ltd, was incorporated in December 1999.

6.3 The founding members of the company are its chairman, Sir Ronald Waterhouse Q.C., who is a former High Court judge and chairman of the Inquiry into Child Abuse in North Wales and is independent of the subscriber associations to the company; the chairman of the Countryside Alliance's Hunting Committee; and the chairmen of all the subscribing Hunting Associations, namely, the Masters of Foxhounds Association, the Central Committee of Fell Packs, the Federation of Welsh Packs, the Association of Masters of Harriers and Beagles, the Masters of Bassett Hounds Association, the National Coursing Club, the Association of Lurcher Clubs, the Masters of Deer Hounds Association, the Masters of Mink Hounds Association, and the National Working Terrier Federation.

Objectives

6.4 ISAH Ltd's stated objectives are:

- to act as an independent supervisory authority for hunting, coursing and terrierwork in England and Wales

- to examine and approve the Rules and Codes of Conduct and supervise disciplinary procedures to which those engaged in hunting, coursing and terrierwork should adhere

- to supervise the organisations which govern the activity of those engaged in hunting, coursing and terrierwork in England and Wales so as to ensure that such organisations enforce compliance with such Rules and Codes of Conduct

<u>The Commissioners</u>

6.5   The work of ISAH Ltd will be carried out by seven Commissioners. Two of these are ex officio in accordance with ISAH Ltd's Articles of Associations, namely, the chairman of ISAH Ltd himself, and the chairman of the Countryside Alliance's Hunting Committee. The other five are appointed by an appointments panel of five persons, separately nominated by the senior officers of the National Farmers' Union, the Countryside Alliance, the Royal College of Veterinary Surgeons and the chairman of ISAH Ltd.

<u>Role</u>

6.6   ISAH Ltd's role and powers are:

- to refer proper complaints to the relevant hunting association for investigation and action

- to examine the outcome of their disciplinary investigations and to impose additional sanctions, within the proper powers of that Association, if it considers insufficient attention has been paid to the public interest, or is otherwise dissatisfied with the Association's decision

- where necessary, to issue a public warning or censure to a member organisation, or suspend, or ban an individual of a member organisation from holding office

6.7   Each member organisation of ISAH Ltd must obtain at the start of the hunting season the agreement of all their member hunts to accept the final authority of the Commissioners, and at the end of each season, provide a written report of the season's activities.

<u>Work to date</u>

6.8   The Commissioners met for the first time on 18 May 2000. They reviewed and pronounced themselves satisfied with the manner in which five disciplinary cases had been handled by the Master of Foxhounds Association (see below). Other member associations did not report any disciplinary cases relevant to this Inquiry. The Commissioners agreed to begin a review at their next meeting of the rules and codes of conduct of their member organisations.

Masters of Foxhounds Association (MFHA)

Organisation of the MFHA

6.9   The MFHA is run by a committee of twelve members who serve for a period of three years each, together with professional help. It regulates foxhunting by its Rules and a Code of Conduct. Terrierwork is controlled by keeping the National Register of Hunt Terriermen. The MFHA also organises seminars regionally on the subject over a three year cycle in order to promote good practice. Other relevant functions of the MFHA include cooperation with MAFF on the handling of animal carcasses (fallen stock), kennel inspections and the administration of point-to-points and equestrian cross country team events. Another important function is the keeping of the stud book for the hounds.

Organisation of MFHA packs

6.10   The main points are:

- a Committee of members runs the individual hunts. It establishes the working policy of the Hunt, looks after the finances and appoints the Masters

- the Master/Joint Masters are mostly unpaid and have ultimate responsibility for the activities of the pack. These include Hunt staff matters, liasing with landowners, and programming and directing hunting days

- the Huntsman controls the hounds during the hunting day and, if a professional, will also be responsible for kennel matters. He or she is assisted by a whipper-in

- the Fieldmaster is either the Master or a nominee and is responsible for stewarding the mounted followers, particularly to prevent trespass and damage

- the Terrierman, in addition to duties on the day of a hunt, is responsible for the general maintenance of the Hunt country, which can often entail work such as path clearing and management of coverts.

Principles of Regulatory Code

6.11   The main principals are:

- recognised hunting is the hunting of a wild animal in its wild and natural state. No fox is to be hunted that has previously been captive or in any way handled

- retention of the good will of the farmers

- Masters of Hounds or their appointed deputies are solely responsible for the conduct of the hunt and their authority is absolute.

Conduct of Hunting

6.12   The main provisions are:

General

- hounds to be prevented from hunting into a built-up area

- hounds to be removed if the fox is hunted to an inhabited building or one adjacent thereto

Terrierwork

- digging-out requires the permission of both landowner and Master

- a hunted fox cannot be dug out from a natural earth other than for the purpose of humanely destroying it. A hunted fox can be bolted from a man-made structure or where digging is not possible

- a handled fox cannot be rehunted

- a fresh fox can be bolted

- Master or his or her appointee to supervise all digging and bolting work which should be carried out by no more than 1- 2 persons and where possible one terrier only

- Master is responsible for activities of terrierman, who must be registered and hold current licence from the MFHA.

Bolting

- hounds to be taken out of sight and hearing

- bolted fox to be given a sporting chance to escape

Earth stopping and Protection of Badgers Act 1992

- all earth stoppers to hold card issued by MFHA

- stopping of setts to be carried out in accordance with section 5 of the Protection of Badgers Act 1992.

196

"Holding Up"

- permitted only as deemed necessary by Master to prevent fox from straying for safety, farming and fox control reasons

Disciplinary Procedures

6.13   The MFHA's current disciplinary procedure was set up in 1998 in order to formalise the previous ad hoc committees that had dealt with complaints of misconduct by members i.e. all current and some former Masters of Hounds.

6.14   The disciplinary steward or his or her deputy, if satisfied with the strength of a complaint, investigates it further and in confidence, so as not to compromise the member if found innocent.

6.15   The current chairman of the disciplinary committee has advised the Inquiry that the greatest difficulty for the steward is to obtain reliable evidence relating to the complaint in hand. He says that this is an inherent problem due to the nature of hunting, and that it may well be necessary in the future for the MFHA to consider means to ensure that reliable evidence of incidents is available wherever possible.

6.16   Once the steward or his deputy has investigated the complaint as fully as possible, a hearing takes place before the disciplinary committee of three. The member accused is present throughout the hearing and is entitled to legal advice at his or her expense. Civil standards of proof are applied and a decision can be made by majority only. The range of sanctions are reprimand, the payment of costs of the Inquiry and the suspension or expulsion from membership.

6.17   The committee prepares a statement giving details of the matter. It is intended for public use and, at the discretion of the MFHA, may or may not be issued to all members. It may also be issued to the press.

6.18   The MFHA has advised the Committee of Inquiry that, subject to members' approval at the annual general meeting on 6 June 2000, an amendment will be made to disciplinary proceedings, allowing, in the more serious cases of complaint, for a member to be suspended on immediate receipt of the complaint until the hearing can be held.

Disciplinary cases

6.19   The MFHA has advised the Inquiry of five disciplinary hearings since January 1999:

- use of an unlicensed terrierman. Sanction: Master suspended until correct licensing in place

- two cases of trespass onto railway lines to retrieve hounds, in one of which two hounds were struck by a train and killed. Sanction: Master reprimanded and instructed to take action to prevent future incidents

- digging-out on land owned by the Forestry Commission contrary to standing instructions. Sanction: Joint Masters suspended from hunting for two weeks and terriermen's licences withdrawn for the next three hunting seasons

- alleged interference with a badger sett. The hearing was delayed pending the outcome of court proceedings on the matter. After the court acquitted the accused, the disciplinary committee nonetheless found the Master guilty of digging-out without landowner's permission. Due to mitigating circumstances the Master was reprimanded only

Other associations governing hunting foxes with hounds

6.20   The Central Committee of Fell Packs (CCFP) and the Federation of Welsh Packs (FWP) have similar governing structures, rules and codes of conduct to those of the MFHA. However, the following points should be noted:

- the CCFP are fully affiliated to the MFHA. The huntsman is responsible for terrierwork. In view of the frequently rocky terrain, the Committee's code of conduct on terrierwork is less restrictive than that of the MFHA. Digging-out or netting are not always an option and, as a result, the Committee allows greater latitude to re-hunt bolted foxes

- the FWP are also fully affiliated to the MFHA and its members are bound by the same code of conduct. Members who hunt quarry other than foxes are bound by the rules of the relevant association. To reflect the history of gunpacks in Wales, the Federation's constitution authorises the use of shotguns.

6.21   The Welsh Farmer's Control Association (WFFC) differs somewhat from the other associations governing hunting foxes with hounds in that its overriding objective is fox control in its members' livestock rearing farming areas. It was founded in 1978 and has about 30 registered packs and hunts very largely without horses. There is some membership overlap with the FXP. It keeps its own list of terriermen who are authorised to work only on a meet by meet basis.

Association of Masters of Harriers and Beagles (AMHB)

6.22   The AMBH was established in 1891 primarily to maintain stud books and to run the annual Peterborough show. The maintenance and improvement of the breeds remains a central purpose of the Association, but nowadays it has assumed the role of the governing body for the registered packs.

6.23   There are 10 packs that hunt both foxes and hares, and the Association's regulations stipulate that, when hunting the former, packs are subject to MFHA regulations. As far as hunting hares is concerned, the Association aims to:

- contribute to hare population management throughout the UK.

- maintain standards of conduct and performance by laying down and enforcing a code of conduct for its members.

Hunting the hare

6.24   The main provisions are;

- a hunted hare must be in its wild and natural state and it must not previously have been held in any form of captivity or had its freedom unnaturally restricted.

- a hare run to ground should either be left, or first got out and killed before being given to the hounds.

- hounds should be called off if a hare is hunted to an inhabited dwelling house.

6.25   The Association reserves the right to terminate the membership of anyone shown to have acted, or who has allowed others to act, in a manner which is prejudicial to the interests or good name of hare hunting.

6.26   The current chairman advises that there have been two disciplinary cases in recent years. In the first, complaints were received that digging out a fox had occurred too close to residential dwellings. The complaints were upheld. The Master was cautioned as to his future conduct and guidelines laid out as to the future activities of the hunt. In the second, the Master of the hunt was cautioned for his conduct towards a female motorist who had accidentally run over a hound.

Masters of Bassett Hounds Association (MBHA)

6.27   The rules and regulations resemble those of the AMBH insofar as they touch on the subject matter of the Inquiry

Masters of Deerhounds Association (MDHA)

6.28   The MDHA was formed in 1951 and is responsible for the three packs of deerhounds that hunt red deer in South West England. It is the governing body of the three hunts and can adjudicate on any matter brought before it. The Association consists of present or acting Masters, chairmen and other officials of member hunts.

6.29   Relevant rules of the association are:

- defining deer hunting to be the hunting of deer in their wild and natural state

- prioritising sick or lame deer to be hunted first, and on non hunting days to instruct Masters and their staff to provide a "casualty" service

- specifying that only an approved type of firearm should be used to kill a deer as expeditiously, safely and humanely as possible

- specifying that every effort should be made to stop hounds from entering a built-up area where they are not welcome. If this should happen, due heed should be taken of the landowner's wishes.

6.30   The Association reserves itself the right to terminate the membership of any member shown to have broken its rules and regulations. Any adjudication of the association must be signed by all members making that adjudication.

6.31   The Inquiry has been advised that there have been no disciplinary cases in recent years.

The Masters of Mink Hounds Association (MMHA)

6.32   Amongst its rules and recommendations, the Association stipulates that:

- missiles, other than shot, must not be used at a mink up a tree and the hounds must be kept at a distance

- a mink run to ground must be dead before handed to hounds

- the Master must take reasonable measures to avoid encounters with otters.

6.33   The Association reserves the right to strike off any member who has been shown to have acted, or to have permitted his or her servants to act, in a manner prejudicial to the good name of mink hunting.

6.34   The current chairman advises that there have been no disciplinary cases during his tenure of office.

The National Working Terrier Federation (NWTF)

Organisation

6.35   In 1984, all the major working terrier clubs in the UK joined together to form the NWTF, with the stated aim of promoting the humane and efficient use of working terriers. Adherence to the Code of Conduct is a condition of membership. There are currently 26 member clubs, comprising 3000-4000 individuals. In addition to disseminating good practice amongst the members, the clubs are also centres for social activity. Since 1997, the NWTF have operated a national identification card scheme and a register of 'accredited' terriermen. This scheme is designed by the Federation as a form of self-regulation, especially for those independent terriermen who are not directly connected with registered hunts. Key aspects of accreditation are that individuals must have been club members for at least two years, well known to other members, and not to have ever been found guilty of any offences under the Protection of Badgers Act 1992, or the 1911 and 1996 animal protection Acts. The accreditation is validated yearly. The Federation also keeps a register of individuals who, it has reason to suspect, would not be suitable for membership of one of their clubs.

6.36   The main provisions of the Code of Conduct in relation to the practice of working with terriers are:

- the objective of properly conducted terrierwork is to provide a pest control service, which is humane, efficient and selective

- particular care should always be taken to minimize any risk of injury to either the quarry or the terrier. The terrier's role underground is to locate the quarry and to bark at it continuously so that it will either leave the earth to be netted, bolted to guns, or reached as quickly as possible and dispatched by shot

- landowner's permission must be obtained prior to any terrierwork

- injured quarry must be dispatched as soon as possible. If, for whatever reason, the quarry is to be transported elsewhere before dispatch, due regard should be paid to its general welfare and comfort

- after digging, the excavated area must be returned to its original condition

- the use of locator collars is recommended so that quarry can be located quickly, and to minimise the likelihood of terriers becoming trapped

- terrierwork must be restricted to legal quarry species only. Familiarity with the Protection of Badgers Act 1992 is essential, as is the knowledge of how to recognise a badger's occupation of a sett.

Rules

6.37   The Federation has the right to strike off any member deemed by the committee(s) to have brought terrierwork into disrepute. Any individual convicted of any offence under the Protection of Badgers Act 1992 or the Protection of Animals Act 1911 will be brought before the relevant committee(s).

6.38   Since 1996, there have been four separate occasions when a total of nine individuals have had their membership terminated because of convictions for badger offences.

The National Coursing Club (NCC)

6.39   The NCC fulfils a similar role in coursing as the Masters' Associations do in respect of hunting. Section 41 of the NCC rule book covers the welfare of the hare at the coursing ground.

- the presence of four "pickers-up'' to dispatch humanely injured hares

- the state of the going and the design of the field must allow the possibility for the hare to escape

- the hare must have sufficient knowledge of the ground.

6.40   A Coursing Inspector must be present at every meeting to ensure compliance with the Club's rules. Provision is made in the rulebook for a range of penalties, including expulsion for those members found guilty of discreditable conduct, which includes mistreatment of the hare.

6.41   There have been no disciplinary cases in recent years. On two occasions meetings have been abandoned when the inspectors were of the opinion that too many hares were being killed.

A STATISTICAL ACCOUNT OF HUNTING IN ENGLAND AND WALES

7.1   The following tables are based on data returned in response to the Produce Studies Limited Survey of Hunts - February 2000

Table 1 - A Statistical Profile of Fox Hunts in England and Wales by Species.

	Fox	Deer	Hare	Mink
Number of hunts	178	3	83	20
Days Hunting	74	97	53	42
Financial				
Total Income	13,034	363	1,427	89
Hunt income per hunting day	986	1247	325	105
Horses Owned	754	39		
Hounds				
Entered Hounds (couple)	5,566	120	1630	176
Unentered Hounds (couple)	1,595	23	442	29
Employment				
Full-time employees	453	14	42	1
Part-time employees	249	11	53	12
Participants				
Subscribers	20,591	1,342	5,245	771
Members of Supporters Clubs	34,723	770	3,398	268

Figures for Hare include Beagles, Bassets and Harriers.

Table 2 - A Statistical Profile of the Average Hunt

	Fox	Deer	Hare	Mink
Income £000's	73	121	17	4
Horses owned	4.2	13.0		
Hounds				
Entered Hounds (couple)	31	40	20	9
Unentered Hounds (couple)	9	8	5	1
Employment				
Full-time employees	2.5	4.7		
Part-time employees	1.4	3.7		
Participants				
Subscribers	118	447	63	39
Members of Supporters Clubs	195	257	41	13
Mounted followers - weekday	30	47		
Unmounted followers - weekday	34	150	15	20
Mounted Followers - weekend	50	90		
Unmounted Followers - weekend	58	300	29	37

Figures for Hare include Beagles, Bassets and Harriers.

Table 3 - A Regional Analysis of Fox Hunts

	Total	SW[551]	South	M&EA [552]	North	Wales
Number of Hunts	178	49	24	28	48	29
Days Hunting per hunt	74	77	73	80	72	69
Total Hunt Income	13,034	3,786	2,179	3,498	2,552	1,019
Foxes Killed						
Total Foxes Killed	13,987	4,444	1,497	2,519	2,853	2,674
Hunt Income per Fox Killed	932	852	1,456	1,389	894	381
Foxes Killed per hunting day	1.1	1.2	0.9	1.1	0.8	1.3
Hunt Income per hunting day	986	1,002	1,240	1,571	735	511
Horses Owned	754	238	124	184	152	56
Hounds						
Entered Hounds (couple)	5,566	1,714	826	962	1,322	742
Unentered Hounds (couple)	1,595	489	222	296	334	254
Employment						
Full-time employees	453	130	68	114	101	40
Part-time employees	249	66	32	65	64	22
Participants						
Subscribers	20,951	5,543	2,666	3,586	5,966	3,190
Members of Supporters Clubs	34,723	11,081	5,724	9,460	4,791	3,667

---

[551] South West
[552] Midlands and East Anglia

Table 4 - Fox Hunts - Averages Total, and within Each Region

	Total	SW[553]	South	M&EA [554]	North	Wales
Income £000s	73	77	91	125	53	35
Foxes Killed	79	91	62	90	59	92
Horses owned	4.2	4.9	5.2	6.6	3.2	1.9
Hounds						
Entered Hounds (couple)	31	35	34	34	28	26
Unentered Hounds (couple)	9	10	9	11	7	9
Employment						
Full-time employees	2.5	2.7	2.8	4.1	2.1	1.4
Part-time employees	1.4	1.3	1.3	2.3	1.3	0.8
Participants						
Subscribers	118	113	111	128	124	110
Members of Supporters Clubs	195	226	239	338	100	126
Mounted followers - weekday	30	29	32	46	26	21
Unmounted followers - weekday	34	33	29	53	33	26
Mounted Followers - weekend	50	53	51	66	43	36
Unmounted Followers - weekend	58	62	54	76	55	44

---

[553] South West
[554] Midlands and East Anglia

Table 5 Income of Hunts by Quarry Species - Average per hunt (£000s)

	Fox	Deer	Hare	Mink
Average Income £ 000s	74	121	18	5
% Subscriptions, donations, caps	56	60	57	66
% Fund Raising	31	32	32	29
% Other Sources	13	8	11	5

Table 6 Expenditure by hunts - Averages per hunt (£000s)

	Fox	Deer	Hare
Average Expenditure of Revenue	69	111	17
% Employment	41	42	38
% Local Expenditure	26	41	24
% Other	34	17	36

Figures for mink are not available in all cases

Figures for Hare include Beagles, Bassets and Harriers.

LEGAL PROVISIONS RELEVANT TO THE SCOPE OF THE INQUIRY

8.1   The topics dealt with by the Inquiry are the subject of a number of legislative provisions and, to a lesser extent, international conventions and European directives.

8.2   These may be separated out into six inter-related strands covering:

- Animal welfare and/or protection

- Pest control

- Food and public safety

- Trespass

- Game and shooting

- Environment and biodiversity.

Animal welfare and protection

8.3   The Protection of Animals Act 1911 provides the modern legal definition of cruelty to animals as the causing or permitting of unnecessary suffering to animals. It goes on to delineate a list of cruelty offences, including beating, kicking, torturing, terrifying, baiting and administering poison except for pest control or other good reason.

- the offences apply to domestic and captive animals or livestock only, and the Act is therefore only partially applicable to hunting with hounds or terrier work

- 'captive animals' are defined as animals held in a permanent, not temporary, state of captivity.

8.4   An amendment to the Act in 1921, and later rulings, clarify the application of the law to captive animals released for hunting or coursing, permitting these activities, provided the animals are not mistreated while in captivity, nor released for hunting in an injured or exhausted state, and once released have a reasonable chance of escape.

8.5   The Abandonment of Animals Act 1960 makes it an offence to abandon animals in circumstances that might lead to unnecessary suffering.

8.6   The Wildlife and Countryside Act 1981 embodies a range of provisions that affect issues of animal welfare and protection. It

- makes the otter a protected animal and thereby indirectly restricts mink hunting in areas of otter habitation and prohibits their further pursuit if they take temporary refuge in an otter holt

- indirectly restricts all forms of hunting with dogs where they may disturb other protected animals (such as sand lizards and smooth snakes when in their hibernacula)

- prohibits the use of self–locking snares, bows, crossbows, explosives other than in firearm ammunition and live animals as a decoy for killing

- makes it an offence to take, or kill, certain mammals by use of a snare, and requires snares to be checked at least once a day

- prohibits the use of certain other methods of killing or taking a range of mammals, none of which figure in this Inquiry

- prohibits the release or escape of mink into the wild since they are not native to this country.

8.7   The Protection of Badgers Act 1992 consolidates legislation over the previous twenty year period intended to protect the badger. It prohibits their injuring, removal, or cruel treatment. The Act also makes it an offence to damage or interfere in any way with a badger sett with the limited exception of temporary stopping up in a specified manner for the purpose of fox hunting. An exception to the Act permits the removal or killing of badgers where it can be clearly shown that they are the cause of damage to property or as an act of mercy.

8.8   The Wild Mammals (Protection) Act 1996 for the first time gave the generality of wild mammals protection under the law by making it an offence to carry out, or permit to be carried out, certain acts, namely, mutilating, kicking, beating, nailing or otherwise impaling, stabbing, burning, stoning, crushing, drowning, dragging, or asphyxiating with intent to inflict unnecessary suffering. The Act also introduces the words 'with intent' thereby introducing the possibility that the offences may be viewed more seriously than those set out in the 1911 Act. Exceptions to the Act are made to cover lawful trapping and hunting, provided the killing of any wild mammal during these activities is done in a 'reasonably swift and humane manner'. It is thought that the Act has the overall effect of placing a higher burden on those carrying out all forms of hunting, in case any elements of a offence pursuant to the acts listed above may be present in their activities, and also to ensure a quick and humane dispatch of the quarry. An additional clause also provides an exception which permits the killing of the quarry by a dog, lawfully deployed for the purpose of the hunting.

8.9   The European Habitats Directive and Related Regulations 1994 ban various methods of killing or taking mountain hares, including the use of gin traps, live decoys , use of tape-recorders, electrical, stunning, or dazzling devices, drugs, poisons, mirrors, crossbows, non-selective nets or traps, gas, smoke and semi automatic and automatic weapons.

Pest control

8.10   The Agriculture Act 1947

- provides a mechanism whereby MAFF can serve notice to control certain pest species, including rabbits, hares, deer and foxes. Currently, a control notice exists on rabbits only

- permits the use of gassing foxes underground, although this method of control is no longer practised since the approval for Cymag ® was withdrawn.

8.11   The Pests Act 1954 restricts the use of spring traps to catch pest mammals to models approved by MAFF.

8.12   The Protection of Animals Act 1911 and other later measures have effectively limited the use of poisons against wild mammals to moles underground, squirrels in the context of forestry, rats and mice.

8.13   Licensing provisions exist to cover pest control measures that would otherwise be prohibited acts under the various animal protection statutes outlined elsewhere in this Appendix.

Food and public safety

8.14   The Food and Environmental Protection Act 1985

- sets up the mechanism by which the Pesticides Safety Directorate must approve pesticides for widespread use

- provides that future non-lethal methods of animal population control will also be regulated by this mechanism.

8.15   Firearms Act 1968 requires the holder and operator of rifles and shotguns to possess a certificate. For a rifle held for pest control, the holder must have written authority for at least one area of land. Many police authorities will inspect the land with public safety in mind before granting the licence.

Trespass

8.16   Certain aspects of the laws of trespass are relevant to the topics covered by this Inquiry:

- wild animals cannot trespass and so no liability arises between landowners for damage caused by, for example, deer or rabbits when passing back and forth over different properties

- a trespass on land is committed by sending or allowing dogs onto another's land without permission . If a dog strays onto property and causes damage, the owner is theoretically liable

- hunting in fresh pursuit of deer, hare or fox with hounds or coursing in fresh pursuit of hare are exempt from the offence of trespassing for game, provided they started off on land where permission had been granted for the activity. They are not, however, exempt from the offence of civil trespass, which also extends to the hounds. Appropriate hunt officials may find themselves liable for the trespass of others following the hunt. This can be particularly relevant to hunting deer with dogs, when trespassing into, for example, a deer sanctuary may occur.

Game and Shooting

8.17   Legislation on this subject is relevant to the Inquiry insofar as the deer and the hare is concerned. It should be noted that deer are classified as wild animals and not game.

8.18   The Deer Act 1991

- Section 1 requires the consent of the landowner or occupier to kill or pursue a deer, or to remove a carcass, although a person is not considered to have committed the offence if they believe that consent would have been granted.

- Section 2 prohibits killing wild-living deer during a close season.

Red Deer	Close Season
Stag	1 May-31 July
Hind	1 March-31 October
Roe Deer	
Buck	1 November-31 March
Doe	1 March-31 October

- Section 3 prohibits killing at night

- Section 4 prohibits killing, or harming deer by various methods except by shooting with a rifle, or hunting with dogs. It further prohibits shooting from a vehicle or using a vehicle to drive deer. The required firearm and ammunition are specified. Partial exceptions to this section are granted for deer on enclosed land, actions carried out with the authority of the occupier of the land, any requirement from MAFF under the Agricultural Act (1947), the prevention of suffering to an injured or diseases deer, and to allow landowners to kill deer where they are causing damage , if this is deemed necessary to prevent further damage.

- The purchase and sale of venison must be by a licensed game dealer and records of such purchases kept.

8.19 Section 14 of the Wildlife and Countryside Act 1981 prohibits the release into the wild of muntjac, sika deer, and sika/ red deer hybrids.

8.20 The Hare Act 1848 was intended to facilitate the killing of brown hares as a pest control measure by removing the requirement for game licences. The Ground Game Act 1880 extended the right to kill brown hare to tenants as a crop protection measure. In a reversal of intention The Hare Preservation Act 1892 prohibited the sale of hare during the breeding season, thereby lessening the economic attractions of killing them.

8.21 Other game legislation affecting hare:

- it is an offence to kill game by the use of firearms during the hours of darkness

- Sunday and Christmas Day hunting of hares is prohibited

- By exemption, a game licence is not required to hunt hares with hounds or beagles.

Environment and biodiversity

The Berne Convention 1979 ('Convention on the Conservation of European Wildlife and Natural Habitats')

8.22 The purpose of this Convention, to which the UK is a signatory, is to provide a broad framework for conservation of fauna and flora within the countries of the Council of Europe.

8.23 Both the deer and the hare are amongst the species listed for protection in accordance with the following provisions:

- the maintenance or adaptation of their population to a level which corresponds in particular to ecological, scientific and cultural requirements, while taking account of economic and recreational requirements and the needs of sub-species, varieties or forms at risk locally

212

- their exploitation to be regulated in order to keep the populations out of danger

- the prohibition of the use of all indiscriminate means of capture and killing and the use of all means capable of causing local disappearance, or serious disturbance, of their populations.

8.24   Exceptions to the application of these provisions are made, intended to protect flora and other fauna, damage to all forms of property, public health and safety, research and education. There is a standing committee, to which all signatories must report every two years full details of all exceptions that have been allowed.

EC Directive (92/43/EC – Habitats and Species Directive)

8.25   The Directive arose as a result of the need of the EC to implement the provisions of the Berne Convention and there is considerable overlap in the main provisions and details.

United Nations 1992 Convention on Biological Diversity

8.26   The Convention introduces a general requirement to manage all aspects of biodiversity in a sustainable manner. There is specific provision to 'eradicate those alien species which threaten ecosystems, habitats or species'.

8.27   The UK's ratification of the Conventions and any associated EC directives has some more general legal impact on the matters under discussion. An important principle established is that legislation should not only serve to protect endangered species and habitats but also to conserve the traditional and commonplace both in terms of animals and ecosystems generally. This may be seen as applying in varying degrees of relevance to such matters as:

- deer management schemes

- encouragement of brown hare populations where they are falling..

- land use that encourages the protection and promotion of such features as hedgerows, ponds, coppices and unfarmed pockets of land.

8.28   The UN Convention also urges signatories to 'respect, preserve and maintain knowledge, innovations and practices of indigenous and local communities embodying traditional lifestyles relevant for the conservation and sustainable use of biodiversity'.

Agreements on International Humane Trapping Standards

8.29   There are two relevant agreements which have predominantly similar terms: the Agreement on International Humane Trapping Standards between the European

Community, Canada and the Russian Federation; and the International Agreement in the form of an Agreed Minute between the European Community and the United States of America on humane trapping standards (Standards for the humane trapping of specified terrestrial and semi-aquatic mammals).

8.30   Neither document affects the UK position at present but future developments could affect pest control methods involving trapping in the future.

8.31   In the first three of these international agreements, the power of national governments to make exceptions from protection provisions for species, even if perceived as pests nationally, is subsidiary to the obligation to maintain their favourable conservation status.

THE INTERNATIONAL PERSPECTIVE

9.1   This note is based on a study carried out for the Inquiry by Professor S.R. and Ms. D.F. Harrop of the University of Kent, to whom the Committee is most grateful. In the time available to them, it was not possible to obtain information from as many parts of the world as would have been desirable. Nor was it possible to provide exhaustive reports on hunting with dogs and its regulatory background on those countries that have been included.

9.2   We have divided the countries considered, somewhat arbitrarily, into four groups:

- countries or states that share a lot in common with England and Wales in respect of hunting heritage, current practice and the legal framework

- countries where the emphasis in the way hunting is practised differs from England and Wales

- countries or states where the English-style of hunting with dogs either hardly exists or, to a greater or lesser extent, has been banned.

- France, a country on its own because hunting with dogs is an extremely popular activity.

9.3   It must be borne in mind that many of the countries discussed in this note have a greater number of quarry species which can be hunted with dogs, but, for the sake of brevity, we have limited our description to the four quarry species which are the subject of our report.

Countries with a similar heritage

9.4   The countries or states where the current practice of hunting with dogs, and its legal and regulatory framework, most closely resemble the situation in England and Wales are Ireland, Scotland, Australia (State of Victoria), Portugal and Italy. Apart from in Scotland, it should be noted, however, that governments in this group of states have assumed a greater supervisory role in recent years.

Scotland

9.5   The Deer (Scotland) Act 1996 prohibits all methods of killing deer other than by shooting. Dogs may, however, still be used to assist in hunting, although English-style mounted hunting with registered packs of deer-hounds is not practised.

9.6   There are ten mounted packs of foxhounds, mostly based south of Edinburgh and regulated by the Scottish MFHA. The Scottish Hill-Packs Association hunts with dogs on foot and receives a government grant for its contribution to fox control in the Grampian region. In addition, fox destruction packs, which often make use of older hounds to chase foxes to waiting guns, operate in hilly areas. Autumn/cub hunting takes place from the third week in August, as in England and Wales, for the stated purpose of fox control. There is no organised hunting of hares or mink with dogs.

9.7   Almost identical legislative measures as those in England and Wales deal with issues of animal welfare, up to and including the Wild Mammals (Protection) Act 1996. At the time this report is being written, a Private Member's Bill, the Protection of Wild Mammals (Scotland) Bill, introduced by Lord Watson, is proceeding through the Scottish Parliament. The central features of the Bill are to prohibit the use of dogs in hunting, searching for and coursing any wild mammal. There is scope in the Bill to grant licences for the use of a tightly controlled dog for stalking, flushing out, retrieving, locating escaped or injured animals and the provision of food for consumption by a living creature.

Ireland

9.8   Hunting with dogs is a well-supported pastime with, for example, over 300 fox packs. The same quarry species are hunted as in England and Wales and there are similar Associations regulating the different packs.

9.9   The Hunting Association of Ireland was formed in 1997 and, in 1998, in response to concern about unacceptable practice in terrier work, negotiated and agreed a Code of Conduct with the Department of Agriculture. The Code is essentially the same as that operated by the MFHA and the other associations in England and Wales which use terriers. One regulation, not mirrored in England and Wales, is that earth stopping is allowed only as a safety measure for humans and other animals, and to assist in the finding of foxes above ground. It should not be for the sole purpose of preventing a hunted fox from going to ground, and, in general, is only to be undertaken on land traversed early on in the hunt.

9.10   Coursing is a popular greyhound sport. Most of the coursing which takes place is "park", in which the coursing takes place within enclosures.

State of Victoria, Australia

9.11   Foxhunting with dogs is widespread in the state of Victoria, where the fox is declared vermin. There are also foxhound packs outside Victoria and some hunting of deer on foot with hounds, mainly in the mountain areas.

9.12   In Victoria, the Prevention of Cruelty to Animals Act 1986 and the Code of Practice 1990 have a considerable impact on the practice of foxhunting, and bring it within the ambit of legislation and state regulation in a manner that is not quite comparable to the situation in England and Wales. The Act makes it a criminal offence to commit an act of cruelty upon any animal. Deliberately terrifying, killing and injuring animals, including wild foxes, are examples of the offence, and may even possibly constitute the more serious offence of aggravated cruelty. Foxhunting is permissible only as an exception to the provisions of the Act, if it complies with a Code of Practice, which has been prepared or altered by the Minister of Agriculture, with the approval of the relevant Governor in Council. Currently, the Code specifies that fox hunters must be members of clubs affiliated with the Hunt Clubs Association of Victoria, or another organisation approved to use horse and hounds for hunting foxes. Generally, the provisions of the Code allow hunting to be carried out in the same manner as recommended by the MFHA for England and Wales. Five differences are worth pointing out:

- it is mandatory that dogs used should be properly selected, trained to hunt the target animal only and not used if they do not kill quickly by instinct

- if a fox not hunted by the pack is marked to ground, the dogs must be immediately removed and the fox left undisturbed

- the welfare of the hounds is a concern of the Code. They must be healthy and not used where there is an unacceptable risk of heat exhaustion/serious injury

- terrierwork remains permissible, although the Code does state that if a fox which has not been hunted by the pack is marked to ground, the dogs must be immediately removed and the fox left undisturbed

- the Code does not address autumn/cub hunting. This is not an activity much practised due to the dry summer terrain of the State.

Portugal

9.13   There is currently only one mounted foxhound pack in existence. All forms of hunting are regulated by the Ministry of Agriculture. Those applying to fox hunting are similar to the MFHA's, although a major difference is that digging-out does not take place. If a fox goes to ground, the hunt is considered finished. In 1999, a Bill to prohibit foxhunting failed to reach the debate stage in Parliament, having met strong organised opposition.

Italy

9.14   There is one mounted fox hunting pack, operating in a form similar to MFHA packs. The fox is regarded as a pest, and therefore the emphasis is on the kill, with both digging out and autumn/cub hunting practised. Act no. 157 (February 1992) reformed previous hunting regulation, preserving the right to hunt, granted by the State, and, in addition, giving the hunter a countryside management role. Hunting is now linked to wildlife planning service and subject to strict guidelines enforced by the Ministry of Agriculture.

Countries with a different tradition

9.15   In the USA and Canada, there are a significant number of mounted foxhound packs but the emphasis is strongly on the 'chase' rather than the 'kill'. The situation is complex because of differences in the laws of the various states and because there are a greater number of potential quarry species.

USA

9.16   The Masters of Foxhounds Association of America was established in 1907 and fulfils the same function as the MFHA in England and Wales. There are approximately 157 packs registered but there are also many unregistered packs, generally preferring to hunt at night. Since the emphasis is on the chase, rather than the kill, if the dogs lose the scent or the fox goes to ground, the hunt is concluded or moves on to another quarry. Digging-out does not occur; nor does autumn/cub hunting as practised in England and Wales. Because fox population levels are less dense, there is not the perceived need to cull foxes and autumn activity is aimed more at the training of horses, dogs and riders in the chase. That the emphasis is not generally on the 'kill' may be less related to welfare matters than the fact that low fox numbers affect its perceived status as a pest. Coyotes, by contrast, are culled as they are seen as a threat to livestock.

9.17   Other points to note are:

- some States have legislation permitting only the chase, not the kill, unless the prey is already injured or wounded

- the welfare requirements of the hounds and good upkeep of the kennels are included in the regulatory regimes of some States

- hunting deer with dogs is prohibited in some States, not others

- Federal legislation reserves the right to prohibit hunting in some areas, if it puts endangered species at risk.

Canada

9.18   There are twelve mounted fox packs in Canada, eight of which are in Ontario, although four of these are drag packs. The fox is not perceived as a pest but, on the contrary, is under some pressure from coyote numbers and, therefore, as in the USA, hunts seek to chase, not to kill.

9.19   The State of Ontario highlights some of the features that distinguish the regulatory background of Canada compared with that of England and Wales:

218

- to be licensed by the Ministry of Natural Resources, a hunt must be registered with the Masters of Foxhounds Association of America or another organisation with comparable standards.

- the terms of the licence do not permit killing or capturing a fox or, possessing or use of a firearm; they also require a pack size of minimum of two, and a maximum of 50, hounds, when hunting, and a minimum of three, and a maximum of 125, participants.

- the regulations recognise that the chase may result in a kill but this is not the purpose of the hunt

- there is not a prescribed closed season, but this is because one is already observed by participants.

Countries where hunting with dogs is not practised or is largely banned

9.20   Countries where hunting with dogs is not practised or is largely banned include Spain, Belgium, Germany, Sweden, Denmark, Finland and Norway.

Spain

9.21   Hunting is regulated in Spain by the regional governments. Permits are, however, invariably necessary. There is no mounted hunting with dogs as practised in England and Wales. However, hounds are used to flush out deer to waiting guns and greyhounds are used widely to catch and kill hares.

Sweden, Denmark, Norway, Finland and Germany

9.22   Hunting in various forms is widespread and highly regulated. There is a substantial amount of welfare legislation in all these countries. There is often the requirement for individuals to pass examinations on the subject before they can hunt. Mounted hunting with dogs or foot packs in the British style is not carried out, and indeed has been banned in Germany since 1936 and, subsequently, both in Sweden and Denmark. However, dogs are still used for flushing out, tracking, retrieving and driving to guns. In Germany, for example, all types of female and young deer and immature red and fallow male deer may be hunted with a rifle having been driven, sometimes for over an hour, by one or several dogs. The same applied to mouflon (wild sheep), red foxes, hare and all game birds. Underground terrierwork is very widespread. It is considered a form of hunting, requiring participants to have passed an examination. In Sweden, game research is financed extensively from hunting fees, and the Hunters' Association has responsibility to keep and collate statistics in relation to animals taken.

Belgium

9.23   Hunting is regulated regionally:

- Brussels: All hunting is banned

- Flanders: A decree in 1991 and subsequent ministerial action has effectively stopped mounted hunting which used to be carried out in the French manner (see below). One foot pack still operates in the French style

- Walloonia: A 1995 decree states that hunting with hounds is to be prohibited from 30 June 2000. Existing packs are currently trying to obtain an extension to their licences.

France

9.24   Hunting with hounds has a very long tradition and remains popular to this day. In 1981, it was the subject of a decree and circular by the Ministry of Environment which gave legal force to a number of rules relating to the code of hunting with hounds. Specifically, they lay down a scheme whereby all packs have to be licensed by the Director of Agriculture in each 'Département' under the advice of the French hunting with dogs association (Association Française des Equipages de Vénerie). Certain types of game which are hunted with hounds, such as the red deer and roe deer, are subject to 'hunting plans', drawn up by local authorities, although hunting's contribution to the global cull quotas of the various species is very small. The French hunting associations acknowledge that their contribution to population control of the quarry species, while helpful, is negligible when set against the contribution of shooting. Animal welfare does not appear to be a matter much regulated or debated, the main opposition to hunting arising out of questions of land rights and usage and the management of wildlife. More recently, there has also been some concern expressed in the French press that hunting activities may be in some instances transgressing the EU Habitats Directive.

- 'Grand Vénerie' (mounted hunting) pursues the quarry with the use only of hounds and no firearms. It is considered the highest form of hunting activity with dogs and currently enjoys a resurgent popularity. There are 400 hunt kennels, nine recognised breeds of hounds and 7,000 hunting horses. The emphasis is on open, woodland hunting rather than negotiating obstacles, and the chase can last from three to four hours. Grand Vénerie has retained more of the historical aspects of hunting than has its English counterpart. This is particularly evident at the end of the hunt, when the deer at bay is often dispatched by the hunter with a sword, lance or hunting knife, rather than a firearm, and rituals around the handling of the carcass will be observed. There are 38 mounted packs (40-50 hounds per pack) hunting red deer in this fashion, 85 (20-30 hounds per pack) that hunt roe deer and 30 packs (80 hounds per pack) that hunt boar. Members pay £1000-£2000 to subscribe.

- 'Petit Vénerie' (Foot Packs) is relatively new to France but has experienced rapid growth in popularity. As with mounted hunting, it is practised without the aid of firearms. In total, there are 240 registered packs, 80 hunting foxes, 115 hunting hare and 45 hunting rabbits. It should be noted that hunting the fox with hounds is new to France.

- 'Vénerie Sous Terre' (terrierwork). This is also widely practised. There are 15,000 hounds attached to 1,750 registered clubs. Foxes and badgers are both hunted. The relevant government regulation foresees that the quarry may be dispatched by the dogs, rather than by digging out, and specifies that at least three dogs should be introduced into the earth.

- Shooting, with the use of dogs and hounds to flush out, stalk or retrieve the quarry, is the most widespread hunting activity involving dogs. Estimates put the number of dogs used for this purpose at around 700,000.

LIST OF ABBREVIATIONS

AMHB	Association of Masters of Harriers and Beagles
BASC	British Association for Shooting and Conservation
BDS	British Deer Society
BETA	British Equestrian Trade Association
BEVA	British Equine Veterinary Association
CA	Countryside Alliance
CLA	Country Landowners' Association
CCFP	Central Committee of Fell Packs
DETR	Department of the Environment, Transport and the Regions
FWP	Federation of Welsh Packs
GCT	Game Conservancy Trust
HHA	The Hare Hunting Associations
IFAW	International Fund for Animal Welfare
LACS	The League Against Cruel Sports
MAFF	Ministry of Agriculture, Fisheries and Food
MBHA	Masters of Basset Hounds Association
MDBA	Masters of Drag and Bloodhounds Associations
MDHA	Masters of Deerhounds Association
MFHA	Masters of Foxhounds Association
MMHA	Masters of Minkhounds Association
NCC	National Coursing Club

NFU	National Farmers' Union of England and Wales
NWTF	National Working Terrier Federation
PACEC	Public and Corporate Economic Consultants
RACE	Royal Agricultural College Enterprise
RSPCA	Royal Society for the Prevention of Cruelty to Animals
WFFCA	Welsh Farmers' Fox Control Association

Printed in the UK by The Stationery Office Limited
On behalf of the Controller of Her Majesty's Stationery Office
Dd 5067685 6/00 521462 19585